WHEN TRUTH GIVES OUT

When Truth Gives Out

MARK RICHARD

OXFORD
UNIVERSITY PRESS

OXFORD
UNIVERSITY PRESS

Great Clarendon Street, Oxford OX2 6DP

Oxford University Press is a department of the University of Oxford.
It furthers the University's objective of excellence in research, scholarship,
and education by publishing worldwide in

Oxford New York

Auckland Cape Town Dar es Salaam Hong Kong Karachi
Kuala Lumpur Madrid Melbourne Mexico City Nairobi
New Delhi Shanghai Taipei Toronto

With offices in

Argentina Austria Brazil Chile Czech Republic France Greece
Guatemala Hungary Italy Japan Poland Portugal Singapore
South Korea Switzerland Thailand Turkey Ukraine Vietnam

Oxford is a registered trade mark of Oxford University Press
in the UK and in certain other countries

Published in the United States
by Oxford University Press Inc., New York

© Mark Richard 2008

British Library Cataloguing in Publication Data

Data available

Library of Congress Cataloging in Publication Data

Data available

Typeset by Laserwords Private Limited, Chennai, India
Printed in Great Britain
on acid-free paper by
Biddles Ltd, King's Lynn, Norfolk

ISBN 978–0–19–923995–5

1 3 5 7 9 10 8 6 4 2

For Eleanor

For Michael

For Nancy

Acknowledgements

I have been working on this project for eight years now. I wish I could remember everyone who gave me comments, asked embarrassing questions, or expressed good-natured hostility about what's to follow. But I can't. I do remember being helped by all of the following: Jody Azzouni, Nancy Bauer, Alex Byrne, Liz Camp, Graeme Forbes, Michael Glanzberg, Patrick Greenough, John Hawthorne, Harold Hodes, Richard Holton, Jim Higginbotham, Jeff King, Peter Ludlow, Robert May, Dick Moran, Bernard Nickel, Paul Pietroski, François Recanati, Susanna Siegel, Scott Soames, Cara Spencer, Jason Stanley, Tim Williamson, Jessica Wilson, Crispin Wright. Thank you.

Portions of Chapter 4 and Appendix II appeared as 'Contextualism and Relativism' in *Philosophical Studies* in 2004.

Contents

Introduction

Nobody thinks that truth is the only virtue talk and thought can have. We want our words to be compassionate, relevant, interesting, clever, convincing, and so on and on. Even when we confine our gaze to talk and thought in which we muster evidence, give arguments, and try to persuade by rational means, there are of course more virtues to which we aspire than mere truth.

But many think that in the sphere of evidence, argument, and rational persuasion truth has a special role to play. Evidence, after all, must be evidence that something's true, right? The first measure of an argument is that its premises ensure, or at least make likely, its conclusion's truth, no? Rationality is the process of uncovering what we should think about or do in the situations we find ourselves in; uncovering this sort of thing is in good part a matter of skillful deployment of means of finding out what is (likely to be) true, isn't it?

In what follows I will try to convince you that while (of course) the truth is important, truth is often the wrong dimension of evaluation for our claims, arguments, or evidence. There is such a thing as getting something completely right—stating the facts in the most stringent sense of 'stating the facts'—which does not involve thinking or saying anything true. There are ways our talk and thought can represent the world, ways which are not vague or semantically deficient, which cannot be assessed for truth or falsity but must be assessed in other ways. And even when it makes sense to assess the claims and counterclaims of a debate for truth and falsity, I will argue, determining what claims are true and which ones are false may be of no help in deciding whose position ought to prevail—because in many cases the truth or falsity of what is under debate turns out to be a relative matter.

I come not to debunk, or minimize the importance of truth; I come to point to some of the things on the shelf beside truth that are just as important. But my project is deflationary in *some* sense of 'deflationary'. Many readers will thus be inclined to measure what I do with the ruler of 'deflationary' or 'minimalist' accounts of truth. So let me introduce what's to come by commenting on such accounts.

*

A familiar sort of minimalism about truth says that the most interesting thing about the notion of truth is that it's just not very interesting.[1] According to this view, we have a concept of truth because it makes it possible to endorse large sets of claims or sentences ('Everything the popes have said about God is true') even when we are unable to enumerate the claims we want to endorse; it allows us to assent to a sentence or claim even when we can only describe it ('The last sentence on page 4, whatever it is, is true'). In a slogan, we have a notion of truth because it allows us to blindly assent to sentences or claims. On such a view, nothing like a conceptual analysis is possible or necessary for the notion of truth. The property of truth has no 'underlying nature'. Beyond the laundry list of equivalences of the form *It's true that S iff S*, there is nothing to be said about truth—at least nothing that isn't of a more or less formal or logical nature, such as that a disjunction is true provided one of its disjuncts is.

Why would someone be attracted to such a view? Well, the argument that truth has no 'underlying nature' is typically a version of the grand old argument from despair. The minimalist despairs of giving an account of truth in terms of coherence, verification, or usefulness. As for correspondence, the minimalist argues that no substantial notion of correspondence is in the offing. Sometimes, of course, when we utter *a is F*, we pick out an object and ascribe it a property; when we do this, what we say is true just in case the referent has the property. In such cases we can make *some* sense of the idea of a sentence, or even the claim a sentence makes, corresponding to the way of the world. But, it is said, we have no reason to think that truth is always to be explained in this way, even when we confine our attention to the simplest sentence forms. After all, the press of usage, absent any 'direct' semantic connection with the world, can result in truth.[2]

Having surveyed all comers and found them wanting, the minimalist despairs of finding any 'underlying nature' for truth, and suggests that the question 'What is the nature of truth?' suffers from a faulty presupposition—that truth *has* one. He sees nothing general to say about truth, beyond the observation that any instance of the schemas *'S' is true iff S* and *It's true that S iff S* (paradoxical instances pushed under the carpet) is true. Once this much is accepted, the idea that truth is simply a device for 'blind assent' looks to be inevitable. After all, we *do* use the truth predicate as a device for blind assent. And if there is not a 'substantial' property associated with it, what purpose other than facilitating such assent could it serve?

---

[1] Representative of the sort of views I have in mind are Horwich (1998*b*) and Soames (1999).

[2] Examples are sure to be controversial, but here is the sort of thing I have in mind. One might well think that no object can be vague, in the sense that it is indeterminate where it leaves off. Many of the objects of ordinary discourse—piles of trash, for example—would have to be vague if they existed. But the sentence 'There are two piles of trash on the highway' is not false or truth-valueless if there is trash piled up in two spots on the highway. From this we might infer that the truth of the sentence is not a matter of anything like the sort of correspondence which makes a sentence like 'The cat is on the sofa' true, but rather of the press of usage appropriating the sentence's assertability conditions as truth-conditions.

But the minimalist's bold conclusions don't follow from his starting point, that there's no general account to be given of what makes a sentence true. Let us grant that there's precious little hope of giving a single, substantive account of what makes each of

(R) This rock is denser than that rock.
(M) $1 + 1 = 2$

true. One might say, for example, that (R)'s truth is a matter of two objects standing in one or another physical relation; (M)'s truth a matter (perhaps) of (something like) the role of that claim in a fruitful practice. It's a fool's errand to try to unify these in terms of correspondence, coherence, or pretty much anything else.

Even if a unified account of what makes sentences true is unlikely, there is still a distinction to be drawn between claims which are appropriately evaluated in terms of truth and falsity, and other claims—between claims which are 'truth-apt' and others. For example, one might insist that a claim like

(C) Sleater-Kinney is a cooler band than The Captain and Tennille.

simply isn't truth-apt. One might say that he who utters (C) is expressing a certain sort of appreciation, one grounded in relations both affective and cognitive between the evaluator, its objects, and their cultural milieu. The proper response to (C), it might be said, is not a matter of determining whether it is *true*: a way of reacting to objects, a way of comparing, liking and disliking things on the basis of their traits and how they affect one—this is not the stuff of *truth*. To agree or disagree with (C), one might say, is to react to, to evaluate the objects with a particular kind of approval or disapproval. There is, of course, feature placing, description, perception of properties involved in such reaction and evaluation; it is not blind, dumb, unreasoned, *ein Trieb* welling up from the id. Indeed, we can argue about (C), give reasons for our opinion, engage in rational dispute about it. But that doesn't mean that the dispute is over a truth: neither of us need be making a *mistake* about such a matter. Where mistakes do not occur, truth does not live.

There are *all sorts* of discursive discourse which have been held to be without truth-value, to be discourses where truth is just the wrong dimension of evaluation. This has been said, to take a somewhat random sample, of conditionals, mathematical claims, one or another range of normative discourse, claims that one promises, christens, finds guilty, etc. Those who say this need not, and often do not, say that such a discourse lacks genuine disagreements, or that one cannot have reasons for what one says in the discourse, or that it is impossible to assent to or deny—blindly or otherwise—the claims of the discourse. According to the minimalist, though, those who say that a discourse, though not truth-apt, involves disagreement, evidence, the trappings of rational enquiry—are not just mistaken, they are (or are perilously close to) suffering from conceptual confusion.

One goal of the present work is to argue that there are wide ranges of discourse which *are* discursive—in which we give (good and bad) arguments, adduce evidence, say what we think, have genuine disagreements—but for which truth and falsity *are not* the appropriate dimensions of evaluation. Insofar as this is so, it undercuts the minimalist's primary contentions about truth. For if we must pick and choose amongst the sentences which state what we think in order to segregate the ones which might be true or false from the rest, then surely the notion of truth *is* of some interest, and there *is* something substantial to be said about it. At the least, one wants to know what it is that prevents the non-truth-apt beliefs from being truth-apt.

One might make one of two responses to this.

First of all, one might simply deny that it is coherent to suppose that something can be a claim—a potential object of assertion or belief—but not be truth-apt. To make a claim, it will be said, is to represent the world as being a certain way. But *representations* are (vagueness aside) correct or incorrect. Furthermore, claims and beliefs are, whatever else they may be, things which function as premises and conclusions in arguments. So—since we can assess arguments as valid or otherwise, and validity is something which can only be understood in terms of *truth*—beliefs and claims just *have* to be the sort of thing assessable for truth. Since more than half of what follows can be understood as an attempt to undermine this picture of saying and belief, I won't address this response at the moment.[3]

I do, however, want to say something about a response the minimalist is likely to make, that our linguistic practice gives the lie to the idea that there are things we might think or say, but not think or be willing to say are true. After all, anyone who agrees with (C) is going to be disposed to say that it's true—it's not as if someone's going to say 'What you say isn't true, but I do agree with it', or 'I believe what you say, but it just isn't true'! He who takes mathematical discourse as being of only instrumental utility will still call mathematical claims true and false when correcting students. She who thinks that conditionals are not truth-apt—because they are devices for performing complex speech acts, or because they serve to express (but not ascribe) judgments of subjective probability—will of course say things like 'All of the claims on page 14 are true', knowing full well that the page is riddled with conditionals. And we obviously need an all-purpose device for indicating that we find all of what someone might say, write, or think acceptable. Since we need such a device, it might be said, and we obviously make use of 'true' for the purpose, surely 'true' is such a device. But then any claim we are willing to use in argument—so, any claim whatsoever—must be evaluable for truth.

---

[3] This response is actually not open to the minimalist. The minimalist denies that the notion of truth can play an explanatory role; the response presupposes that validity is to be explained in terms of truth.

The response is that (a) we *use* 'true' as a (universal) device of blind assent, so (b) that is what it must be—and it can be so only if any claim we might want to make or dispute is potentially true or false. But how is (a) supposed to make (b) plausible? Let us mine the work of arch-minimalist Paul Horwich for bridge premises. According to Horwich, (i) meaning supervenes on use, where a word's use is to be identified with some relatively small set of 'basic' properties which (along with the 'basic' properties for other expressions) suffice to explain all the facts about how a word is used in a population; (ii) the explanatorily basic properties about the word 'true' as it's used in English are just those determined by our disposition to assent to instances of *It's true that S iff S.*

Do (a), (i), and (ii) commit us to (b)? Not at all. The claim that use determines meaning is (as Horwich intends it) the claim that expressions cannot differ in meaning without differing in (the relevant dimensions of) use.[4] This doesn't imply, or even suggest, that one can read the semantics of an expression—in particular, its extension—off of the meaning-determining facts of use. It is as basic a fact as there can be, that we apply 'water' to liquids with a certain array of perceptible features. But no one, I think, now thinks that whatever has these features—that whatever our use commits us to calling 'water'—must be water. Why can't something similar be true of 'true'? Error can be ingrained, even to the point where it infects our most central beliefs, and thus—on most any reasonable story about conceptual identity—our concepts.

Do (a), (i), and (ii) at least imply that anyone who has the concept of truth will accept, or act as if he accepts, truth as a device of disquotation for and agreement with declarative discourse?[5] No. After all, we can rise above our dispositions and not give in to them. I may be disposed to assent to 'It's true that $2 + 2 = 4$' whenever I am disposed to assent to '$2 + 2 = 4$' without always following through on that disposition. If I hold certain views about truth and mathematics (and hold, say, that mathematical discourse is merely instrumentally useful), I will at least on occasion resist the disposition to assent to the claim that it is *true* that two 2s are 4, even when I grant that two 2s are of course 4.

Does it at least follow that linguistic competence requires that I accept, or act as if I accept, truth as a device of disquotation for and agreement with declarative discourse?[6] No, it does not. For one thing, it would seem that linguistic competence requires only that I be aware of the fact that people expect one another to be disposed to use the truth predicate as if it were such a device. Whether I will in fact use it as such a device in a particular situation where I

---

[4] See, e.g., Horwich (1998a: 67–71).

[5] To say that truth is a device of disquotation is to allude to the fact that one can—since one can always invoke a biconditional of the form

'S' is true iff S

—always infer S from 'S' *is true.*

[6] Jody Azzouni made this suggestion in conversation.

may think the use would be a misuse will depend on any number of factors—for example, on whether I judge it worth getting into a philosophical argument when all I want to do is indicate that I disagree with most everything the person who writes *The Times's* ethics column has to say.

The minimalist may at this point insist that without a truth predicate, blind assent is impossible. But why should we think that? Consider all the ways we can agree or disagree with one other. For example:

I accept/agree with/disagree with/reject all that she said.
What he said is a good/bad way of thinking about the issue.
To believe what he has to say about the matter is intellectual suicide—but then it's your intellect.
I can get behind that.
I'm down with that.
You can trust/rely on anything she has to say on the subject.

And so on and on. Why must it be inevitable that these idioms are to be cashed out in terms of truth?

I agree that we typically use the idiom of truth when we blindly agree or disagree. That's the way we talk. Minimalism is a philosophical position that offers an explanation of the way we talk, a way to understand what's going on when we use the word 'true'. The explanation isn't a priori; certainly there's no reason to think that every claim we are disposed to unreflectively accept just has to be correct. (I think Quine once said something like that.) As I see it, we—mistakenly or simply out of convenience—use 'true' in cases in which we shouldn't; we act as if there is a single dimension of evaluation for all our discourse when, in fact, there is not. It is not as if there is no trace of the view I am suggesting in the thought of the hoi poloi, many of whom will if pressed admit to strong opinions about 'matters of taste' but have reservations that those opinions are true or false.

You're entitled to some sense of where this train is going before you climb on board. Here's an itinerary.

The first three chapters look at some of the ways in which the performative aspects of our talk—what we do with our words—bear on whether and when our talk should or can be evaluated in terms of truth and falsity. Chapter 1 explores the idea that the performative and expressive components of our thought and talk may push talk and thought which might otherwise be evaluated as true or false to a place where truth is just the wrong dimension of evaluation. The idea, if you like, is that sometimes the performative and expressive trump the semantic.

The case I look at is the use of racial and ethnic slurs as well as other words whose primary purpose seems to be to hurt, to menace, to subjugate. The chapter begins with a puzzle: On the one hand, epithets seem to have clear application conditions. It is a *linguistic* mistake to call a Frenchman a Limey. This makes it seem that they must be true of their targets. On the other hand, if someone slurs in saying something—a bigot says 'Only [insert slur]s live there'—we do not want to say that what was said is true. For if I think what the bigot said is true, I think that only [insert slur] live in the relevant place. But only a bigot would think that.

A philosopher of language is likely to try to explain this in terms of faulty presuppositions (slurs introduce a presupposition that their targets are contemptible), or conversational or conventional implicatures that are false, or with the hypothesis that a slur on people of kind K means something like *despicable because of kind K* (and since no one could be despicable for that reason, the slur is true of nothing). No such account, I think, gets at the heart of the matter.

Someone who says 'Only [slur]s live there' certainly says something, something he believes. But to identify what he says we must look at more than what semantics usually looks at. The performative and expressive aspects of slurring are just as much components of the 'sense' of the slur as is the fact that the slur is used to classify a certain group. Because of this, thinking of someone as a * (* a slur on people of kind K), is thinking of him in a different way than thinking of him as a K. Furthermore, these performative and expressive aspects of a slur involve representation, though in a somewhat different way than do other words. For one way to represent someone as contemptible is to show contempt for them, just as one way to represent something as deserving of fear is to be afraid of it. The thoughts at issue not only express contempt, they represent their targets as contemptible because of (for example) their ethnicity or race. They therefore misrepresent them, as no one is contemptible for that reason. So these thoughts are not true. But it would be wrong to think that they are therefore false. If they were, we could adjust the mistake made in an utterance of *If Bob married a *, he's unhappy* simply by pointing out that though Bob married a *, he's quite happy. But we can't do this, because saying this is still displaying contempt and thus (mis)representing. The upshot is that slurring speech, though expressing beliefs and (mis)representing the world, is simply not truth-evaluable. It involves error and must therefore be rejected. But to say this is not to say that what the racist says is *false*.

A striking fact about slurs is that they can sometimes be used without the user being liable to censure. This is true of the appropriation of a slur by its targets, of some uses of slurs in indirect speech and narrative, and of other uses. This raises the question of whether the evaluative and performative elements associated with slurs are or are not essential to their meanings and to the concepts they express. The same question arises for terms like 'lust', 'chastity', and 'Samaritan'—'thick terms', as Bernard Williams called them, terms which 'mix classification and attitude'. Do we, for example, change such a term's meaning when we succeed in using it without the taint of its conventional evaluative dimension? Chapter 1 essays the beginning of an answer to such questions. It defends a view of word meaning and concept individuation on which whether something is 'part of a way of thinking' or of a word's meaning depends as much on contextual and social factors affecting the person who asks if this word meaning or concept is the same as that, as it does on 'purely interior' facts about a thinker or speaker.

Chapter 2 begins with the following puzzle. Sometimes, when we talk about talk—when, for example, we talk about paradoxical sentences such as the liar—we seem to 'get things right', but our getting it right *can't* be a matter of our saying something true. A liar sentence is, of course, not true—that's something we can prove, and we thus know. But of course what a liar sentence says is—well, that it's not true. Something similar holds of the claim that applications of vague predicates to their borderline cases are without truth-value. If Jo is a borderline case of baldness, it seems it's not true that he's bald, and not true that he's not. And it seems to pretty much everyone that Jo's bald iff it's true that he's bald. But contradiction ensues if all these things are *true*.

Chapter 2 develops the idea that there are more ways to 'get things right' than simply by asserting something—that is, by committing to its truth. One can, for example, *deny* the claim that the liar is true, where denial is understood as *sui generis* and not reducible to assertion of a negation. If we see the connectives like 'not' as sometimes contributing to the sense of what one says with a sentence, sometimes acting as force indicators—encoding information about the act being performed—we can make sense of the idea that someone could 'get it right' without speaking the truth.

Frege objected to the idea of a *sui generis* speech act of denial on the grounds that it made many inferences mysterious. If in giving the argument

If not A, then B,
Not A,
So B,

I am making a denial with the second premise, the argument looks to be invalid: 'not A' in the first premise isn't being used to deny anything, and so it looks like 'the sense' of second premises isn't the same here as 'the sense' of the conditional's antecedent. So, the argument isn't valid. Peter Geach famously picked up this point to criticize the emotivists, J. L. Austin, and others who saw sentences which routinely figure as premises or conclusions of arguments as doing something other than enabling assertion. What sense, after all, can an emotivist make of

If cheating is bad, Jim won't do it
Cheating is bad
So Jim won't do it   ?

According to the emotivist, one isn't saying something with the second premises; one is expressing disapproval for cheating. But whatever 'cheating is bad' is doing in the conditional, it's not expressing disapproval of anything. (Indeed, it's hard to know *what* it could be doing there on an emotivist view.)[7]

Much of Chapter 2 is given over to responding to Frege. I first show that if we think of the connectives and quantifiers as sometimes playing the role of force indicators, it's very easy to explain what's going on with a sentence like *It's true that Jo is bald iff Jo is bald* or *If that sentence is a liar sentence, what it says isn't true.* The trick is to think of a family of speech acts, of which assertion and denial are the simplest, as being systematically associated with sentences, the association being systematic because the (force-indicating) meanings of connectives and quantifiers combine with each other in a simple, systematic way. Concentrating first on the issues raised by the puzzle about paradoxical and vague sentences, I show how we can think of a semantics for a language like English as associating with each sentence a 'commitment' to the truth or non-truth of various collections of claims. Logical validity is a matter of 'commitment preservation' (fulfilling all the commitments associated with the premises means fulfilling those of the conclusion), of which the standard definition of validity, in terms of the truth of premises guaranteeing the conclusion's truth, is a special case.

The general moral of Chapter 2 is this: The simplest sentences of our language are vehicles for expressing various sorts of commitments. Sometimes these are commitments to the truth of a claim; sometimes they are other sorts of commitments. Devices for compounding sentences such as the connectives have a use on which they function to produce vehicles for expressing complex commitments systematically related (by those connectives' meanings) to the commitments expressed by the sentences the connectives combine. Commitments, whether to a claim's truth or to something having nothing whatsoever to do with truth, can stand in relations which deserve to be called logical. And so the idea that a discourse—if it involves reasoning, evidence, argument, and the rest of the trappings of rationality—must be a discourse whose claims are true or false is seriously off the mark. Chapter 3 applies these ideas to Geach's criticisms of the emotivists and others. I try to show that a straightforward generalization of the (semantics of the) language presented in Chapter 2 provides an account of validity for arguments involving normative premises which an emotivist just slightly less crude than Ayer could have adopted.

The second half of this book takes up relativism about truth and the status of opinions about 'matters of taste'. By 'relativism' I mean the view that what we say or think is at least sometimes true only relative to something determined by the interests or standards of thinkers. One goal of Chapter 4 is to show that pedestrian facts about when we judge people to disagree, along with widely accepted views about how the interests of speakers affect the interpretations of their words, entail relativism. A second goal is to argue that relativism, in and of itself, is a relatively benign view—accepting it, even as true of the majority

---

[7] See Frege (1918) and Geach (1965).

of claims we make, does not require that we allow that any opinion is as good as any other, or that when a claim is 'true for me, false for you' there cannot be reasoned argument between us, or even good reason for one of us to come around to the other's opinion. We do not have to embrace an 'absolute' notion of truth simply because we want to insist that some views are wildly unreasonable, or that there is often or even usually a best way to think about a matter.

Pretty much everyone allows that gradable adjectives (such as 'rich', 'red', 'rotund', and 'religious') vary in extension across different contexts with the interests and purposes of conversants. David Lewis famously and convincingly argued that conversational 'rules' and processes (such as 'accommodation') demand such variation. But we very often take people in different contexts, contexts with different standards for applying such adjectives, to have a genuine disagreement—as when, say, Didi and her blue-collar friends think the million-dollar-lottery winner to be rich, Naomi and her blue-blooded friends think that such a person is obviously not rich. But if they disagree, they are saying the same thing with 'Mary is rich'; if application varies with context, each speaks truly.

After exploring some ways of trying to non-relativistically reconcile these facts and finding them wanting, I sketch a version of relativism which makes sense of the facts. On it, truth is something a claim sometimes has only relative to the standards conversants adopt or presuppose. None of the standard charges of incoherence directed at relativism apply to this view—it's not self-defeating (*it* is not relatively true), it doesn't entail that there are 'true contradictions'. And quite plausible views of the nature of concepts—ones which ground concept identity (partially) in such things as functional roles, 'partial definitions', or a 'core extension' and a prototype structure—provide a natural model of thought and meaning on which such relativism is to be expected.

A likely place to look for relative truth, it seems, is in matters of taste. Our detailed conceptions of who is handsome, who sexy, what is hip, what L7, what is boring, what perverted—these typically differ. My judgment of who is sexy, hip, or perverted seems to answer to my considered opinions on the matter; likewise for yours. But we nonetheless will argue about whether someone is sexy, whether a certain activity is perverted—we take ourselves to disagree, and think the disagreement (sometimes) worth argument. And this sounds like a setting in which genuine relativism might flourish.

Chapter 5 argues that this isn't the best way of thinking of these matters. The primary reason, I argue, is that while we recognize that we may disagree about these things, we also acknowledge that in (some) such matters neither of those who disagree need be making a mistake. And this is not something that the relativist—at least not the relativist of Chapter 4—thinks possible. If Didi thinks Mary is rich, and Naomi thinks that Mary is not rich, Didi thinks that Naomi is *wrong*, for Didi thinks it's *false* that Mary isn't rich. Didi can acknowledge that Naomi's opinion is valid given Naomi's standards, but for Didi to acknowledge that is not for her to acknowledge that Naomi's opinion is true. Chapter 5 defends the intelligibility of disagreeing with someone about a matter of taste while allowing that those with whom one differs are not making a mistake about the matter.

I have tried to write a book that philosophers outside of philosophy of language would find interesting and provocative. (I *wanted* to write a book that non-philosophers would find engaging.) To these ends, I have tried to keep this book as non-formal as possible. Chapters 1 and 4 contain nary a symbol, and ought to be accessible to anyone with a modest grounding in philosophy and a feeling for how analytic philosophers think about meaning. Chapter 2 contains some technical material. It is, after all, in part about whether logic lives only where there is assertion; it's pretty hard to discuss that question in any detail without—well, talking about logic. I've tried to confine the technical material there to a single section, and give, immediately following that section, a non-technical gloss of it. Chapters 3 and 5 are mostly free of formalism; what formalism they contain is roped off from the main go. For the most part, the chapters of this book can be read independently of one another, save that Chapter 3 presupposes the material in Chapter 2.

The argument in Chapter 2 is, I think, relevant to some formal issues, in particular the issue of whether it's possible to 'express all the semantic facts' about a language in that very language. If the story told in that chapter is correct, it perhaps helps us make a little headway on understanding the senses in which this is (or isn't) possible. I have confined the discussion of these matters to an appendix, in the hope that so structuring the discussion might scare off fewer of those I hope will read at least some of this. A second appendix connects the discussion of relativism to current debates about the semantics of knowledge ascriptions; it is separated from Chapter 4 because it is perhaps of less general interest than the material therein.

1

Epithets and Attitudes

A word is a slur when it is a conventional means to express strong negative attitudes towards members of a group, attitudes in some sense grounded in nothing more than membership in the group. A slur on Asians, for example, is a word which speakers know (and as competent speakers are expected to know) is used to insult and display contempt for Asians merely because that is what they are. What makes a word a slur is that it is used to *do* certain things, that it has (in Austinian jargon) a certain illocutionary potential. Given what slurs are used to do, it is no surprise that their use often achieves extreme effects on their targets—humiliation, subjugation, shame.

Slurs can be used without displaying contempt or causing hurt.[1] This happens, for example, when a slur is appropriated by its targets: it is an insult to no one, save perhaps the homophobe, for gay people to call themselves queer. A slur can be self-ascribed to record one's status as a victim of discrimination or worse. There need be no racism in an epithet's use by comedians to make fun of or criticize various attitudes and behaviors of both he who slurs and he who is slurred. One may use a slur in order to teach someone that it is a word which shouldn't be used. And an epithet can sometimes be used non-offensively in indirect discourse or narrative to portray someone else's racist remark or attitude.[2]

I will for the most part concentrate on uses of slurs which are offensive. My primary interest is the relation between such words' illocutionary and perlocutionary properties—their potentials for performing acts and achieving effects—and their more straightforwardly semantic properties; in particular, their potential for contributing to the truth and falsity of what a sentence says.

It seems undeniable that racial and ethnic slurs have application conditions. If I point at Prince Charles and say 'He's a Frog', I have—over and above any

---

[1] I am here indebted to conversations with Nancy Bauer and Margaret Klenck, comments from Robert May, and to the discussion in Randall Kennedy (2002).

[2] Strikingly it is not always possible for us, even when we want to, to use a slur in these ways without being subject to censure. No matter how honorable my intentions, I cannot join in the appropriation of slurs on African-Americans—at least not without something very much like an invitation from a target of the slur to so use it. (A nice discussion and example of this is given at the end of chapter 1 of Kennedy 2002.) Reports of slurring speech in which the slur is used are in some situations no less offensive than direct use of the slur, no matter how benign the reporter's intention.

moral breach—made a linguistic mistake, one of the same sort as I make if I point at him and say 'He's French'. Linguistic competence requires knowing that the French, not the English, are called 'Frogs', the English, not the French, are called 'Limeys'.[3]

Normally, if it makes sense to speak of a predicate being misapplied, and there are cases in which the predicate is not misapplied, there are going to be simple sentences in which the predicate is applied to an object which are true, and other such sentences which are false. At first blush, this would seem to be true of slurs and epithets: 'Frog' is a derogatory term for the French, and a derogatory term for the French is a term for the French. But if S is a term for the French and f is in fact French, then if I point at f and utter *He is an S*, I speak truly.

Appearances notwithstanding, one has a strong intuition that this can't be right. Let S be some odious racial slur. Imagine standing next to someone who uses S as a slur. Perhaps you are in front of a building where targets of the slur live or work; the racist mutters *That building is full of Ss*. Many of us are going to resist allowing that what the racist said was true. After all, if we admit its truth, we must believe that it is true that the building is full of Ss. And if we think that, we think that the building is full of Ss. We think, that is, what and as the racist thinks. This certainly seems to make us complicit in the racist's racist attitude, and thus to some extent racists ourselves.

One hears it said that the racist's utterance is true, but objectionably couched.[4] I don't think invoking the idea of unacceptably expressed truth helps here, for we cannot draw the right sort of line between thinking that it is true that S and thinking that S. The thoughts you think true, whether you like or not, are *your* thoughts. If you understand the racist and think what he says is true, you agree with him—you think (say) that the house is full of Ss. And we just saw where that leads: if you think this, you think of the people in the house as the racist does when he slurs. But if you think of people as the racist does in slurring, you are being racist.[5]

In what follows, I discuss the intuition that we cannot ascribe truth to utterances such as the racist's. I first consider some attempts to bolster the

---

[3] Of course the application conditions of epithets are vague; in the case of racial epithets, the use of the terms is arguably embedded in a mistaken view that races are 'real kinds'. Neither of these facts casts doubt on the claim that understanding such terms requires recognizing that their use is subject to correction for misapplication. Vague terms have application conditions, even if those conditions are vague. And the fact that, for example, jade is not a true kind doesn't mean that we cannot speak of right and wrong applications of 'jade'.

[4] Alan Gibbard, for example, has said this. Such views are discussed in Sections 1.3 through 1.6.

[5] There are lines one can plausibly draw here. On many views of thought, the thought that *S* is distinct from the thought that it's true that S, since only the latter must involve the notion of truth. And so, Donald Davidson notwithstanding, one may think that S without thinking that it's true that S, simply because one may have thoughts without having the concept of truth. One may plausibly say that someone who knows what it is for a thought to be true could think that S without thinking that it's true that S, because one may have beliefs in an area of discourse one thinks isn't truth-apt.

intuition with tools from the philosopher of language's tool kit, by saying (for example) that slurs have application conditions that nothing can satisfy, or saying that a slur introduces a faulty presupposition. No such account, so far as I can see, is terribly plausible.

I then sketch what I think we should say. As I see it, to think or talk slurringly of a person is, among other things, to have certain attitudes towards him, including evaluating him negatively and having contempt for him because one takes him to be of a certain race, ethnicity, religion, etc. The difference between thinking that Prince Charles is English and thinking that he is a Limey is, in part, that one is contemptuous of him when one thinks him a Limey, and thus *thinks* of him negatively when one thinks him a Limey. The attitude—the contempt—is *part of what one thinks.* Furthermore, to have an attitude of contempt towards someone because of their race or ethnicity is, *inter alia*, to represent one's target in a certain way: as contemptible because of his race or ethnicity. Such a representation is incorrect: no one is contemptible for such a reason. So what one says cannot be true. But the right attitude to take towards someone who slurs another is not that they have made a mistake that renders their thought false. Rather, we should reject the very way of thinking the thinker used in his thought. Not all representation is aptly evaluated in terms of truth and falsity. So, at any rate, I shall argue.

Slurs are 'thick terms', terms whose use, as Bernard Williams put it, 'mixes categorization and attitude'. Of such a term one wants to know exactly how (if at all) the attitude contributes to the thought expressed by using the term, whether the term could be understood by someone lacking the attitude, and under what conditions (if any) the presence of the attitude blocks the thoughts expressed by using the term from being true or false. I take up some of these questions at the chapter's end, arguing that in some ways everybody who has weighed in on these issues has gotten things wrong. Those (like Williams and John McDowell) who think that certain attitudes are in some way essential to some thick concepts are wrong; but so are those who say the attitudes annexed to a thick term neither help individuate the thoughts expressed with the term nor contribute to how the term represents. As I see it, whether two people express the same thought with a sentence is something which turns as much upon the interests of and social pressures upon the person *asking* whether the thoughts are the same, as it turns on facts independent of the situation in which we ask whether what one person

---

But while we can deny that anyone who thinks that the Frogs are a haughty lot must also think that it's true that they are, can we deny the converse? It is not clear to me how one goes about doing this.

Neither, it seems to me, is there much hope in suggesting that I might know what your utterance says, be so related to it that I could say what you say by using the very words you do, think that what you say with your words is true, but not think the thought in question because I refuse to 'mentally token' (or audibly token) your words. I'm sorry: If you understand me when I utter 'George Bush is a goddamn demagogue' and think to yourself 'How true, how true', you too think that Bush is a goddamn demagogue, whether you are willing to blaspheme or not.

says or thinks is the same as what another person does. For that matter, whether a thought is true or false can be as much a matter of the context in which it is asked *Is that true?* as it is of how things are independently of the asking. So, at any rate, shall I argue.

1.1

A slur and its 'neutral counterpart' have, as we might put it, the same tar-gets—they are applied to exactly the same objects. But perhaps the slur is not *true* of targets.

How could this be? The meaning of a slur, like that of any word, depends on how it is used. A slur is a device which is used to express contempt for, to deride, and to insult its targets. It is mutual knowledge among speakers that slurs have such a use. Now while we expect that the nature and details of the negative attitudes expressed vary across the users of slurs, there is arguably rough uniformity in attitudes among those users. And so there is arguably a relatively small number of things normally conveyed by a slur's use, from which anyone who understands the slur will tend to draw its interpretation. I venture that most adults if they were asked about the attitude of a person who slurs African-Americans would come up with pretty much the same simple list: such a person despises or hates African-Americans because of their race, or believes that they are inferior because of their race.

This, one might propose, imbues slurs with a descriptive meaning beyond whatever descriptive meaning they have in virtue of applying to their target class. When the use of a slur is a conventional expression of an attitude A towards an object, held because the object is F, the slur comes to mean something like *worthy of A because F*. Because it has this sort of connection with the expression of racial hostility, a slur directed towards African-Americans means, to a first, rough approximation, something like *black and despicable because of it*.[6] But of course no one is or even could be despicable because of their race or ethnicity. So, the partisan of this view concludes, while the slur has application conditions, nothing does or could satisfy them. The same sort of thing is true of other epithets used to belittle on the basis of race, ethnicity, religion, sexual orientation, etc. Call such a view *DS*, for *defective satisfaction conditions*.

One might object to DS that it is possible to use a slur without insulting, demeaning, or evincing a negative attitude towards its targets. This happens, for example, when the slur is appropriated by its targets. If the slur's meaning is

---

[6] It is no objection to such a view, in my opinion, to suggest that shades of meaning are being obliterated here, as Jennifer Hornsby (2001) seems to suggest of a kindred story. For one thing, the view gestured at in the text can accommodate differences in application conditions so long as such differences are underwritten by differences in mutual expectations.

preserved in the appropriation—in particular, if there is no change in meaning relevant to truth-conditions—the fact that the targets of a slur can and often do find ways to defuse it by adopting it seems to show that DS is wrong.

The objection is inconclusive, for it is not at all clear that, for example, 'queer' preserved its meaning upon appropriation by the gay community. Before appropriation, it was arguably *conventionally* used to express hostility and homophobia: a good dictionary would have marked it as derogatory. After appropriation, it was not—at least not by the appropriators—used to express hostility or homophobia. A good dictionary will today note that the word has a use which is not derogatory. There is a case to be made that in appropriation there was a meaning change.

In any event, the objection misses the point of the original worry about slurs and truth. Suppose illocutionary facts do not enter into meaning: that a word is used, even conventionally used, to insult or denigrate, let us momentarily suppose, is not a fact about a word's meaning, but 'simply about its use'. Suppose that the same is true of whatever 'expressive' properties a word might have, so that the fact that a word is used to exhibit or otherwise to give vent to an emotion or evaluation is 'pragmatic, not semantic'. (I do not think this is a sensible way to use 'meaning', but let this be granted for a paragraph.) If we grant this, we are well on the way to agreeing with the objector that there is nothing more to the meaning of a slur beyond what is common to the use of the bigot and the use of the appropriator. But one can *still* argue that when someone utters a sentence with a slur and intends thereby to insult, denigrate, or disvalue on the basis of group membership, what the sentence says is not truth-apt. For at issue is whether the illocutionary or the expressive have the power to trump the semantic, so that the fact that a sentence is used in a certain way changes the terms on which it can be evaluated. If we decide to slice meaning so that the illocutionary is not part of meaning—so that it is 'merely pragmatic'—we need to acknowledge the possibility that there might be a determinant of truth and falsity beyond what a sentence means and 'the way the world is'. To object to DS from the possibility of using a slur without its standard performative or evaluative baggage misses this point.

DS depends upon a sort of sociolinguistic hypothesis, that speakers expect that they can read the attitude of a slur's user simply off the fact that he uses it. That hypothesis might be true of some epochs but not of others. My limited sociolinguistic take is that in my country's recent past DS may *not* have been true of a great many slurs, including some pretty odious ones. Forty or so years ago it was not uncommon to hear people use slurs on the playground and at the dinner table. People—including people one would not have taken to have dislike or contempt for the targets of a slur—apparently thought little or nothing of telling jokes in which such slurs occurred. They would use them to talk about their target classes. It was not, I think, implausible that many users of slurs were not consciously invested in or committed to hatred, moral condemnation, or belief in the inferiority of the targets of slurs. Rather, the use of slurs reflected a complicated web of attitudes, including discomfort about or fear of what seemed pronounced physical and cultural differences, as well as a lamentable tendency to talk as others did.

I think people generally recognized that this was so—that is, they did not assume it was clear what attitudes to read off the fact (but only the fact) that someone used a racial or ethnic slur in conversation. I am *not* denying that many users of slurs were invested in hatred and contempt. Rather, I am questioning whether those who slurred were routinely conscious of such attitudes and whether there was a widespread presumption that whoever used slurs must have had such attitudes.[7]

So I'm suspicious of DS as a *general* explanation of our reluctance to ascribe truth to slurring speech. And there are other reasons to question it. For one thing, DS conjures satisfaction conditions out of illocutionary action in a somewhat puzzling way. Someone addressing an Anglo audience who uses a slur on Asians typically thereby denigrates and insults Asians. So much is clear. But why should we think that he *asserts* that they are inferior or worthy of contempt? After all, do I *assert* that you are a jerk, a loser, or worthy of contempt if I stick out my tongue or give you the finger? Do I, for that matter, *assert* that you are a jerk, a loser, or worthy of contempt if in frustration I yell at you 'Jerk!!! Loser!!!!'? Do I *assert* that a certain bicycle chain is an object of my frustration, or deserves to be cursed, if, after a half hour of being unable to tighten it properly, I remark 'BLANKETY BLANK PIECE OF **BLANK**'? Of course not. Why should we say anything different about slurs? What is obnoxious about a slur is what is typically *done* with it.

Furthermore, DS doesn't explain one of the most striking things about slurs, something they share with other devices of invective and insult. Slurs typically 'scope out': their use is insulting and denigrating even when they are embedded. If * is a slur on Jews, then uttering 'Bob didn't marry a *; he married a Baptist' is as offensive, and offensive for the same reasons, as is uttering 'Bob married a *': each sentence signals a negative evaluation of Jews. Almost any embedding of a sentence in which a slur is used is offensive; someone accused of anti-Semitism for uttering 'If Bob married a *, then so did Ted' cannot plead that he only said 'if'. It's not clear why this should be if the odium associated with such slurs is located in their satisfaction conditions. Indeed, if that was all there was to be said about the terms, then it should be perfectly all right to endorse such things as the last-mentioned conditional, for such sentences would be non-problematically true, having antecedents which couldn't be.[8]

---

[7] For some relevant discussion in the philosophical literature see Appiah (1990) and Garcia (1996). There are a number of books containing sometimes lengthy transcripts of conversations with 'ordinary people' from this era concerning their racial attitudes which give some sense of how easily slurs were used; see, e.g., Wellman (1977).

[8] Someone might suggest that we can explain our reticence to ascribe truth to claims made with slurs by supposing that the satisfaction conditions of slurs are vague. If slurs have vague satisfaction

1.2

In this regard slurs resemble expressions like descriptions and clefts. The use of a definite description *the F* signals an assumption that there is a unique F. The assumption 'scopes out', insofar as the description's use signals this assumption even when the description is inside a negation, a conditional, or a question. Likewise, for the cleft construction *It was X who F-ed* and the assumption that someone F'ed.

Descriptions and clefts not only signal speaker assumptions, they introduce conversational presuppositions. If I say 'It was Cheney who plotted to steal the oil', I signal my assumption that someone plotted to steal the oil. If no

conditions, presumably this is because, given a slur S, while it's true that S's satisfaction conditions are A or they are B or . . . or they are Z (for more or less non-vague conditions A through Z), it's not determinate that S's satisfaction conditions are A, and not determinate that they are B, and . . . not determinate that they are Z. One way to spell this out makes the indeterminacy one among conditions false of a slur's targets. So it would go if someone said that (a) it is indeterminate whether a slur on target T meant *inferior because of ethnicity T*, indeterminate whether the slur meant *worthy of contempt because X, Y, Z* (X, Y, Z being stereotypes of target T), indeterminate whether it meant *less pleasant to be around because of ethnicity T*, but (b) it is determinant that the slur means *inferior because of ethnicity T*, or it means *worthy of contempt because X, Y, Z*, or it means *less pleasant to be around because of ethnicity T*.

This view is liable to the two objections at the end of this section. The view is conjuring satisfaction conditions out of illocutionary acts just as much as more straightforward views which assign determinate satisfaction conditions to slurs; the view makes mysterious the fact that we find the denial of a claim made with a slur just as offensive as the claim itself. (For if it is determinate that sentence S means A or means B, and A and B are both definitely false, surely S is definitely false, too.)

Someone might say that it is not just vague *what* the satisfaction-conditions of slurs are, but vague *whether* anything satisfies them. If it is vague whether 'queer' as used by the homophobe means *homosexual* or means *contemptible because homosexual*, such a view would be true of 'queer'. This would presumably make a use of *He is queer* applied to a gay person truth-valueless (because it would be indeterminate whether it means the true *He is homosexual* or the false *He is contemptible because homosexual*), and it would make such a use of *He is not queer* also truth-valueless (this being indeterminate in meaning between the false *He is not homosexual* and the true *He is not contemptible because homosexual*).

There are at least three reasons to be unhappy with such a view. First of all, it leaves us with no explanation of why we resist ascribing truth to a wide range of claims made with slurs. One's reaction to the homophobe who says 'Sean isn't queer, but I think maybe Bob is' does not depend on the sexual orientation of Sean and Bob—but on the current view what is said would be true if Sean were not gay, but the speaker believed that perhaps Bob was. There is a use of 'real man' on which it (seems to) mean something like 'not gay'; one wants to say that the problem with 'Real men aren't queers' is the same problem we find in a sentence like 'He is queer'. But the former—at least on natural accounts of truth of vague talk—would turn out true on the current view. The second problem with this view is that it continues to conjure satisfaction conditions out of illocution. The third, and I think primary, problem with this view is that it misdiagnoses the (probably) genuine vagueness of slurs. It probably *is* vague what 'queer' means in the homophobe's mouth—there are any number of things which bring the homophobe to fear and dislike the gay person, and settling on one of these as 'the meaning of "queer"' obscures this. But the idea that the homophobe 'sort of means' nothing more with the term than 'homosexual' is surely wrong: the term, as the homophobe uses it, is *definitely* derogatory.

one objects, the assumption 'becomes part of the conversational record'. This means that subsequent conversation will be governed by the assumption that someone so plotted: I and my audience may use the claim as a premise in argument, a counterexample to others' assertions, etc. Perhaps slurs—at least in their core uses—not only signal negative assumptions on the part of the speaker, but—when no one objects to their use—introduce a negative presupposition about the slur's target into the conversational record.[9]

That the use of a slur signals the *speaker's* belief or assumption that a particular group deserves negative evaluation isn't enough to explain why we are loath to ascribe truth to a sentence in which it is used. A speaker's uttering 'I think Eastern Europeans are contemptible' signals such an assumption, but I will accept the utterance if I think the utterer sincere. But if a slur not only signals a speaker's assumption but makes it a conversational presupposition if no one objects, that explains the intuition with which we began. For when a presupposition we reject accompanies a sentence's use, we resist calling the sentence true. And if a slur presupposes that its target is contemptible because of race or ethnicity, it presupposes falsely.[10]

What is it for something to be presupposed? Let's follow Robert Stalnaker, and say that someone in a conversation presupposes claim p provided he assumes or believes—or at least is disposed to behave as if he assumes or believes—all the following: p; that other conversants assume or believe p; that conversants recognize that he is making these assumptions, or has these beliefs.[11] A conversational presupposition is something all the members of a conversation presuppose.

---

[9] If this is correct, slurs are *really* pernicious devices. For when all the members of a conversation presuppose p, it typically becomes mutual knowledge in the conversation that all presuppose it. So if my not objecting to your using a slur inscribes on the conversational record that its targets are contemptible, it inscribes on the record that I assume that they are contemptible. If slurs are devices for introducing presuppositions in the way that descriptions and clefts are, they are devices which through our silence make us complicit in the bigotry of others.

[10] Some say that when a sentence's use has a false presupposition, the use is neither true nor false. Others say that presupposition failure in and of itself does not cause a sentence use to lack truth-value. Since my conclusion will be that slurs don't trigger presuppositions to begin with, there is not much point in our wading into the waters of this dispute.

[11] Stalnaker (1974: 49–53). (The definition in the text is adapted from Stalnaker's definition of what it is for a *speaker* to presuppose p; the adaptation consists in replacing 'addressees' in Stalnaker's definition with 'conversants'.) The invocation of dispositions is to handle cases in which (for example) a speaker uses a description ('I can't be at the meeting; I have to pick up my wife's sister at the airport') realizing that the audience may not know or assume that it denotes, but expecting this to become part of the conversational record once he uses it. This sort of use is a central case of presupposition; Stalnaker suggests it can be captured by identifying presupposition with a *disposition* to behave in conversation as if the relevant beliefs or assumptions are present.

I myself am inclined to analyze these cases differently from Stalnaker. I would say that I do not presuppose *in the sense of presuppose for the purposes of the conversation* that I have a sister when I say out of the blue 'I must get my sister', but I will presuppose it after I have said it, provided no one objects; I will, in that case, also expect you to as well. If we say this about such cases, we can leave presupposition as a disjunctive attitude (belief or assumption), instead of identifying it with a disposition. This is relevant to the issues which n. 12 raises. Since these issues are something of a sidebar, I do not explore them here.

We should linger on the notion of assumption. Assumptions are assumptions for particular purposes, and 'assume' here is elliptical for something like 'assume for the purposes of a conversation'. We will assume or presuppose all sorts of things we do not believe, or even that we disbelieve. So it goes in proof by *reductio*, or in a conversation in which we humor someone's delusions. To assume p for conversational purposes doesn't require much, if anything, beyond being willing to let go remarks made by others which entail p, to allow p's use as a premise, and so on.

What we come to assume for conversational purposes we often assume automatically, without conscious fanfare. One just *does* assume (say) that there is a positive solution to the equation on p. 331, having read 'suppose the equation on page 331 has a positive solution'. No conscious decision is made, no bell audible to consciousness rings. Given the bloodless nature of assumption (its not involving belief), its ability to fly below consciousness, and its more or less automatic nature, one can't dismiss out of hand the idea that a slur's use might routinely inspire a negative assumption about its target.[12]

The idea we are pursuing is that slurs introduce negative presuppositions about their target into the conversational record when no one dissents. There are two ways to spell it out. One might first of all say that this is in fact the typical result of a slur's use: normally, an unchallenged use of a slur is followed by auditors presupposing something negative about the slur's targets. Call this hypothesis *DF* for de facto.

DF is surely false of contemporary uses of slurs addressed to their targets, or used with the knowledge that a target is in the audience. There is little reason that I can see to think that the target of a slur typically shares, or can be made to assume for conversational purposes, the negative attitude of someone bigoted towards him. This is not to say people are not sometimes bullied into 'accepting' an insulting remark or its presuppositions, nor that it isn't sometimes the wisest course for a slur's target to 'let it pass'. Rather, it's to say that a slur's target will not normally make negative assumptions about himself when slurred, and so DF is not even roughly true of 'second-person' uses of slurs.[13]

---

[12] Does the fact that I don't believe and could not be brought to believe that Hispanics are contemptible speak against the idea that when someone uses a slur on Hispanics in my presence I automatically assume that Hispanics are contemptible? Certainly we would need some argument that this is so. Assumption, as I have been trying to point out, is something which occurs in a mental area where non-deliberate behavior is rife. It is not clear that one's moral beliefs will have the power to prevent the sort of quasi-automatic effect which assumptions are. Perhaps they do, but if they do, this is a surprising fact for which we need evidence.

Relevant here, perhaps, is the fact that there is nothing wrong per se with assuming the claim that Hispanics are contemptible: If I assume this in order to perform a *reductio* on a racist's beliefs, I haven't done anything wrong. Whether an assumption is to be condemned turns in good part on *why* the assumption is made.

[13] Suppose we are in a historical era where bigots are in power and the mere sign of opposition on the part of the target will be dealt with harshly. Then most targets may well be disposed to behave as if they assumed that they were inferior when slurred, such behavior being the safest way

Is DF true of slurs not addressed to nor made in the presence of their targets? It depends upon the historical and cultural context. If prejudice is endemic, something like DF may well be true. But if we are looking to DF to explain *our* reluctance to ascribe truth to slurring talk, it must be true of current practice. This seems implausible to me. What can a speaker who uses a slur and is not challenged conclude, about whether he would be challenged if he were to start making derogatory assertions about the slur's target? This depends on the particular case. In *many* cases, people who might let a use of an epithet pass would not let the direct voicing of the attitudes underlying the epithet pass unchallenged. So the unchallenged use of a slur normally does not lead to our presupposing the user's attitudes towards the target.

A slur might not *in fact* introduce a negative presupposition, but still be something which is *supposed* to do so. A description of a slur's meaning would, on this view, mark it as a word which has this purpose, so that a competent speaker would know that if no one objects to a slur's use, the user and other conversants are entitled to assume that all presuppose something negative about the slur's targets. Call this hypothesis *DJ* for *de jure*.

I assume that most contemporary speakers don't want words with the properties that DJ ascribes to slurs. One wonders how there could be such words if most speakers don't want them. Suppose it is known that most people do not think group G contemptible, and known that people are not inhibited by fear from saying that they do not think this. Are you entitled to think that if you insult or belittle the members of G and I do not choose to call you on it, I am willing to let you do it again, that I would let you go on to voice claims about inferiority or the like, or that I share your contempt for G? Surely not. But then it is not clear how the sort of expectations necessary for DJ can be in place when prejudice is not widely shared.

As I see it, DJ misdiagnoses 'how slurs work'. Is it *the rule*, or at least a good rule of thumb, that someone who uses a slur is trying to slip an assumption into the conversational record? Surely not. A pretty good rule of thumb is that someone who is using these words is insulting and being hostile to their targets. But there is a rather large gap between doing that and putting something on the conversational record. If I yell 'Smuck!' at someone who cuts me off, or say 'That smuck who just cut me off should lose his license', I insult and evince hostility. Am I entitled to assume, if you don't say 'He's not a smuck', that you assume that

to behave. It seems to follow that in such a situation the use of a slur in the presence of a target would be followed by the target's presupposing that he was inferior.

This may seem odd, but I think it is the right result. To assume q for purpose P is to be prepared to allow q to play a particular role, that role depending upon P. For example, to assume that Iraq has a stockpile of WMDs for the purposes of charting public policy is to be prepared to take seriously reasoning about public policy whose premises imply that it is likely or certain that Iraq has stockpiled WMDs. To assume X for purposes of conversation is to be prepared to let people reason from X in conversation, not to challenge X, etc. And it is a fact that one *can* make people make pernicious assumptions for many purposes, conversational ones included, via intimidation.

the person in question is a smuck, or are hostile towards him? Surely not. One doesn't have a conversational obligation to demur, if one disagrees, from whatever slings and brickbats one's conversational partners performatively launch. (One may, of course, have some other obligation to demur.) In this regard, the 'content of an insult' is different from what is asserted and from a conventional presupposition. One *does* have a conversational obligation to demur from these if one disagrees. For if one does not, *they* go on the conversational record.

Slurs are not conventional means of inserting contemptuous attitudes into a conversation's record. They pattern with terms of insult and invective—'dweeb', 'smuck', and so on—when the latter are addressed to someone or used as insulting prefixes. If anything is conventional about a slur, it is that its third-person use gives vent to a malevolent attitude, its second-person use insults and denigrates.

1.3

Perhaps the intuition with which we began is wrong, and racial and ethnic slurs *are* true of their targets. Perhaps they are, as Alan Gibbard puts it, terms which combine

classification and attitude. . . where the local populations stem from different far parts of the world, classification by ancestry can be factual and descriptive, but, alas, the terms people use for this are often denigrating. Nonracists can recognize things people say as truths objectionably couched.[14]

I dismissed this idea at the start of this discussion. But perhaps it deserves another hearing if appeal to satisfaction conditions and presupposition failure are unable to explain how the sentences we have been considering can fail to be true.[15]

The idea of a concept which combines 'classification and attitude' is of course Bernard Williams's idea of a 'thick concept', a concept whose application is 'determined by what the world is like. . . [and] usually involves a certain valuation'.[16] Canonical examples are terms for virtues, vices, and sins. Since the

---

[14] Gibbard (2003a: 300). I should mention that what I have elided here is the claim 'Racial epithets may sometimes work this way'.

[15] At this point the philosopher of language is thinking—Aha, now comes the discussion of the idea that while utterance of *He is an S* will be true, if aimed at a target of the slur S, there is a 'pragmatic' explanation of why we reject such utterances. As the savvy philosopher of language knows, such explanations usually invoke some broadly Gricean mechanism, holding that (a) the utterance suggests or conveys (but doesn't 'strictly and literally say') some claim which (b) we take to be false, while (c) we are so intent on rejecting this claim that we don't differentiate rejecting it from rejecting what the sentence 'strictly and literally says'.

I *will* discuss this idea, but only at the end of the chapter. My reason for deferring discussion is that it is hard to see what is wrong with this explanation unless and until we have the right explanation—which the next sections attempt to sketch—on the table.

[16] Williams (1985: 129).

application of such terms is determined by what the world is like, Williams says, they can be true of what they are applied to. So, to fix on an example, when Augustine said that his early life was unchaste, he spoke truly, his command of the criteria of chastity being after all impeccable.

Gibbard thinks that Williams is wrong about concepts like chastity—they are not true or false of anything—but that he is right about the concepts expressed by racial slurs. What, exactly, is the difference? Gibbard tells us that '[i]f how people classify with a thick term depends on their attitudes and their attitudes are faulty for their situation, then they do not get it right or wrong with their classifications'.[17] According to Gibbard, poor Augustine's classification of his behavior as unchaste depended on his 'faulty attitude', and so he can't be credited with speaking the truth. What exactly it would be for a classification to depend on an attitude, faulty or otherwise, is something to which I will return below. For the moment, though, let us concentrate on the idea that when a slur on Jews is used by an anti-Semite, the attitude expressed is faulty, but the classification made does not depend on the adjoined attitude. The *classification*, after all, could be pulled off with the word 'Jew'. So, Gibbard thinks, sentences using the slur can be true though 'objectionably couched'.

Gibbard's picture seems to be something like this. There are certain things— classifications, let us call them—which people make when they speak or think. At least some of the time, classification can be separated from the way in which it is made: the anti-Semite and the rabbi make the *same* classification when one uses the slur and the other speaks of the Jews. Classification, however it is made, is necessary and sufficient for the question of truth to arise: when and only when a classification is made, do we have something which—issues of vagueness put to the side—is true or false.[18]

I think this is a bad picture. I take it that what is in the first instance true or false are the things we think and say, the things with which we are concerned when we remark that X said *that A*, or Y thinks *that B*. When we think or say something which is true (or false), we do indeed classify. But classification (in the sense of the last paragraph) is to be explained in terms of the concepts or 'ways of thinking' which we employ when we think and say things. It is *because* the anti-Semite thinks of someone in a particular way when he slurs him, *because* we think of a person in another way when we think of him as a Jew, and because these two *different* ways of thinking of a person are related in certain ways, that we are entitled to say that there is a

---

[17] Gibbard (2003*a*: 302).

[18] This is oversimplified. There is classification in the command *Take out the trash!*, but the command is not a truth bearer. What I mean to ascribe to Gibbard is the idea that simply to classify is—vagueness aside—to do something which is either true or false.

It sounds a bit odd, I suppose, to say that someone like Augustine doesn't manage to classify behavior when he calls it chaste. This *is* however, Gibbard's view: 'if we reject Augustine's concepts, we cannot coherently credit him with achieving classification' (Gibbard 2003*a*: 298).

sense of classifying in which the anti-Semite and we are making use of the same classification.[19]

There are obviously significant similarities between thinking of someone as a Jew and thinking of him in the slurring way the anti-Semite does. In an important sense, the application of each concept is guided by the world in the same way. There is a kind of mistake which one makes if one applies either way of thinking to a non-Jew; there is a kind of success, complimentary to the mistake, which one achieves if one applies either to a Jew. 'Classification' is a good name for the activity liable to such successes and failures. Classification so understood is a prerequisite for truth, since what involves no classification is no candidate for truth.

But why think, as Gibbard does, that classification is *sufficient* for truth or falsity? The classification itself is a bloodless thing, something that cannot be identified with thinking of an individual as a Jew, or as the slurring anti-Semite does, for the classification is something made when one thinks of someone in either of these ways. Whatever truth belongs to a classification is truth it inherited from the thought expressed in making it.[20] To point out that the anti-Semite is 'classifying' correctly—and remember that 'classify' here is a *technical* term, one which is not synonymous with everyday terms like 'think of' and 'conceptualize'—seems no more relevant to the question of whether he has said something true than does the fact that the anti-Semite has successfully targeted his prejudice.

1.4

But why *not* allow the thought expressed in uttering *He is a* * to be true, when the individual classified is a target of the slur *? Well, to say that a thought is true is, *inter alia*, to approve of it, to endorse it: if I say your thought is true, I am saying that you are representing the world aright. To say that your thought is true is to endorse it *as* representing the world correctly. But when the anti-Semite thinks slurringly of Jews, he is not representing the world aright. We cannot approve of representing or thinking of people in the way in which he does, for we would approve of thinking of people as inferior merely because of their religion. It is wrong to represent anyone in that way.

---

[19] Why say these are different ways of thinking of someone? Because to think that Jews observe the sabbath on Saturday is not, automatically, to think that *s do so. But if the two ways of thinking were the same, to think the one would be to think the other. Remarks below about individuating what is said are, of course, relevant to this argument.

[20] This way of speaking may make it sound as if the point depends upon reifying what is said. I don't think this is so. I believe the argument here is just as good (or just as bad . . .) if we begin by insisting that it is particular uses of sentences (and particular mental states) which are in the first instance true or false.

I just suggested that we cannot endorse the anti-Semite's slurring performance as true, as it involves misrepresentation. Do not infer that I therefore think we must pronounce it false. To say that the anti-Semite's claim, that *s do not observe Lent, is false is to say that he made a particular kind of error, a kind of error which can be corrected *merely* by adjusting the way he classified or quantified, or by judicious use of negation. But this is not the case. If it were, we could fix the problem which prevents us from ascribing truth to

(B) If Bob married a *, then so did Ted.

by correcting the speaker along the following lines: Well, that's false, for Bob did marry a *, but Ted did not. The kind of error—the kind of misrepresentation—involved when one thinks of someone in slurring fashion is not the sort of error which can be corrected merely by reclassifying. Sometimes—this is one of those times—someone may represent the world but, because of the kind of representation employed, truth and falsity are simply the wrong terms in which to evaluate the representation. We do not reject (B) because it is false, but because it involves a way of thinking of Jews that is just not a way that one can think accurately about them. Negating (B) is not enough, for thinking (what's said by) (B) negated is *still* thinking of Jews in an odious, inaccurate way.

Some will find my way of looking at thought and representation curious: How can it be that a thought represents things as being *so* (things contain a group despicable because of ethnicity), and the (truth-functional) *denial* of that thought represents things as being the same way? But surely it's not at all mysterious that this sort of thing might happen. We all accept the idea that a claim and its negation may both involve commitment to a representation's being accurate—this is just the sort of thing that happens when a claim carries a presupposition, for a claim's presuppositions project to its negations. For the reasons given in Section 1.2, saying that the (mis)representation involved in thinking that *s are F, or in thinking that *s aren't F, is a presupposition (in the semanticist's somewhat technical sense of 'presupposition') seems wrong. Still, quite clearly, when one uses a slur, over or under a negation sign, one *is* thinking of the word's targets in a negative way.

Some will find my way of looking at thought and representation curious: How can it be that there is a *representation* that is in no (relevant) way vague, but is neither true nor false of its target? Given a representation—*Things are thus and so*—mustn't we always be able to ask, Are things like that, or are they not? And unless vagueness (or the problems attending liar sentences) intervenes, mustn't there be an answer to this? But the answer to this question determines whether the representation is true (as things are as it represents) or false (as they are not).

There are two things to say in response to this, though they are things that it will take most of this book to spell out.

First, we can agree that whenever we have representation we can ask whether the representation is accurate and expect that there is an answer. We can do this even when the representation is vague. We can say of the borderline case of baldness that he is not bald (denying the claim that he is bald) and that he is not not bald either (denying the negation of this claim). To say that we can coherently deny a claim and its negation presupposes that denial is a *sui generis* speech act, not to be identified with the assertion of a negation (or any other assertion), the denial of a claim being appropriate when the claim is not true—when it is false or without truth-value. As we will see in the next chapter, there are compelling reasons for thinking of denial in this way. Given that we can deny both p and its negation when p is without truth-value, this is just what we should do with the representations involved when one person says that all *s are Fs, and his companion says, no, at least one * isn't F. We should reject both of these claims, just as we should reject both the claim that Jo is bald, and the claim that Jo is not bald, when Jo is a borderline case of baldness.

The second thing to be said here is that there are good reasons, quite independent of our current worries about epithets, to think that some representations are not to be evaluated in terms of truth and falsity. As I will argue in Chapter 5, the natural way of thinking about claims, that various activities are cool, people attractive, or foods disgusting, is to understand them as not being candidates for truth or falsity, not even relative truth or falsity. We may just disagree about whether Johnny Depp is good-looking: you think he is, I think he's not. In such a case, though we really disagree, neither of us need be making a mistake. But then, though I *represent* Depp as not attractive, and you *represent* him otherwise, our representations aren't true or false. They can't be, for if they were, at least one of us would be making a mistake.[21]

I will be accused of punning in the last few paragraphs on 'wrong' and 'incorrect'. It might be morally wrong, someone will say, for the anti-Semite to think or say that X is a *; it does not follow that it is not true that he is a *. There are two sorts of normativity at issue, moral and semantic. Now I agree that saying that it is morally wrong to think p is not saying that thinking p is misrepresenting the world (and thus not thinking anything true). These are different kinds of normativity and I am not (at least I think I am not) confusing them. What I am claiming is that to think of someone as the anti-Semite does *is* to misrepresent them in a way that deprives what is said of truth.

When the anti-Semite thinks of someone in his anti-Semitic way, he thinks in a way that expresses, that vents his negative attitude towards Jews, and thereby shows contempt for and denigrates them. To *do* these things is to misrepresent Jews. It is to misrepresent them not because one is using a word that means something like *contemptible because Jewish*. Rather, it is to misrepresent Jews because one is doing certain things—e.g. expressing negative attitudes and

---

[21] I stress that the material in the last two paragraphs is not intended as a full response to the worry that preceded them; it is instead an indication of how Chapters 2 through 5 will develop a view responsive to that worry.

contempt elicited by religion—the doing of which is one way to represent Jews as worthy of contempt. To have or display contempt for someone, to think badly of them by having such contempt, *is* to think of them, to represent them, as worthy of contempt.[22]

I imagine some will deny that there could be a genuinely *representational* fact whose explanation depends upon pointing to an evaluative or affective component in someone's way of thinking about an object or property. Whenever a thought is *about Z* or a concept is *true of Z*, it will be objected, there is an explanation of this that makes no use of the evaluative or the affective. And if so, it will be said, I am wrong to say that just to perform, to evaluate, or to have an affective reaction is thereby to represent.

I think this objection is just wrong. Suppose that a certain scenario—invading Iran, say, to root out its stockpiles of WMDs—causes me to be afraid every time it is mentioned. It is not that I think 'Ooooh, that's SCARY'. Rather, there is something about the mere mention of it that makes me afraid for myself and my children. It *could* be, of course, that I subconsciously cognize the proposition that the scenario is frightening. But there is no reason to suppose that this will often, or even typically, be the case. Does the pogonophobe reason his way to his phobia by thinking 'How do beards frighten me? Let me count the ways . . .'? Of course not.

Whatever the mechanism of my fear, that I have this reaction to the scenario in itself means that I *represent* it as frightening. Note, in support of this, that we typically treat such fear—as well as phobias—in the way we treat all representations: as subject to criticism (or congratulations) for irrationality (or for the recognition of genuine danger). The upshot, as I see it, is that there is nothing confused in thinking that the affective is responsible for representational properties. And I do not see why we should say anything different about the evaluative or performative. That someone thinks, evincing contempt, **s are different from us* means that the person *represents* the people he is thinking about as contemptible. To evaluate someone or to display value-laden emotion towards him *is* to represent him in a certain way.

---

[22] There are some subtle issues here concerning acts and attitudes. Suppose that Smith has a belief he expresses so:

*s don't observe the sabbath on Sunday.

He may have this belief even when he is not expressing it or consciously entertaining it. When he is not expressing or entertaining the belief, he is not *displaying* contempt for anyone. But the belief, even when not being expressed or entertained, presumably involves the same way of thinking of Jews as it does when it is expressed. Is it, then, a mistake to say that the relevant way of thinking involves *expressing* contempt?

It is still true that Smith is contemptuous of Jews, even when he is asleep. The way he represents them (even while asleep) is a way of representing them which represents them as contemptible; to have a belief such as this is to have contempt for the Jews. So long as this is accepted, the points in the text are correct, even if we are loath to say that a way of thinking itself expresses an attitude.

1.5

I will be accused of a conceptual confusion. It is one thing, it will be said, to represent someone as being thus and so; it is a different thing to have or show contempt for him or to evaluate him, positively or negatively. The contempt or the evaluation may, of course, be based on a representation. I may evaluate you negatively or be contemptuous of you because I represent you as a Republican and disvalue all that is Republican. But the evaluation and contempt are distinct from the representation. Likewise, the *representation* involved in thinking of someone as does the anti-Semite has nothing to do with—that is, is completely separate from—whatever evaluation or performance may accompany it. The story I just told, however, crucially depends on the idea that to make an evaluation, to have or to express contempt, is (in part) to represent someone in a certain way. So, anyway, might someone object.

I want to concede something to this objection. Not that I am confused, conceptually or otherwise, but that when we consider a way of thinking which involves an evaluative outlook, it is usually—perhaps always—possible to separate the evaluation involved in the way of thinking from the classification involved in it. This is obvious for ways of thinking associated with slurs and epithets. Every slur, so far as I can tell, has or could have a 'neutral counterpart' which co-classifies but is free of the slur's evaluative dimension. Presently I will argue that something similar is true of thick terms in general.

Of course the objector will not be satisfied with *this* concession. According to the objector, the anti-Semite's negative attitude towards Jews is contingently conjoined with the way he thinks of Jews when he thinks of them slurringly. So the thought he has, when he thinks that *s do not observe Lent, can be separated from the negative attitude. To my mind, it is an embarrassment for this more or less Humean picture that it is apparently committed to saying that there is 'nothing negative' in the way of thinking of Jews involved in the anti-Semite's thought. For if the thought is independent of the negative attitude, it must be possible to think the thought without having the attitude.

There is something odd about the objection, that since affect and categorization are clearly separable in the case of slurs, affect does not help individuate the beliefs expressed with slurs. The conclusion just doesn't follow from the premise. Why should the fact that an evaluation is a 'separate existence' from a categorization show that the two can't go together to make up a single entity? Does the fact that one can think of Aristotle as the author of the *Metaphysics* without thinking of him as the author of the *Nicomachean Ethics* (and vice versa) show that the sense of the name 'Aristotle' for a particular individual could not be given by 'the author of the *Metaphysics* and the author of the *Nicomachean Ethics*'?

All this raises the question, What makes it the case that a certain way of thinking, of an individual or an attribute, is constituted by a certain set of components? When one reads Frege one walks away with a picture of ways of thinking as tidy, sound-bite sized packets of information, neatly roped off from the mass of one's beliefs: this man thinks of Aristotle as *the teacher of Alexander the Great who wrote the* Metaphysics, that woman thinks of him as *the unobservant Greek philosopher who had the temerity to write that women had fewer teeth than men.* Surely our mental landscape is not cleanly segregated into discrete packets of sense. The information we take to be information about a single individual is (presumably) a vast jumble, not necessarily sorted in terms of importance or likelihood of accuracy. There are few, perhaps no, connections among 'pieces of representation' which would make this aspect of a representation of an individual connect analytically with that aspect. Furthermore, our reaction to and mental take on an individual or attribute will almost always mix together description, affect, wish, expectation, and so on.

We do, of course, think about, compare, and identify the beliefs of different people. And the way we do this is often best understood by individuating beliefs in terms of those small, sound-bite-sized ways of thinking to which I just alluded. But when we do this, *we* are imposing order on the jumble of the mental landscape. When we look at others and ask ourselves if they share our beliefs, we make—we must make—choices, dependent on our interests and situation, about whether another thinks of a particular individual as do we, and thus about when the mentality of the other contains a belief contained within our own.

There is, I think, great plausibility in the idea that our practices of identifying beliefs and other attitudes across people rely in part on such more or less one-off identifications of ways of thinking across thinkers.[23] And it is also plausible that when we ask what someone else said, or whether we agree with what they think, we often (but not invariably) individuate and identify in ways which effectively insert into sense—insert into the thought—the evaluations, conatus, and feelings we and others have towards objects and activities. My point is not theoretical or normative, but descriptive. It is made by thinking about cases.

Consider those two renowned experts on sin, Pope Paul VI and Simon Blackburn. Those who have been titillated by Blackburn's recent celebration of carnality know that he will have none of the prudishness, shame, and haughty condemnation of sensuality which exemplifies the attitude of the author of *Of Human Life.* When he wrote that encyclical, the Pope was well aware of the sexual landscape of the sixties. He was appalled. He condemned the behavior of the time—he said it was lustful. Is this something with which Blackburn agrees? The Blackburn, who writes of orgasm

---

[23] I have argued elsewhere for this—e.g. in Richard (1990: ch. 3).

it is as close to ecstasy—to standing outside ourselves—as many of us get . . . it fills our mental horizon . . . This abandonment deserves more than a moment's attention. It is a good thing if the earth moves.[24]

Of course Blackburn does not think these things are lustful.

My description of the views of the professor and the prelate are, I think, perfectly natural. I expect that you will find the description natural even if you happen to know that the title of Blackburn's book is *Lust*, and that the book is a celebration of, and extended argument with the Christian tradition over, that for which it is named. And, as a matter of fact, if one looks at the way the Church and the don define the subject, it is pretty clear that they are talking about exactly the same thing. Blackburn takes lust to be

the enthusiastic desire, the desire that infuses the body, for sexual activity and its pleasures for their own sake[25]

The Church posts the following definition on the web:

Lust is disordered desire for or inordinate enjoyment of sexual pleasure. Sexual pleasure is morally disordered when sought for itself, isolated from its procreative and unitive purposes.[26]

Both Blackburn and the Church think that the behavior I alluded to before was lustful; what they differ on is whether this is a reason to condemn it.

Wait! Didn't I say before that we can say that Blackburn and Pope Paul VI disagreed about whether the activity was lustful? Indeed. We can say that. And we can say that they agreed that it was lustful—just not in the same breath. In some cases, for some purposes, we individuate concepts and beliefs so that they incorporate affective attitudes. In other cases, for other purposes, we individuate concepts and beliefs so that they do not incorporate the affective. When we individuate in the first way, we say that people whose evaluations differ as do Simon and Paul's disagree about whether a certain behavior is lustful. When we do not, we do not.

1.6

I have suggested that the identity of concepts is to an extent constructed by us. It is determined 'in the context of the observer' whether the evaluative attitude annexed to the racist's use of a slur is a 'part of' the concept expressed by the slur. To say this is *not* to say that it is a matter in which, in typical situations, we have a choice. It is, rather, to say that it is facts about our interests and

---

[24] Blackburn (2004: 24–5).   [25] Ibid. 19.
[26] <http://www.Vatican.va/cathecism> sect. 2351.

relations—conversational, social, and so on—which control how we may or must individuate the concepts of others in thinking about their beliefs.

If I am right about this, one expects—*I* expect, at any rate—that given the right conversational or historical situation, it will be possible to detach the evaluative component from a thick concept. And if that is right, then one expects that no matter how closely a thick concept is currently associated with a certain evaluative attitude, it is in principle possible for someone to use the concept to categorize things without having the evaluative attitude towards what is classified. One can always, if you like, perform the sort of divorce Blackburn performs in wresting lust from Christian condemnation.

It has been said that the evaluative component of at least some thick concepts cannot be detached from them. Of thick concepts in general, Williams writes:

How we 'go on' from one application of a concept to another is a function of the kind of interest that the concept represents, and we should not assume that we could see how people 'go on' if we did not share the evaluative perspective in which [a thick] . . . concept has its point. An insightful observer can indeed come to understand and anticipate the use of the concept without actually sharing the values of the people who use it. . . . But in imaginatively anticipating . . . the observer also has to grasp imaginatively its evaluative point.[27]

Gibbard seems to concur—he thinks, for example, that Augustine's classifications 'depend on his attitude'. McDowell has on occasion suggested that many thick concepts apply to objects in virtue of those objects meriting a particular affective reaction. If this is so, then presumably creatures who do not have the relevant affective reaction to at least some of the right objects could not have the concept, somewhat as someone blind from birth could not have the concept of pumpkin orange.[28]

It is reasonable to think that if Williams et al. are right, I am wrong. For suppose that applying a concept to an object required taking a certain evaluative viewpoint. There would then be a strong case for saying that the relevant evaluation was essential to the concept. And this seems to be what Williams, Gibbard, and McDowell have in mind. They think, roughly put, that to think of something as chaste one must see it as good because it reflects a certain set of values. If this is so, then it is not 'up to us' as to whether a positive evaluation

---

[27] Williams (1985: 141–2).

[28] For McDowell's views see the essays in part II of McDowell (1998).

Some will object to McDowell and Williams that we may acquire concepts by being members of linguistic communities whose members already have the concepts, another's word being as good as his concept. I am not sure what either would say to this: perhaps they would draw a distinction between 'parasitic' and non-parasitic concept possession, with the former sort of concept possession being said to be of little interest; perhaps they would distinguish being in a position to echo others' words and being able to think their thoughts.

My reservations about Williams's and McDowell's views do not rely on the idea that concepts, like colds and other viral scourges, are spread orally.

should be annexed to a mental structure which we describe as a person's concept of chastity.

I have two comments. First of all, I think it is worth insisting on something which Williams at least seems to have quite clearly seen: *Any* ethical or moral perspective is liable to criticism, even very radical criticism, 'from the inside'. That is: No matter what coherent cluster of thick terms someone might begin with, it seems possible that one might (coherently) come to doubt that the evaluations associated with those terms were proper. Suppose that one could not acquire the concepts of lustfulness, modesty, chastity, and the like without occupying something like the Christian perspective with regard to sex. (I tend to doubt this, but let it pass for the second.) We can certainly imagine someone acquiring these concepts and then thinking that in applying them they were misevaluating. Imagine that Augustine underwent a second conversion, to a way of looking at the world on which the fact that an act manifested lust was not a reason to condemn it, that an act or trait evinced a dedication to not being sexually provocative was not a reason to praise it. Augustine being Augustine, we can imagine that he would try to bring as many of the benighted as he could into his new perspective. The obvious way to do this would be to try to convince them that they were making mistakes in evaluation: that the fact that an act was lustful was not, in and of itself, a reason to condemn it; the fact that an act was chaste was not, in and of itself, a reason to praise it. Surely Augustine could say this sincerely, meaning to and succeeding in contradicting what Catholics thought, when they thought that something's being lustful (or chaste) was a reason to condemn (or praise) it. And in doing this he would not be saying anything incoherent or self-contradictory: it just wouldn't be responsive to Augustine to insist that he was laboring under a 'conceptual confusion'.[29]

---

[29] I suppose I owe some account of what an 'evaluative perspective' is. As I understand the notion, an evaluative perspective is a complex of classificatory and evaluative dispositions, the sort of thing which is constituted by dispositions such as the dispositions to:

classify an act as unchaste if it is sexually provocative and such that a normal person would know that is sexually provocative;
classify an act as lustful if it makes manifest a desire for sexual pleasure ('for its own sake');
condemn an act if it is believed to be either unchaste or lustful.

(Actually, what I intend is to identify evaluative perspectives with functional states which are defined by 'Ramsifying' on (the names of the thick terms in) collections of disposition descriptions like those displayed in the text.) Such perspectives are, of course, vague affairs, and I assume that if we thought it necessary to flesh out the notion, we would do it in a way that allowed people to share an evaluative perspective when there was sufficient overlap between their dispositions to deploy thick terms. The evaluative perspectives we actually find occupied by humans will usually provide some necessary and some sufficient conditions for applying their thick terms; real examples will probably rarely if ever supply necessary and sufficient conditions. I shall assume, along with Williams, Gibbard, and McDowell, that we understand what it is to 'imaginatively participate' in such a perspective without actually having the dispositions which constitute it. There is, I suspect, no one way in which one might do this—one might feel moved in the way those who occupy the perspective are moved, but intellectually distance one's self from it; one might have a combination of dry intellectual appreciation for what the perspective requires along with a motivational echo of

I see the moral here as this: No (thick) concept is immune from being used by someone who has dropped its evaluative trappings, in the way Blackburn has abandoned disvaluing lustfulness and Augustine in our toy example has abandoned valuing chastity. And since *we* can describe what would be happening in such a situation, *we* can correctly identify a conceptual structure as realizing a certain thick concept *without* making it essential, for a structure's realizing the concept, that it involve any particular evaluative attitude. For we can say, as I just did, that someone like Augustine would *not* be laboring under a conceptual confusion in saying what he said about lust.

I promised two comments on the idea that a particular evaluation might be somehow essential to a particular thick concept. Here is the second. It seems to me that conceptual identity can be in part a matter of conceptual history and social relations. Whether, for example, a certain concept I now exercise is the same concept that Thomas Aquinas exercised three-quarters of a millennium ago is determined in part by contingent historical relations between his mental life and mine. It seems to me, furthermore, that sometimes a concept can be misapplied, even in what seem to be central cases, for a very long time before we come to see how it is to be correctly applied.

Now if one puts these facts together, it is puzzling why someone would hold the blanket (almost a priori) view that a thick concept's evaluative component is in some interesting sense essential to it. We can, after all, make dramatic mistakes in applying our concepts. We can begin by misapplying them, misled by demagogues, wishful thinking, or plain bad theory, and then come to get it more or less right. Or we can begin by applying it aright, and then get it wrong. Why should this be so only with regard to the 'descriptive' parts of our concepts? We think—I think, anyway—that Thomas and Paul just had it wrong about lust. I think that Augustine just had it wrong about chastity. If I generally choose not to use the word 'chaste'—well, that is in part because it's not common in these parts to use 'chaste' in a neutral manner. But there is all the distance in the world between constant conjunction and essentiality.

1.7

I say that when someone slurs, what he says is not true, not false. I do not say that the slurring representation is to be denied truth-value simply because it is 'expressive' or performative. I think that sincere utterances of 'I promise to meet you' or 'I find the defendant guilty as charged' are first and foremost performances. But I have no animus against the idea that they may be true for all

the perspective; perhaps one can occupy a position via simulation, somewhat as the virtuous actor tries to occupy the mind of the evil character.

that. Rather, I deny slurring talk truth and falsity because to ascribe it such we must represent as does he who slurs, and to so represent is to represent wrongly.

One can represent 'performatively' or 'evaluatively' with invective milder than a slur and say something true. Consider 'asshole'. It would be an interesting exercise, no doubt, to try to spell out the meaning(s) of this word without using invective; I shall not try. We know well enough what it is for someone to be an asshole—there are plenty of them around, and all of us are occasionally assholes ourselves. Suppose that Smith is an asshole and he is at the door. If I say, referring to Smith, 'That asshole is at the door', I display contempt for Smith by calling him an asshole. *That* does not prevent what I say from being true.

Both 'asshole' and slurs are devices used to display contempt for people in virtue of their possessing certain properties.[30] The difference between the terms is that there is nothing intrinsically misrepresenting about the reaction voiced by 'asshole': the way assholes behave merits contempt. To represent an asshole as an asshole is to represent things as they are.[31]

There are, of course, a variety of epithets, and a variety of sorts of uses of epithets. What we should say about a use of an epithet will vary from case to case. Suppose, for example, that Farmer Bob says, referring to his horse, 'I've had that nag there for ten years'. Suppose he has had the horse for ten years, and that the horse has done nothing to merit his contempt. Are we to say that Farmer Bob does not say something true?[32]

It depends. One might, after all, say—as my dictionary seems to say—that 'nag' has a use on which it is synonymous with 'old, inferior, or worthless horse'.[33] Then if Bob's comment is simply an assertion, with no performative element, it's false.[34] If Farmer Bob made jocular use of 'nag', as we make jocular use of 'son of a bitch' when we use it to refer to a friend, then the remark is true. In any case, there is reason to think that Bob's utterance is truth-valueless only if Bob is expressing (unfounded) contempt. And if he is, well then he *is* misrepresenting the horse, isn't he? If one thinks of the horse in the way he is thinking of it, one misrepresents it, in expressing unfounded contempt. And then the argument of previous sections seems to apply.

I say that when the bigot slurs, what he says is not true, not false. But is that always the case? When the bigot slurs and is sincere, he says something, he expresses something he believes. Suppose the bigot, suspecting that the person he sees in front of him is classified by the slur *, says 'Well, I believe that he, Smith, is a *'. He says he believes that Smith is a *; he does indeed believe it. So isn't

---

[30] One could debate this. It is probably somewhat vague (indeed, somewhat variable across users and uses) what attitudes and evaluations are being expressed with 'asshole'. That doesn't effect the root point here.

[31] The last two paragraphs are in response to queries by Jim Higginbotham.

[32] Tim Williamson asked essentially this question.

[33] *Random House Dictionary of the English Language*, college edition.

[34] I assume that ten years old isn't old for a horse.

what he says true? But if it is, then it can't in general be that when someone slurs in saying something, what they say is not true. But if this is not in general so, why suppose it is in the cases discussed earlier in this chapter? The reasoning before was that what was said, since it employed slurring, involved a misrepresentation which deprived it of truth. Why wouldn't the same misrepresentation, and ensuing lack of truth, occur in the present case as well?[35]

Call the speaker *B*. We might ask three questions about B's utterance of 'I believe that Smith is a *':

1. Does B believe *that* [namely, what B says with 'Smith is a *']?
2. Does B believe that Smith is a *?
3. Does B speak truly, when he says 'I believe that Smith is a *'?

I agreed that B believes what he says he believes; the answer to (1) is 'yes'. I have granted that B believes what he says; what B says is that Smith is a *. I'm willing to infer that B believes that Smith is a *, answering (2) affirmatively. But then, since B said that he believed that Smith is a * and that's true, B spoke truly, right?

No. It is perfectly possible that when *we* say 'B thinks that Smith is a *' we speak truly, even if B does not speak truly when *he* says 'I believe that Smith is a *'. For, as we observed at the beginning of this chapter, it *is* possible to use an epithet without slurring. Attitude reports appear to be one place where this is possible, even for those who are not in a position to publicly appropriate a slur's use. Given that B slurs and I do not, and that whether one slurs affects the identity of what is said, it follows that B and I do not express precisely the same thought with our uses of 'Smith is a *' in this case. Likewise, it is possible that (niceties about the difference between B's use of 'I' and our use of 'B' to the side) the thought B expresses with 'I think that Smith is a *' is not precisely the thought that we express with 'B thinks that Smith is a *'. It is not as if in answering (1) and (2) affirmatively and (3) negatively we are committed to saying that some thought is true and not true.

There is an obvious difference between my thinking what I think and B's saying and thinking what he thinks: I do not slur (and thereby misrepresent) Smith; B does. If we take the performative and expressive aspects of an utterance to enter into the individuation of what the utterance says—and the burden of the last sections has been that we often can, even *must*, do this—this means that we need not, must not, *identify* what B says, in his slurring performance, with what we think to ourselves when we homophonically translate it. So even if we are correct to think that B believes what he says—correct to think that B thinks that Smith is a *—it doesn't follow that B's slurring performance is something we need approve by giving it the dignity of 'truth objectionably couched'.

One has a strong intuition that B is expressing a belief that he has, when he utters 'I think that Smith is a *', and thus that it must be true that B thinks that

---

[35] This objection comes from Scott Soames.

Smith is a *. I think this intuition is veridical. What is wrong is the—admittedly quite natural—move from this intuition to the conclusion that when B speaks, he speaks truly. As I see it, we make the move because we have been taught, when thinking about matters of truth, to prise away any performative or expressive aspect of the utterance (indeed, of the thought) we are evaluating. But this, I think, is a mistake. If we could only regain our pre-Fregean semantic innocence, we would, I think, find it plainly incredible, that it is irrelevant to which way of thinking is associated with a word's use whether that use expresses contempt. If we accept that B and we are expressing different ways of thinking of Smith with *, we should be ready to accept that the 'truth status' of a sentence in which * occurs may differ, when we use it and when B does.[36]

I say that sentence uses in which the user slurs say nothing true or false. One might complain that the cost of saying this is too high. Shall we, it will be asked, say that slurs have no extensions, or shall we instead say that the truism, that a sentence of the form *a is F* is true just if what *a* names is in the extension of *F* is not true? Shall we say that the anti-Semite who utters 'I promise to give back the money I took from the *s' cannot keep his promise (because to keep a promise to *V* requires that one makes true what's said by one *I will V*), or shall we instead tell a novel story about what it is to keep a promise? One worries that whatever we say, we will end up complicating or reformulating the semantic account of our language, replacing relatively simple accounts of reference, truth, promise keeping, and so on with more complicated ones. And this is a theoretical cost.[37]

There are several things to be said in response to this. The first is that it's not clear that the 'theoretical cost' incurred here is all that large. Is it, for example, all *that* great a complication in theory to say that when a term's use has a performative or evaluative dimension, we need to distinguish between the things of which it is true and the things to which linguistic conventions sanction its application? Is it all that great a complication to go on to say that if these two sets do not coincide—and so there is something defective about the relevant

---

[36] One might object to what I have said in the following way. You allow us to move from 'B uttered "Smith is a *" and believed what he said' to 'B believes that Smith is a *'. The inference is all right if the use of 'Smith is a *' under 'believes' in the conclusion says what it says when uttered by B. But your point here depends on *denying* that the sentence as used by B says what we say with it in indirect discourse.

In response: Forget slurs for the moment and think about proper names. If Thornton says 'Derrida naps', saying that Jacques Derrida naps, I can echo him and ascribe an assertion to him, saying 'Thornton says that Derrida naps'. This is so even if the 'ways of thinking' of Derrida that Thornton and I associate with the name 'Derrida' are *wildly* different; it is so even if Thornton's way of thinking of Derrida contains elements that I do not ascribe to Derrida and vice versa. The inference mentioned in the last paragraph does *not* depend upon ascriber and ascribee expressing *precisely* the same thing with the sentence used to express and ascribe; rather, it requires (putting things intuitively) that the ascribee's utterance on this occasion can be *translated* by the ascriber's utterance. For further discussion see Richard (1990: chs. 2, 3) and Richard (2006).

[37] Stephen Davis and Tim Williamson made remarks that suggest this sort of objection, though they are not responsible for the particular spin I have given it.

sentence uses—compliance with a promise or an order is to be explained in some way other than in terms of truth?

Secondly: while we of course don't want to needlessly complicate our theories, we also don't want them to be so simple-minded that they distort our picture of what we are theorizing about. The conclusion that what is said in slurring speech is neither true nor false comes rather directly from the everyday observation that to think what someone like B thinks, when he thinks that the person in front of him is a * or thinks that the person is not a *, is to think wrongly because it involves misplaced contempt and hostility. As I see it, we can avoid this conclusion only if we oversimplify the phenomena semantic theory is primarily about—thought and its expression—by artificially ignoring the performative and emotive dimensions of thought and talk when we theorize.

1.8

Those versed in the ways of analytic philosophy of language are perhaps puzzled by my failure to consider 'the most obvious' explanation of our reluctance to ascribe truth or falsity to what is said by slurring. This is an explanation in terms of one or another 'pragmatic' mechanism of the sort Paul Grice famously made us aware a half century ago. My excuse for deferring discussion of this is that my doubts about such explanations turn on what I think is the proper story to tell about slurring. That tale has been told, and it is time to take up the idea that the right account of the phenomena we've been discussing lies in pragmatics.

Grice's ideas presuppose a distinction between what a sentence's use says ('strictly and literally') and what it implies. The rough idea can be brought out by noting, with Grice, that (normally) to utter 'Bill produced sounds which closely matched the notes of "Sunday, Bloody Sunday"' implies, but does not *say*, that Bill sang 'Sunday, Bloody Sunday' poorly. According to Grice, what a sentence's use says is closely tied to the sentence's literal meaning; an important mark of the distinction is that an utterance might be true (false) when what is implied is false (true), but an utterance's truth-value must be the truth-value of what the utterance says. Not only did Grice provide this distinction; he offered an elaborate theory of how a sentence use might come to imply something it did not say.

Grice used the distinction and the accompanying theory to defend various accounts of the meaning of words that interest philosophers—the little words of logic ('or', 'if', 'all', etc.), 'know', 'true', and some others—against objections that the accounts predicted sentences in which the words occur to have truth-values that pretty much no one thought they had. The crux of the defense was to note that what is implied is often—perhaps most of the time—of much greater conversational moment than what is strictly speaking said. Thus, it is to be expected that we will focus on what is implied, not necessarily on what is said, in evaluating an utterance. An example: we tend to reject a conditional *If A then B* if we see no connection between the A and the B. Some have said that this shows that to assert a conditional is to assert *inter alia* a connection between its antecedent and consequent. This is contrary to what the logician teaches, that *If A then B* comes to no more or less than *Either not A or B*. Grice observed that we suppose (absent contrary evidence) that a speaker has reason to say whatever he says; but one has reason to assert *Either not A or B* only if one has some reason to think that A's being true in some way brings B's being true in its wake. Since it is manifest to speaker and hearer that one would assert the conditional only if one thought there was this sort of connection, asserting the conditional implies that A and B are so connected. Thus, the intuition that uttering *If A then B* conveys the existence of such a connection is just what we would expect *given* the logician's account of its meaning and the just-mentioned facts about conversation.

Thus goes the Cliffs Notes summary of Grice's 'Logic and Conversation'. What does all this have to do with epithets and attitudes? Well, someone might propose that when S is a slur and N is its neutral counterpart, *He is an S* is true just in case *He is an N* is true. But a use of the former sentence has an offensive implication, in Grice's sense of implication, on which we understandably fix. We are so concerned to reject it, the suggestion would be, that we miss the fact that the offensive implication is a by-product of the assertion of something which is true. What to make of this suggestion depends on the details; I will consider the two most likely stories.

The first is that uses of slurs carry what are sometimes called 'particularized conversational implicatures'—ones which are made in a one-off fashion (as opposed to the putative 'generalized' implicature about A's bringing B in its wake carried by the conditional *If A, B*). A standard example of a particularized implication is this: I ask 'Where can I buy gas?'; you say 'There's a gas station a mile south of here'. Given the context in which your utterance occurs, you imply, but do not say, that one can purchase gas a mile south of our location. The implicature occurs (as do all conversational implicatures) because, given the assumption that you are following 'the rules of conversation' (try to say true things you have evidence for; be orderly; be perspicuous; be helpful; etc.), the best explanation of your utterance involves supposing that you want me to infer, from your making it, that one can buy gas a mile south of our location.

Why do I say it is implausible that slurring involves conversational implicature? Well, this sort of implicature occurs, so to speak, because it solves a problem posed by someone's utterance: What must they want us to think, given what they said and that they are 'playing by the conversational rules'? The problem is solved by seeing what follows from the assumption that you are playing by the rules, that you said what you did, and other things obvious to everyone. But whatever interpretive problems slurring might cause, it is not clear how appeal to maxims of conversation will help solve them. For nothing much seems to follow from the facts that you insulted the slur's targets by slurring them and that you are trying to be conversationally relevant, helpful, orderly, and so on—at least nothing much follows that couldn't be inferred from one or the other of these facts alone. In particular, simply to say *He is an S* (S a slur) is to express the thought that the relevant person is an S, and to convey that one accepts this thought. To think *this* thought is to think the person worthy of contempt. So *simply* to say that a particular person is an S is to represent that person as contemptible. It is what the person says and thinks, when he slurs, that we want to reject. We don't need to drag a Gricean mechanism in to understand this. One of course wants an explanation of how the speaker could speak as he did, when he slurs another. It seems a bit meshuga to look for it in the principles of conversation.

One might somewhat more plausibly say that while it is 'part of the meaning' of a slur that its target is contemptible (or inferior, or . . .), this is not part of the truth-conditional content of such terms; the term of art here is 'conventional implicature'. The idea of conventional, non-truth-conditional implicature is grounded in Grice's remark in 'Logic and Conversation' that

> If I say (smugly), *He is an Englishman; he is, therefore, brave*, I have certainly committed myself, by virtue of the meaning of my words, to its being the case that his being brave is a consequence of (follows from) his being an Englishman. But while I have said that he is an Englishman, and said that he is brave, I do not want to say that I have *said* (in the favored sense) that it follows from his being an Englishman that he is brave.[38]

Grice offers no explanation of why he does not want to say this, but one can see why he might: To use 'therefore' in the way in question might be said to *perform* an act of drawing a conclusion; drawing a conclusion is not *saying* that one is doing so, or saying that one is doing so validly. Because the purpose of 'therefore' is to indicate that one is drawing a conclusion, this is 'part of its meaning', and the implicature is thus rightly said to be conventional. Some might think that something similar is true of 'but': its purpose, it might be said, is to *draw* a contrast; drawing a contrast is not saying that one is there, but it does in some important sense imply that there is one to be drawn.

In the case of 'but' and 'therefore', the argument for a conventional implicature is that the words are marked for *doing* certain things beyond the humdrum semantic tasks of referring, predicating, quantifying, and so on. It is thus manifest that their use imparts some information, that one is doing the thing for which the words are marked. But, of course, if it is manifest that one is (sincerely) drawing an inference or contrast, it is manifest that one thinks the inference is valid, the contrast there to be drawn. Thus, the use of these words conveys the (perhaps mis)information that the inference is valid, the contrast genuine. Since the information conveyed is not encoded (simply) by the reference, predication,

---

[38] Grice (1967: 22).

quantification, etc. which occurs as one utters the sentence, that information is not 'part of what is strictly and literally said'.

One might think that the racial epithets fit this pattern quite well. After all, they are conventional means of expressing derogatory attitudes towards their targets. They are marked for *doing* something beyond the humdrum semantic tasks of referring, predicating, and so on. So, one would expect, their use imparts (non-semantically) certain information. Just as drawing an inference, from A to B, conveys that one is justified in doing so—conveys that the inference is valid—so, one might say, displaying contempt for someone on the basis of race or ethnicity implies that one is justified in doing so—implies that they are contemptible because of race or ethnicity. We thus reject the utterance in which the slur is used. Not paying close attention to the distinction between what is said and what is implied, we mistake this for rejecting what the sentence 'strictly and literally says'.

I do not wish to deny that there can be—that, indeed, there is—information conventionally associated with a (use of a) sentence, conveyed by it('s use), which does not enter into determining whether the sentence('s use) is true or false. I do not want to deny that when someone utters *He is an S*, S a slur, linguistic convention (in particular, the fact that the slur is marked as a device of derogation) puts the hearer in a position to see that the speaker thinks, and would be happy to have the hearer think as well, that the target of the slur is contemptible. But I do deny that it is by appeal to this fact that we best explain our reluctance to say that (when the slur is aimed at its target) what is said is true.

A slur is a device made to denigrate, abuse, intimidate, and show contempt. Such is its conventional potential. But because of this it is also a device that is used to portray, to represent its targets. The racist *thinks of* the targets of a slur S as Ss. (Indeed, he wants us and the targets themselves to think of them(selves) in this way.) There is of course a connection amongst the functions of the slur. To refer to someone as an S (S a slur targeted on T) is to *show* contempt for him on the basis of his being a T; to think of someone as an S is to *think* of him as contemptible. The thought that one is having, when one thinks *He is an S*—the thought that sentence, in virtue of what it means, gives vent to—is a thought in which the relevant individual is represented as contemptible. So, at any rate, I have argued in the second half of this chapter. *That* thought must be rejected—not by asserting its negation (and thereby continuing to represent the individual as an S), but by its outright rejection.

It is our recognition of this that leads us to reject the thought that someone is an S. That is, it is our rejection of the thought that *He is an S*—what the sentence *says*, in as strict a sense of 'says' as you like—that is responsible for our reaction. But a sentence that strictly speaking says something that is not to be accepted as true—what such a sentence strictly speaking says is not true.

1.9

I have, in some ways, pronounced the intuition with which we began—that slurring speech cannot be true—both right and wrong. I have, in some ways, said that Gibbard's verdict on such speech—that it may be true, though 'offensively couched'—is both wrong and right. For I have suggested that in different situations we might individuate the way of thinking expressed by a slur differently. If we include the contemptuous attitudes annexed to that way of thinking—something I have been arguing it is possible and permissible, sometimes even required, to do—we have a thought we should not call true or false. But it may be possible, in some situations, to think of this way of thinking as only accidentally involving the relevant attitudes. If we can do this, we can presumably ascribe truth to a thought employing this way of thinking—if, at least, there is nothing wrong with it beyond the attitudes conjoined to it.

I close by observing that this last possibility is very often one that seems not to be open to us. It is just not open to me to unilaterally detach the affect, hatred, and negative connotations tied to most slurs and use them interchangeably with their neutral counterparts. Whether I like it or not, I am unable to use most slurs without showing contempt for their targets. I would say that the same thing is true of approving of or ascribing truth to uses of slurs by others. It might be that in another place and time, if few or no people had the attitudes now associated with a slur, I could ascribe truth to what someone said using it without in effect endorsing the attitudes expressed, just as Blackburn can today call something lustful without thereby condemning it. But at this juncture, at this particular point in history, I can't.[39]

[39] It may seem that I have said nothing which applies to most racist talk. Most racism is achieved without the signaling of contempt with specific devices. The professor who remarks, when a colleague laments the paucity of minority students in the philosophy program, 'Well, one has to have strong quantitative abilities to do well in philosophy, and on the whole they don't' would normally and correctly be taken to have made a racist remark. (The example is a variant of one due to Cara Spencer.) Does anything I've said apply to this kind of case?

I think so. Assuming that 'they', as used here, contributes a certain way of thinking of a group of people to what's said, the question to ask here is whether the way of thinking is like those associated with a slur in the relevant regard: that is, is it a way of thinking of someone which 'fronts' denigration and contempt in the way a slur does? If so, the right thing to do is not logic chop or engage the man on a descriptive level (arguing, say, that he is confusing training in standardized test taking with intellectual ability). The right thing is to reject the way of framing the targets of the thought. Some claims are claims we ought to reject not because they are false but because to seriously take them or their denials up requires thinking of the world awrong.

2

When Truth Gives Out

Some say the notion of truth constitutes the core of any adequate account of thought and talk. Others say it's an anemic, practically contentless notion unable to carry an explanatory load. I say neither of these pictures is right.

The first picture is in fact a portfolio whose pages are loosely connected by the ideas that language and thoughts are vehicles of representation and that representation is explained in terms of truth and reference. Linguistic meaning is often identified with truth-conditions; understanding with knowledge of truth-conditions. To say something (at least 'the central case' of saying something) tends to get identified with asserting something—with putting a thought forward as true. Donald Davidson, famously and perhaps with hubris aforethought, denied beliefs to creatures without the concept of truth. Lots of philosophers who wouldn't go that far still see belief, since it is a representation of 'the way the world is', as bound to truth. One hears, for instance, that it is a mark of conceptual confusion to claim to believe something while denying the thing believed to be true. And of course truth is central to the way we've been taught to think about what makes for a good argument: deductively valid argument is defined in terms of truth, an argument being deductively valid when the truth of its premises guarantees that of its conclusion.

The second picture is drawn by deflationists and minimalists, who tell us that the most interesting thing about truth is that it's not very interesting. A typical minimalist story goes as follows:[1] The old idea was that truth must have some kind of essence—correspondence to the facts, rational coherence, some property tied to the outcome of enquiry. Such views are wrong, the minimalist says, for there is no one thing, or even handful of things, which make for truth. Truth has no essence, no illuminating, punchy definition. What there is to be said about truth—*all* there is to be said about it—has been said when we have said that

It's true that snow is white just in case snow is white.
It's true that Muck is south of London just in case Muck is south of London.
It's true that all one needs is love just in case all one needs is love.

---

[1] I use 'minimalism' and 'deflationism' interchangeably. There are several varieties of minimalism among which I won't distinguish. The story about to be told is perhaps closest to that told by Paul Horwich (1998*b*).

and so on and on. To have the concept of truth is to be disposed to accept such equivalences. We have this concept only because of our occasional need to comment on claims en masse ('Nothing the Pope has to say about abortion is true') or to endorse or dispute a claim when we cannot, or do not want to, identify it ('The claim at the bottom of page 12 is true'). Truth thus plays only a formal, somewhat logical role.

The deflationist, thinking the notion of truth to be so slight, thinks it cannot do any explanatory work. And thus he rejects the centrality of truth in an account of thought and talk: Meaning is not to be identified with truth-conditions; understanding is not knowledge of truth-conditions; principles of logic, though often formulated using the notion of truth, are not principles about it or explained in terms of it.

As said, I don't think either attitude—neither that which sees truth as *the* central notion in an account of thought and talk, nor that which sees it as a thin, formal notion—is tenable. My worries flow from a belief that much of what we say and think isn't to be evaluated in terms of whether it is true or false. My goal is to seduce you into agreeing that claims and beliefs can 'get it right' or 'get it wrong' without being true or false.

The idea that what we say and think needn't be the sort of thing which is to be evaluated for truth threatens the idea that truth stands at the center of an explanation of meaning. If many of our (literal) assertions and beliefs aren't 'truth-apt', we can't identify meaning with truth-conditions, understanding with grasp thereof, or representation with representation of how things truly are. How much of a revision is called for depends upon how much and how important the cases in which truth is displaced turn out to be. But something which is called into question almost immediately is the idea that the *basic* notion of validity is one on which validity is a matter of the truth of premises providing a guarantee for the truth of a conclusion.

The idea that what we say, that that for which we give arguments, needn't be truth-apt also undermines the minimalist's picture of truth. The minimalist's view is that the truth predicate's function is to provide a means of 'blindly' assenting to or rejecting claims (i.e. assenting to or rejecting claims without identifying them by means of clauses of the form *that S*). It can serve this purpose only if—only to the extent that—for any claim p, p is equivalent to the claim *p is true*. Indeed, it can serve this purpose only if we are all aware, at some level, of this equivalence. The minimalist thinks there are such equivalences; he holds, in fact, that 'claims of the sort *It is true that S* . . . are trivially equivalent to S and that this equivalence is in some sense definitional of truth'.[2] Minimalism requires (loosely speaking) that the claim that S and the claim that it's true that S 'come to the same thing', at least for anyone who has the concept of truth. If minimalism is correct, there must be a sort of incoherence in the idea that it

---

[2] Thus Soames (1999) at p. 231.

could be that (for example): The Pope said that abortion is wrong; abortion *is* wrong; but it's not *true* that abortion is wrong.[3]

But this sort of thing is not incoherent if there are ranges of discourse which are not truth-apt but in which we express beliefs, are able to give reasons, and so forth. And if there are such stretches of discourse, one thinks that there *is* something substantial to be said about truth. For one expects an account of how it comes to be that the claims of some declarative, belief-expressing discourses are truth-apt while the claims of others are not. The idea that there are ranges of discourse that aren't truth-apt but which express beliefs also undermines the idea that the truth predicate's function is merely to provide an all-purpose device of blind agreement. If the Pope's pronouncements about abortion aren't true or false, one can still agree with them blindly—one can say 'I agree with/endorse/accept/am down with what the Pope has said'—but one shouldn't call them true or false.

So what is an example of an arena of judgment and belief which can be right or wrong while neither true nor false? The example I'll focus on in this chapter is talk about talk that is without truth-value. In particular, I'll focus on talk about the application of vague predicates to their borderline cases and talk about paradoxical sentences.

Vagueness is sometimes characterized in terms of borderline cases, a vague predicate being one that has or could have such cases. *Roughly*, a borderline case for a predicate is an object of which we feel uncomfortable saying the predicate is true, and uncomfortable saying that the predicate is false, and feel so not because we lack some knowledge about the object or the predicate's meaning.[4] A borderline case for 'bald' is someone who we would typically say is 'sort of' bald, but he is not (or not definitely) bald *and* he is not (or not definitely) not bald. If one takes 'Well, he's not bald, and he's *not* not bald either—he's sort of in the middle' at face value, recognizing that this reaction isn't the result of linguistic or factual ignorance, one will say the claim that such a person is bald isn't true (he's not bald), and isn't false (he's not not bald either). Paradoxical sentences—a standard example is

(L)   Sentence L is not true.

—are sentences which we can *prove* don't say anything true or false.[5]

What is puzzling about these sentences is *not* that they apparently say things which aren't true or false. What is puzzling is that we can (and feel compelled to)

---

[3] See, again, Soames (1999), at pp. 249–50, where the impossibility of all of these being assertible is said to be 'a feature of any acceptable theory'.

[4] This way of characterizing the notion of a borderline instance is contentious, as the discussion below will indicate.

[5] After all, if (L) says something true, it is true. And what it says is that it's not true. So contradiction ensues if it says something true. Suppose, on the other hand, that it says something false. What (L) says is: *This is not true: sentence L is true.* But if a claim *not p* is false, then claim p is true. So sentence L is true. So L says something true. But what is true is not false. Contradiction once again. (It should be noted that the proof assumes that (L) says only one thing.)

say various things about them and about what they say which *seem* to be right but which *can't* be true. Suppose Jo is a borderline case of baldness and that application of a vague predicate to a borderline case results in a claim neither true nor false. Then what we say when we utter

(J) Jo is bald.

is not true. But what we say in uttering (J) is that Jo's bald. If that's not true, then it's not true that Jo is bald. But how can *that* be the right thing to say, if saying that Jo's not bald is also saying something that's not true? A related point can be made about talk of what it would take for (J) or the claim it makes to be true. We know, after all, what it takes for sentence (J) to be true:

(JT) 'Jo is bald' is true iff Jo is bald.

The problem is, it's hard to see how (JT) can be the right thing to say about sentence (J). Its right-hand side—which is sentence (J)—is *ex hypothesi* without truth-value. But how can its left-hand side differ in 'truth status' from its right? Presumably it can't, as the sentences flanking the 'iff' seem trivially equivalent. So we seem to have a biconditional flanked by truth-valueless sentences; on the normal ways of telling the story about such biconditionals they aren't true.[6] But if (JT) says something that's not true, we shouldn't say it, right?

One might try to avoid these problems by telling a story on which sentences like (J) and (L) either don't say anything, or say something that is either true or false. One might, for example, suggest that 'bald' is invariably true or false of an object (or at least of the sorts of things which could sensibly be said to be bald or otherwise to begin with); borderline cases of 'bald', it might be said, are individuals who are such that we can't determine their status.[7] One might say of sentences like (L) that while they of course seem to say something, there is in fact nothing they say. I will say a little about such views below, but don't want to get sidetracked in an extended consideration of them. One of the principle motivations for such views is the feeling that we land in unsolvable logical and

---

[6] In particular, this is how things turn out when the connectives are given a 'strong Kleene' account. On such an account,

−*A* is true if *A* is false, false if it is true, and undetermined otherwise;
(*A & B*) is true if both conjuncts are, false if at least one is, and undetermined otherwise;
(*A v B*) is true if at least one conjunct is, false if both are, and undetermined otherwise.

Other connectives are understood as defined in terms of '−' and '&'. (The idea behind the treatment is that a sentence with some truth-valueless components will get the truth-value v, if any way of assigning truth-values to its valueless atoms gives v as a result; otherwise, such a sentence is without truth-value.)

[7] The best-known contemporary development of this view is given in Timothy Williamson (1994). Williamson's principle argument against the view that 'Jo is bald' is truth-valueless if Jo is a borderline case of baldness is discussed in Richard (2002).

An extended defense of the idea that sentences like (J) make claims without truth-value is given in Richard (forthcoming *a*).

semantical puzzles if we say that vague terms are neither true nor false of their instances, or—holding on to the validity of

(LT) 'Sentence L is not true' is true iff sentence L is not true.

—allow that a sentence like (L), or someone who utters such a sentence, manages to say something. If this chapter (and Appendix I) are successful, they show that no such puzzles arise.

The kind of problems (J) and (T) present are pervasive in any language in which sensible sentences can say things which aren't truth-valued; they have nothing in particular to do with vagueness or paradox. Consider, for example, the triviality

(T) If a sentence says something and what it says is true, then the sentence itself is true.

Suppose that S is a sentence of English which indeed says something, but the thing said is neither true nor false. (T) is true only if all its instances, including

(TI) If S says something and what it says is true, then S is true.

are true. But, once again, on standard accounts of how truth is determined in languages with 'truth-value gaps'—i.e. languages in which a sentence may say something that's not true or false—(TI) will itself be without truth-value.[8]

Here is the arc of this chapter. I first briefly discuss and reject some strategies which might be thought to defuse the problems just raised. I then introduce the approach I think we should take, suggesting that not all saying is asserting. When I say correctly that (J) or (L) is not true, I'm not *asserting*—i.e. committing to the truth of—anything. Rather, I'm *denying* a claim—that Jo is bald, that (L) is true. Denial is *sui generis*, in the sense that it can't be defined in terms of assertion; denial is (roughly speaking) appropriate when the claim denied is not true—either false or without truth-value. As I'll show, a straightforward generalization of this idea allows us to explain how uttering (LT) or (JT) can be saying the right thing: what one is doing, in uttering these, is performing yet another sort of speech act, one (roughly) appropriate when the claims yoked by the 'if and only if' have the same status: both are true or neither is.[9]

There is a well-known objection to the idea that denial is a *sui generis* speech act, due to Frege. Clumsily put, the objection is that the idea—that what we (sometimes) do with 'not' is not to assert but to deny a claim—is an idea that would make it impossible to do logic or at least impossible to do it sensibly. Peter Geach observed that Frege's objection generalizes to pretty much any view which

---

[8] A view will entail this if it says that conjoining something true with something without truth-value yields a sentence without truth-value, and a conditional with indeterminate antecedent and consequent is itself indeterminate.

[9] The idea that sharply distinguishing assertion from denial helps make sense of what is going on with paradoxical sentences surfaces in Terence Parsons (1984).

takes things that are premises in arguments to be non-assertoric. After spelling out versions of such objections to my own proposal, I undertake to answer them. I show how we can naturally and rather simply give a semantics for a language whose sentences are conventional means to make assertions, denials, perform the sort of biconditional speech act alluded to above, and so on. The semantics associates with sentences various 'commitments'—in the first instance, to the 'truth status' of various claims. Asserting p, for example, commits one to p's truth; denying p commits one to p's being either false or without truth-value. We can assess such commitments, not for truth or falsity—that would lead, in cases like that of (J), (JT), (L), and (LT), to paradox—but for a property I call *appropriateness*. Logic can be—*should* be—based on this property, an argument being valid if whenever all the commitments associated with its premises are appropriate, so are the commitments associated with its conclusion. This chapter ends by showing that this answers Frege's worries about denial. Chapter 3 takes up Geach's worries about (for instance) emotivist accounts of normative language.

The material in this chapter is relevant to a good deal of the literature on truth and the liar paradox, and to questions in philosophical semantics, such as whether it is possible to 'do the semantics of a language within the language itself'. Because addressing these questions gets pretty technical pretty fast, and because they are a bit orthogonal to our main concerns, I have segregated what I have to say about these topics in Appendix I.

2.1

One way to dissolve the problem posed by sentences such as (J) and (L) is to deny that they say anything to begin with. But it's hard to credit the idea that serious utterances of sentences like (J) and (L) fail to say anything. Suppose, for example, Jo is a borderline case of baldness, so that 'Jo is bald' is without truth-value. Presumably Jo *might* have been bald; and, if so, then 'Possibly, Jo is bald' is true. But what truth can this express, save one which obtains in virtue of the fact that the claim that Jo is bald—i.e. the claim made by (J)—might have been true?[10]

One sometimes hears it said that liar sentences such as (L) are for one or another reason silly or senseless. This is an odd idea, if only because the parts of such sentences are properly interpreted—their names name, their predicates have (intensions and) extensions, their quantifiers quantify—and they are put together in the way a sensible sentence is put together. Furthermore, there doesn't seem to be anything silly or senseless about saying that a sentence in a particular location is false (as in 'The sentence on the board in room 17 is false'), or about

---

[10] Such an argument is given in Williamson (1992).

Bob and Ray when Bob says that Ray has never said anything true about him, and Ray says that everything Bob has said of him is true. But if, as it happens, the sentence on the board in room 17 is 'The sentence on the board in room 17 is false', that sentence is neither true nor false; the case of Bob and Ray commenting on each other's veracity is like this, too. In each case something which *could* be true seems to be said; in each case the assumption that what is said is true or false leads to contradiction.[11]

One might allow that both (J) and (L) make claims, trying to dissolve the problem they pose by saying that 'not' is ambiguous, sometimes expressing 'choice negation' other times expressing 'exclusion negation'. Each kind of negation is an extension of the familiar two-valued negation: the choice and exclusion negation of a truth is a falsehood, the choice and exclusion negation of a falsehood a truth. But while the choice negation of something without truth-value is also without truth-value, the exclusion negation of something without truth-value is itself true.

	Choice Negation	**Exclusion Negation**
p	$\sim$**p**	$\neg$**p**
true	false	false
false	true	true
no truth-value	no truth-value	true

How, exactly, is this supposed to help? Does it, in particular, allow us to explain how (JT) and (LT) apparently can be used to convey sound information about the conditions under which (J) and (L) are true? Let's use '$\sim$' to express choice negation, '$\neg$' to express exclusion negation. Consider, again,

(JT) 'Jo is bald' is true iff Jo is bald.

With a little art, we can construe this as a truth by interpreting it in terms of exclusion negation. *A iff B* is equivalent to *If A, then B; if B, then A*. And a conditional is equivalent to the disjunction of its antecedent's negation with its

---

11 Charles Parsons (1984) suggests that what claims there are to quantify over and to assign to utterances shifts across contexts; in a situation in which we reason to contradiction from a liar sentence, our reasoning misfires because there is no claim which is expressed by the sentence in the domain of our quantifiers. Tyler Burge (1979) develops a similar view.

Consider a variant of sentence L:

(M) Sentence M expresses a proposition that is not true.

On Parsons's view as I understand it, it is often the case that there is an object x (for example, sentence (M)) and a property P (expressing a truth) such that (although there is no category mistake involved in ascribing P to x, and it is possible for us to think about x and to ascribe P to objects like x), we cannot, as a matter of fact say or think that x has P. For if we could say or think this—that is, that sentence (M) expresses a truth—we could say or think that it does not. And if we can do that, there is something that sentence (M) says; namely, that it does not express a truth. Parsons does not, in my opinion, make it plausible that a principle like *For any object x and property P such that we can refer to x and ascribe P to objects like x, we can think that x has (or lacks) P* fails.

In any case, whatever its merits as an account of the liar, there seems little hope of using Parsons's account to solve the problem posed by sentences like (J).

consequent. If we take the negation in question to be exclusion negation, we interpret (JT) as

(JTE) Either ¬ (J) is true, or Jo is bald; either ¬ Jo is bald, or (J) is true.

If (J) is true or false, this is true. If (J) is without truth-value, its exclusion negation and that of '(J) is true' are each true. So given that the disjunction of a truth with something without truth-value is true, (JTE) is true. Effability regained.

This is all very nice, but it falls apart once we try to apply it to (LT). We need to decide how to understand the 'not' which occurs in (L)—is it choice or exclusion negation? If we interpret this as choice negation, (LT) is not true. If we interpret it as exclusion negation, things are no better. For in this case (L) must have a truth-value—at least it must given that '(L) is true' says something. (Since we are now allowing that (L) says something, it's hard to see how the sentence of which (L) is the negation—i.e. the sentence '(L) is true'—could fail to say anything.) But if (L) has a truth-value, either '(L) is true' has the same truth-value, and paradox ensues, or (LT)'s sides do not have the same truth-value, and we have no account of how (LT) can be a sound thing to say. So we are unable to explain why it is so obviously the right thing to say, of '¬ (L) is true', that it is true iff (L) is not (i.e. ¬) true.[12]

2.2

If Jo is a borderline case of baldness, he is not bald. If so, it is a fact that Jo is not bald, and one can state that fact by seriously uttering

(0) Jo is not bald.

---

[12] Does distinguishing between choice and exclusion negation at least solve the problems raised in Section 2.1 about talk about vague talk? I don't think so. Suppose Jo is a borderline case of baldness, but that I can truly say that Jo is not bald—which I can, if I can use 'not' to express exclusion negation. Since the inference schema

(D) S.
So it's definitely the case that S.

would seem to be truth-preserving, I can also truly say that it's definitely the case that Jo is not bald. But if it's definite that Jo is not bald, then surely he is *not* a borderline case of baldness. And of course there's nothing special about Jo: *nobody* can be a borderline case for 'bald'. So it looks as if claiming that 'not' can express exclusion negation is tantamount to claiming that vague predicates don't have borderline cases.

Some—Timothy Williamson is an example—would deny the validity of (D). But they are driven to do so by the view that applications of vague predicates to borderline cases have truth-values (though we are unable to determine what those values are); thus, such theorists reason, to say that someone is definitely (not) bald is to make an epistemic claim. Those who acknowledge that (J) is truth-valueless, if Jo is a borderline case of baldness—those, that is, to whom the remarks in the text are addressed—have no reason to deny, and generally do not deny, the trivial validity of schema (D).

And if Jo is a borderline case of baldness, it is a fact that it's not the case that Jo is not bald. And one can state that fact by seriously uttering

(1) It is not the case that Jo is not bald.

Now I do not lapse into incoherence simply by stating the facts. So I cannot be asserting—that is, putting forward as true—the claims that Jo is not (truth functional) bald and that Jo is not not bald, for asserting both of these is incoherent. It is hard to credit the idea that I would be asserting some *other* claims in seriously, non-figuratively uttering (0) and (1). So there must be a kind of utterance *besides* assertive utterance which counts as a 'stating of the facts'.

What sort? Serious utterance of (0) when it's assumed that the claims that Jo is bald and its negation are without truth-value amounts to *rejecting* or *denying* the claim that Jo is bald.[13] To reject a claim p is not to assert that p is not true; it is not to assert p's negation. It's not to assert anything at all, but to do something which is appropriate (given that one's goal is to 'express all and only the facts') just in case p is not true.[14]

It is tempting to think of rejection as 'the dual' of assertion, with truths about rejection coming from ones about assertion by changing the polarity of appropriate parameters. Thus, rejection of p is appropriate iff p is not true; its assertion iff it is true. But we must proceed cautiously here. If I assert p and q follows from p,[15] I am committed to the truth of q, in the sense that I am committed to q's being assertible. But if I reject p, and q follows from p, I certainly am not thereby committed to the falsity of q, as q (and p) might simply be truth-valueless. I am, instead, committed to the non-truth of q, in the sense of q's being 'rejectable'—i.e. something which is to be rejected, not asserted.

If I assert p and I assert p's negation, I am to be censured, for I have committed myself to a distribution of truth-values which cannot be realized.[16] Not so if I reject p and its negation. In the case of (what's said by)

(2) Sentence 2 is not true.

for example, it is clear that I should reject it as well as (what's said by)

(3) Sentence 2 is true.[17]

---

[13] I use 'rejection' and 'denial' in this and the next chapter as names of one speech act. In Appendix I, however, 'rejection' is used in another way, to name a speech act distinct both from denial and from the assertion of a negation.

[14] This is hardly a definition. Indeed, it can't even illuminate someone who doesn't understand rejection, since what I've said is OK only if 'p is not true' here expresses the rejection of p's truth.

[15] That is: if, of necessity, if p is true, then so is q. Note that we cannot assimilate *claim q follows from claim p* to the classical derivability of something expressing q from something expressing p.

[16] 'Distribution' in the sense in which each partial function from propositions to truth-values is such a distribution. I am liable to censure, roughly, because anyone in a position to grasp the objects of my assertions is in a position to know that the distribution of truth-values I'm committed to can't be realized.

[17] I will in what follows sometimes slur the difference between a sentence and the claim it makes/proposition it expresses.

Is there inconsistency in rejecting both (2) and (3)? Certainly nothing inconsistent has been *asserted*. Do I incur impossible commitments, in rejecting both of these? Given what was said above, my commitments in this case amount to *rejecting* any q such that (2) or (3) follows from q. Such commitment would be censurable if it were unrealizable—that is, if the distribution of truth-values to which I am committed could not be realized. But we know that this distribution is realized—neither (2) nor (3) is true, after all, and so nothing from which they follow is true either.

Rejecting a claim is censurable (in the way in which accepting a contradiction is censurable) if I am committed to asserting what I reject, or if the claim rejected follows from something to whose assertability I am committed. Asserting p while rejecting it is no better than asserting p and its negation. Asserting $p \vee q$ and asserting $-p$ commits me to the assertability of q; thus I cannot reject it. Of course, just as multiple assertions may make a rejection censurable (asserting $p \vee q$ and $-q$ commits me to not rejecting p), so patterns of assertion and rejection may make further assertions and rejection censurable (asserting $p \vee q$ and rejecting q makes both rejecting p and asserting its negation censurable).

The purpose of 'fact-stating' discourse is to 'say how things are'. Part of saying how things are is characterizing the distribution of truth-values to propositions. Given that there are propositions which are neither true nor false, I can in principle give such a characterization if I am able to either assert or reject a proposition. I cannot do this if I am limited to assertion. So limited, I can't incur an appropriate commitment to the status of (1) through (3); silence no more implies dissent than it does assent. In order to 'state all the facts'—to say how things are, with the claims that Jo is bald and that he is not, or to say how it goes with a liar sentence—I must assert some propositions and reject some others. In uttering (1) through (3) I am saying how things are, I am 'stating some of the facts'. And this means that I am *saying* something, even if I am asserting nothing.

When it is a fact that a proposition or sentence is without truth-value, one can state this by rejecting the claim that it has one. Of course that means that one can give accurate information without asserting anything true. Some might think that that claim sounds very odd. But surely one *can* do this: Contemplate the construction of a Kripkean truth predicate for English.[18] What happens to sentence (2) at the end of this construction? Well, nothing: that is, it is not put in the extension of 'true'—and so is not true—and it is not put in its anti-extension—and so is not false. So the liar (and thus what it says) is neither true nor false. *Surely* I have given you perfectly accurate information in saying all this. And I have done this in English. But if that's so, then (on pain of a contradiction being accurate) I have not said anything that's true.

---

[18] This is discussed in Appendix I. For those who don't know what I'm alluding to, read the sentence so: Consider what happens when we give an account of the meaning of the word 'true' on which it turns out that sentences such as (2) never receive a truth-value.

2.3

There are objections to the idea that 'not' is sometimes used to signal a *sui generis* speech act of rejection. The best known are due to Frege and Geach. In 'Negation' Frege considers a pair of arguments of the forms

(A)	If not B, then not M.	(B)	If R, then not M.
	Not B.		R.
	So not M.		So not M.

Frege observes that we cannot interpret 'not B' in (A)'s initial premise as involving denial, for uttering 'If not B, then not M' doesn't require denying anything. He concedes that one could make sense of the idea that an argument such as (A) is valid, when its second premise is uttered in denial, but argues that to do so is pointless: It would, first of all, go against the intuition that 'both inferences proceed in the same form' (they are both instances of *modus ponens*); it would require unnecessary complication, since we would have to posit a use of 'not' expressing truth-functional negation, a use of 'not' signaling denial, and yet a third use in sentences like 'If not B, then not M' when that sentence is paired with the denial of B in *modus ponens*.[19] Following Frege, Geach writes:

> where an ostensively assertoric utterance of 'p' and 'If p, then q' can be teamed up as premisses for *modus ponens* . . . the two occurrences of 'p' . . . must have the same sense if the *modus ponens* is not to be vitiated by equivocation; and if any theorist alleges that in its ostensibly assertoric occurrence 'p' is really no proposition at all, it is up to him to give an account of the role of 'p' that will allow of its standing as a premiss. This task is pretty consistently shirked.[20]

Substantially, the same worries can be raised without reference to validity. Suppose we say that in uttering 'Jo is not bald', Jo being a borderline case of the bald, I am best construed as denying that he is bald. It would seem that no matter what the status of Jo's hair, uttering

(4) If Jo is not bald, then someone is not is bald.

is in order. But how are we to construe the utterance of (4) when Jo might be a borderline case of baldness? In this case what is expressed by (4) is without truth-value, and it is not appropriate to assert what is not true. But if a serious utterance of (4) is not assertive, what is it? One *might* say that uttering (4) is (sometimes) performing an act of 'conditional rejection', with the rejection in this case conditional upon the rejection of the claim, that Jo is bald. But even

---

[19] Frege (1918), in Geach and Black (1970). This argument is to be found at pp. 124–5 and 129–31.
[20] Geach (1965).

supposing the notion of conditional rejection makes sense, the suggestion is just wrong. The reading of the consequent of (4) on which it is in order is one (partially) symbolized

(4′) For some x: x is a person and not: x is bald.

To utter this is *not* to deny, of any particular person, that he is bald. It is *not* to deny that there are bald people. There is *no* claim of which it is a denial, conditional or otherwise.

We have the following (not unrelated) problems:

(I) Explain what it would be for an argument of (A)'s form to be valid, when its second premise is used in denial—and do this so that we are not committed to the absurdity, that in uttering its first premise one is denying something.

(II) Reconcile, if possible, the claim that (A) and (B) may be of the same form even if (A)'s second premise is uttered in denial.

(III) Explain how we are to interpret the first premise of (A) in case (II).

(IV) Explain what could possibly be meant by saying that a serious utterance of (4), or a denial of the truth of a liar sentence, was correct or appropriate, if what is meant is not that the utterance is an utterance of something *true*.

Perhaps these seem to you like problems that only a logician could love. But a lot hangs on whether these kinds of problem are soluble. Geach's *primary* target was those who claim that various stretches of discursive discourse—stretches which *look* as if they involve assertion—in fact involve no such thing. The target was, for example, an emotivist like A. J. Ayer, who claimed that when someone says 'you ought to keep your promise', he isn't *asserting* anything; he is expressing one or another sort of approval of promise keeping.[21] Geach's point, turned against such a view, is that *surely* someone who says 'You ought to honor your father, for you ought to honor your parents, and if you ought to honor your parents you ought to honor your father' is giving an argument, one which from a logical point of view is good, and good for the same reason as an argument like 'You will break your foot, for you will fall off that ladder, and if you fall off that ladder you'll break your foot'.

But how could someone like Ayer make sense of the idea that the former was an argument, much less a good one? If it's a valid argument, the sense of 'You ought to honor your parents' must be the same when it's uttered alone and when it's uttered in 'If you ought to honor your parents you ought to honor your father'. On Ayer's view, uttering the former is sort of like enthusiastically saying 'Three cheers for honoring your parents!', thereby expressing one's approval for filial obeisance. So if this is a (formally) valid argument, wouldn't one have to be doing the same thing—i.e. expressing the same approval—in uttering the

[21] See Ayer (1936), esp. ch. 8.

conditional? But of course one isn't doing this in uttering it, any more than one is approving of execution in saying 'If you ought to execute traitors, you ought to execute mass murders'. Of course Ayer would just deny that reason or argument had anything to do with what we label as moral argument. But this is so unbelievable it's not really worth considering. So, at least, Geach thought; so, I think, should we.

What hangs on how we deal with problems (I) through (IV), then, is whether views like those of the emotivists—or of anyone who sees stretches of argument-loaded discourse as non-assertive—can make sense of the facts of use. You don't need to be a logician to think this a problem worth thinking about.

2.4

This section begins to sketch a response to Frege and Geach. I first lay out some assumptions and introduce a bit of jargon.

I assume the idea that assertion and rejection are *sui generis* speech acts is clear enough to theorize upon. Each kind of act results in a distinctive commitment to 'how things are' with the proposition which is the object of the act. I take these two kinds of commitment as primitive, the positive commitment to a claim incurred by assertion, the negative incurred by rejection, though I will say a good deal to explicate them here and in Appendix I. Such commitments can be appropriate or otherwise; as a first approximation, we say that a positive commitment to a claim is appropriate iff the claim is true; otherwise, the negative commitment incurred by rejecting it is appropriate.[22]

Say that a *first-order commitment* is a set of such positive and negative commitments. It can be represented by a set of pairs, each pair a mating of the relation of assertion or of rejection with a claim. Alternatively, a first-order commitment can be represented as a pair $<s, s'>$, where s and s' are sets of claims. The pairing represents that commitment which involves a positive commitment to each member of s, and a negative commitment to each member of s'. (I will switch from one representation to another, as convenient.) Such a commitment is appropriate iff each of its constituent commitments are.

A *second-order commitment*—what I sometimes call a *pattern* of first-order commitment—is a commitment to at least one among some class of first-order commitments being appropriate. Suppose, for example, I am inclined to think that the claims p and q are either both to be rejected or both to be accepted. Then I have a second-order commitment to the appropriateness of at least one of the following first-order commitments:

---

[22] Because liar-like pathology can arise with sentences which speak of appropriateness (e.g. 'It is not appropriate to deny what this sentence says'), a correct characterization of appropriateness is more complicated. This is taken up in Appendix I.

{<assert, p>, <assert, q>};
{<reject, p>, <reject, q>}.

Evidently, second-order commitments can be represented as classes of (representations of) first-order commitments; a second-order commitment {C1, C2, . . . Ck} is appropriate just in case at least one of its constituent first-order commitments is.

Suppose sentence S expresses the claim p. Assertive utterance of S is an assertion of p. It thus expresses a positive commitment to p, and thus expresses the first-order commitment {<assert, p>}. It also expresses the second-order commitment {{<assert, p>}}. Suppose one wanted to reject p. One use of 'It's not the case that S' expresses rejection. When so used, an utterance of this sentence expresses the first-order commitment {<reject, p>}, as well as the second-order commitment {{<reject, p>}}.

Suppose that I seriously utter

(5) If Jo is not bald, then the woman in the corner is not bald.

knowing that Jo is the woman in the corner and perhaps a borderline case of baldness. If Jo is a borderline case of baldness, this won't have a truth-value. So I shouldn't be taken to have *asserted* anything. And I am certainly not rejecting anything either. So what am I trying to get across? A plausible answer, I think, is that I'm trying to convey that either a positive commitment to the claim that Jo is bald is appropriate—it's something that can be safely asserted—or a negative commitment to the claim that the woman in the corner is bald is appropriate. What I am doing is expressing a second-order commitment, one represented so:

{{<assert, that Jo's bald>}, {<reject, that the woman in the corner's bald>}}.

Quite generally, I propose, serious sentence utterance—sentence utterance intended to be 'fact-stating', the sort of utterance philosophers have in mind when they speak of assertive utterance—is utterance which expresses a second-order commitment. To be a competent speaker of a language such as English involves knowing what sort of commitment is (conventionally) expressed by serious utterance of its sentences. Thus, a semantics for a language like English must associate with its sentences the patterns of first order commitment (i.e. the second-order commitments) which its sentences conventionally express.

If this is right, then it is simply not true that in order to say something, in the everyday, pre-theoretic sense of 'say something', one must assert or (reject) some claim. To say something is to incur a second-order commitment; it should be clear (just from the way in which we represent second-order commitments) that the class of such far outruns the class of possible assertions and denials. And if to say something is to endorse a pattern of second-order commitment, then to utter something of the form *x said that p* is to utter something true just in case (what) x (names) seriously uttered a sentence which has the commitment conventionally associated with p.

We're accustomed to treating 'say' as simply the version of 'assert' one uses with the servants. And thus I expect some resistance to the view I've just put forward. So let me try to convince you that it is well-nigh forced upon us by familiar facts. Even knowing full well that an instance of *'S' is true iff S* threatens paradox, we are loath to abandon it. The reason we lavish so much attention on a sentence such as

(6) 'Sentence (L) is not true' is itself true iff sentence (L) is not true.

is that what sentence (6) says of the liar sentence (L) is so obviously the right thing to say about it. But of course it is *not* right to *assert* the material biconditional '"Sentence (L) is not true" is itself true ↔ sentence (L) is not true', for that commits us to its truth, and *that* commits us to a contradiction, given an undeniable identity and seemingly undeniable inference rules. The thing to do, in the face of all this, is not give up serious utterance of (6), or tinker with our rules of inference, but to give up the idea that a serious, 'fact-stating' utterance of a sentence like (6) must be assertive, in the sense in which asserting a claim involves commitment to its truth. Rather, to utter (6) is to commit to one the following patterns of assertion and denial being appropriate:

(P1) Assert that 'Sentence (L) is not true' is true.
      Assert that sentence (L) is not true.
(P2) Reject the claim that 'Sentence (L) is not true' is true.
      Reject the claim that sentence (L) is not true.

And, indeed, one of these patterns *is* appropriate.[23]

One might object—echoing Frege—as follows. For any sentences A and B there is a claim true iff A and B are materially equivalent to one another. We can, and often do, make such claims in English, using 'if and only if'. Similarly for claims which are truth-functional negations, conditionals, and conjunctions of other claims, and sentences in which 'not', 'if. . . then', and 'and' are used. Thus, the view being sketched requires us to hold that these expressions suffer from a rather odd sort of ambiguity, between a 'sense' on which they contribute to force, not content, and one on which they contribute to content, not force.

That the view I am sketching must posit such an ambiguity is surely correct; the question is, how damning is this? We have an argument that the words in question carry the 'force determining sense'. For what sentence (6) says is the right thing to say about sentence (L); but this is so only if 'iff' carries the

---

[23] To answer a question which might occur to the reader after the next section: I assume that the 'not's in these patterns are truth-functional.

force-determining sense therein. If we have an argument that the words carry the other sense too, well, then we should conclude that they *are* ambiguous.[24]

2.5 (A)

The issues Frege and Geach raise are first and foremost issues in logic. To answer them we need at this point to do some (fairly elementary) logical investigation. Some people don't like to get bogged down in the details of this sort of thing. If your eyes tend to glaze over after the 32nd symbol, you might just skip section 2.5(a); section 2.5(b) gives a short, non-technical summary of the material herein.

Consider a version of sentence logic which contains atomic letters, truth-functional connectives '$-$', '$\&$', '$\lor$', '$\to$', '$\leftrightarrow$', and expressions 'not', 'and', 'or', 'if... then', and 'iff'. We think of these last devices as 'commitment operators'—expressions which applied to something expressing a second-order commitment yield something expressing such a commitment. The language contains any sentence generable from its atomic letters using the truth-functional connectives—that is, it includes all the sentences of conventional sentence logic. Let us call such sentences *unforced sentences*, as they lack occurrences of any of the force-indicating commitment operators. The language will also contain every 'forced sentence' obtained by closing the class of unforced sentences under 'force-functional compounding'.[25] For example, the language contains the sentences

---

[24] So I respond to Frege's and Geach's objection to postulating an ambiguity in 'not'; see Frege (1918), Geach (1965: 260).

As Jeff King pointed out to me, 'ambiguity' is probably not the happiest word to use here, since (lexical) ambiguity is multiplicity of sense. The use of 'not' as a force indicator, however, is not a use on which it has a different sense from its truth-functional use (at least not in anything like Frege's sense of 'sense'); it is a use on which it signals the performance of a certain sort of speech act. Knowing no better word to use here, I shall continue to speak of 'not' et al. as being ambiguous.

I say that 'not', 'iff', and so on are sometimes used to contribute to sense, sometimes to contribute to force; I will call the connectives, when they play the latter role, 'force functors'. It may be that 'force' is not the happiest word to use here. The standard account of force has it that force is something that in one way or another attaches to a *single* proposition: I may (on one version of the standard view) express the proposition that snow is white with assertoric force (making an assertion), or interrogative force (thereby asking if snow is white), or imperative force (thereby commanding that snow be made white), etc. But the use of 'iff' discussed above (to take an example) is not a use on which it is used to signal that a *single* proposition is put forward in a certain way, but rather to signal the assumption of a certain sort of commitment that can be characterized in terms of assertion and denial. I think it reasonable to say that the view that I sketch in this chapter makes use of a sort of generalization of the notion of force, with forces being things that apply to sequences of propositions. Knowing no better term to use here than 'force', I will simply continue to use it.

[25] That is to say: The language includes the smallest class S of sentences such that

Any unforced sentence is in S.
If A, B are in S, so are *not A; (A and B); (A or B); (if A, then B); (A iff B)*.

(C) A ↔ − B.
   A iff − B.
   A iff not B.
   A iff not − B.

Force indicators may thus have both truth-functional connectives and force indicators in their scope.

Should we go on to allow for sentences such as

(D) A ↔ not B.

in which force indicators occur within the scope of truth-functional operators? The issue is *not* whether we can make sense of the idea that we might seriously utter the English sentence

(E) Amanda is rich if and only if she is not poor.

using 'not' as a force indicator, not a truth-functional connective—that is, using 'not' in the way in which it is used in 'Amanda is not poor' when that sentence is uttered as the denial of the claim that Amanda is poor. The semantics below will make sense of *this* idea, by showing how the (conventional) force of a sentence like (E) is systematically determined by the meanings of its parts, even in the case in which both 'not' and 'if and only if' are interpreted as force indicators. The issue, rather, is whether we can make sense of the idea that we might speak a language of which something like 'Amanda is rich ↔ she is not poor' is a sentence, in which '↔' is *stipulated* to express truth-functional equivalence, and 'not' is *stipulated* to be a force indicator.

It is not clear that such sentences are sensible, or that there is anything to be gained by trying to engineer a sense for them. Certainly the sentences are of dubious coherence if we think of the meaning of the truth-functional connectives as given by truth tables. If this is the way in which '↔''s meaning is given, there seems nothing for the sentences flanking the connective to do, save to (try to) contribute a truth-value by contributing a proposition. One expects them to do this by contributing the truth-value of the proposition of which their unembedded utterance would be an assertion. But 'not B' on the view we're sketching is not a vehicle for making an assertion. We could, of course, simply read 'not' as '−' when embedded under '↔', but this is effectively conceding that we can't make sense of the result of embedding a force operator under a truth-functional one.

In any case, it is not clear why we should *want* to make sense of sentences such as (D). Consider an English sentence, some of whose uses might be thought candidates for involving the embedding of a force operator under a truth-functional one; for example:

(F) If sentence (L) is the strengthened liar, then sentence (L) is not true.

It is difficult to imagine what we might want to convey with this sentence other than something which would be appropriate to convey when and only when we should either reject the claim that (L) is the strengthened liar or reject the claim that (L) is true. But (as I shall show) we can convey this sort of thing without embedding commitment operators under truth-functional operators. We thus do not extend the language to include the likes of (D).[26]

A semantics for the language proceeds in three steps. It assigns claims to the unforced sentences. It characterizes truth for such claims, and thereby truth for unforced sentences. Finally, it defines the notion, *the second-order commitment associated with the sentence S (relative to an assignment of claims to propositional letters)*. We won't worry about the nature of the claims assigned to unforced sentences; simply identify the claim expressed by such a sentence with the sentence itself. A characterization of truth for unforced claims is then an assignment of truth-values to atoms, along with an induction extending the assignment to all unforced sentences. The assignment of truth-values to atoms may be partial since we allow for meaningful sentences—i.e. ones which make claims—without truth-values. Let us suppose that truth is assigned using Kleene's strong truth tables, so that, for example,

$-A$ is true if A is false, false if it is true, and undetermined otherwise;
(A & B) is true if both conjuncts are, false if at least one is, and undetermined otherwise;
(A v B) is true if at least one disjunct is, false if both are, and undetermined otherwise.[27]

Let c be a first-order commitment (representable as) $<s1, s2>$, s1 and s2 sets of propositions. We say that someone *fulfills* c provided that she asserts each member of s1 (and rejects no member of s1), and rejects each member of s2 (and asserts no member thereof). When c is a second-order commitment, one fulfills c just in case one fulfills one of its constituent commitments. For semantic

---

[26] There are two ways in which a force operator might occur within the scope of a truth-functional operator. Besides that just discussed, we may complementize a sentence containing a force operator—moving, say, from the sentence 'Not(Jo is bald)' which is used to deny that Jo is bald, to 'That not(Jo is bald)'. This last names the claim made by (i.e. second-order commitment incurred by) an utterance of 'Not(Jo is bald)'—that is, the claim made when one denies that Jo is bald. We can embed such a complement clause in a predicate of claims and apply a truth-functional connective to the result, as in

It is true that not(Jo is bald).

(Martin believes that (it is true that snow is white iff snow is white)) ∨ Martin is an idiot.

In denying that there is any need to manufacture a sense for the sort of embedding discussed in the text, I am *not* denying that sentences like those just displayed are sensible or without truth-value. Such sentences are briefly discussed in Appendix I.

[27] I generally omit clauses for the conditional, biconditional, and existential quantifier, as well as the clauses for the corresponding force operators; in all cases the omitted operators can be treated as if introduced by standard definitions.

purposes, we individuate commitments in terms of their fulfillment conditions. As a prelude to assigning commitments to sentences, we give a partial inventory of sorts of commitment.

1. For each pair $<s1, s2>$ of sets of claims there is a F(irst) O(rder) C(ommitment) c which one fulfills just in case one asserts every member of s1 and rejects every member of s2 (and asserts no member of s2 and rejects no member of s1). For each such c there is a (unique) S(econd) O(rder) C(ommitment) c^* which one fulfills iff one fulfills c. We call such c^*s *basic* commitments.

2. Let C be a set of SOCs. There is a unique SOC c^* such that one fulfills c^* just in case one fulfills each c in C. We call c *the conjunction of C*.[28]

3. Let C be a set of SOCs. There is a unique SOC c^* such that one fulfills c^* just in case one fulfills some c in C. We call c *the disjunction of C*.

4. For each SOC c, there is a (unique) SOC which is the *inverse* of c. If c is the SOC incurred by asserting the proposition p—that is, if c is the SOC represented as $<\{p\}, \Phi>$ (Φ the empty set)—the inverse of c is the SOC incurred by denying p—that is, the SOC represented as $<\Phi, \{p\}>$. Analogously, the inverse of $<\Phi, \{p\}>$ is $<\{p\}, \Phi>$. If c is the conjunction of the commitments in the set C, there is a unique inverse c' of c, such that one fulfills c' iff one fulfills the inverse of at least one member of C. If c is the disjunction of C, there is a unique inverse c' of c such that one fulfills c' iff one fulfills the inverse of each member of C. Finally, if c1 is the inverse of c2, c2 is the inverse of c1.

We now give a definition:

C_S, the commitment associated with sentence S, is defined as follows:

A. If S is an unforced sentence expressing a claim p, C_S is the basic commitment associated with $<\{p\}, \Phi>$.
B. If S is the 'force disjunction' of the set Γ of formulas (namely, the result of disjoining the members of Γ with the force operator *or*), C_S is the disjunction of commitments associated with the members of Γ.
C. If S is the force conjunction of the set Γ of formulas, C_S is the conjunction of the commitments associated with the members of Γ.
D. If S is the force negation of T, then C_S is the inverse of C_T.[29]

---

[28] We are entitled to speak of *the* conjunction of two commitments because commitments are individuated simply in terms of fulfillment conditions. Analagously for disjunctions and inverses. (Uniqueness can be proved inductively.) Notice that there is nothing in the present conception of commitment which would prevent a commitment from, for example, being a basic commitment, a conjunctive commitment, a disjunctive commitment, and the inverse of some other commitment.

[29] Strictly speaking, the definition should be relativized to an assignment of propositions to atoms. The characterization in the text of the operations of disjunction, conjunction, and inverse is informal. It is straightforward to define them explicitly. Disjunction can be identified with union. In

As an illustration, we calculate the SOC associated with 'p iff q', which, given that 'iff' and 'if... then' are introduced via standard definitions, is an abbreviation for '(either not p or q) and (either not q or p)'.[30] Write

$A(\phi)$ for *One asserts (and does not reject)* ϕ;
$R(\phi)$ for *One rejects (and does not assert)* ϕ.

The SOCs associated with 'not p' and 'not q' are, respectively, ones which one fulfills iff

$R(p)$, $R(q)$.

Thus, the SOCs associated with 'not p or q' and 'not q or p' are, respectively, ones which one fulfills iff

$R(p)$ or $A(q)$; $R(q)$ or $A(p)$.

Thus, the SOC associated with 'p iff q' is one which one fulfills iff

$(R(p)$ or $A(q))$ and $(R(q)$ or $A(p))$.

Since in fulfilling a commitment one cannot assert and reject a claim, the SOC associated with 'p iff q' is one which one fulfills iff either one asserts p and q (and rejects neither) or one rejects p and q (and asserts neither).

Say that a sentence of the language is in *normal form* if it is a force disjunction of force conjunctions of unforced sentences and their force negations, the force negation of a formula A being *not A*, the force disjunction (conjunction) of A and B being *A or B* (*A and B*). Fix an interpretation of the language, and consider the class of SOCs expressible by sentences of the language. Each SOC will be expressed by a sentence in normal form. (To see this, recall that each FOC c is represented as a pair $\langle s1, s2 \rangle$, the first element of the representation being the claims which must be asserted to fulfill c, the second element those which must

---

order to define the other operations: When p is a proposition, neg(p) is its negation. If a is the n-tuple $\langle a1, a2, \ldots, an \rangle$ and b is the n-tuple $\langle b1, b2, \ldots, bn \rangle$, $a + b$ is $\langle a1 \cup b1, \ldots, an \cup bn \rangle$; if a is as above and C is a collection of n-tuples $\{b1, \ldots, bk\}$, then $a + C$ is $\{a + b1, \ldots, a + bk\}$. Then CONJ, the conjunction operation, is a binary operation on SOCs defined so:

CONJ $(\{c\}, C) = c + C$
CONJ $(C' \cup \{a\}, C) = a + \text{CONJ} (C' C)$.

Generalized conjunction is defined in terms of CONJ. Inverse is defined:

CONV $(\{\langle a, b \rangle\}) = $ the set of pairs $\langle a', b' \rangle$ such that either
　　　　　　　　a' is the empty set and $b' = \{p\}$ for some p in a, or
　　　　　　　　b' is the empty set and $a' = \{p\}$ for some p in b.
CONV $(\{c1, \ldots, ck\}) = \text{CONJ}(\text{CONV}(c1), \ldots, \text{CONV}(ck))$.

[30] The rest of the paragraph indulges in harmless use/mention confusion to facilitate comprehensibility.

be rejected to fulfill it. The force conjunction of the members of s1 with the force negations of the s2's is a normal form for the SOC corresponding to c. Now suppose that c is a SOC expressible in the language. If c is expressed by an unforced sentence, the remarks just made about FOCs and their corresponding SOCs show that c has a normal form. A normal form for the disjunction of a set C of SOCs is given by the force disjunction of the normal forms of its constituent SOCs. A normal form for the conjunction of SOCs c1 and c2 can be obtained from normal forms for c1 and c2 in the obvious way;[31] a normal form for the conjunction of a set C of SOCs can be obtained by an iteration of the process of generating a normal form for a two-termed conjunction. Normal forms for inverses are obtained in the obvious way, by force negating a normal form and using (principles corresponding to) DeMorgan's laws and double negation to drive the negation through.[32])

Define *Sentence T is a normal form for sentence S* in the obvious way. It's trivial to show that for any sentence A one fulfills the commitment associated with A (relative to an assignment of claims to unforced sentences) iff one fulfills the commitment associated with a normal form of A.[33] A normal form for a sentence expressing the SOC c thus perspicuously encodes (via its disjuncts) a class K of FOCs such that one fulfills c iff one fulfills some member of K. It is obvious that for any finite set of atoms and (partial) distribution D of truth-values thereto there is a sentence of the language which expresses a commitment appropriate to exactly those situations in which D is realized. Such is the sentence which results from (force) conjoining those atoms made true in D, the (truth-functional) negations of those atoms made false in D, and the force negations of the remaining sentences along with the force negations of their truth-functional negations. Thus, someone speaking the language has, for any distribution of truth-values to (finitely many) propositions, a way of indicating that truth-values are so distributed—namely, uttering one of the sentences of the language which expresses a commitment appropriate to that distribution.

---

[31] Making things painfully obvious: For each disjunct d in the normal form for c1, form all the results of force-conjoining d with a disjunct d' of c2; then force-disjoin all the resulting conjunctions.

[32] Thus, for example, a normal form for

not (−p v q) iff not (r & −s)

is

((−p v q) and (r & −s)) or (not (−p v q) and not (r & −s)).

[33] In brief. Pick an effective procedure for associating a unique normal form with each sentence. The proof is then by induction on the number of occurrences of force operators in a wff. The induction step is a bit messy, but straightforward. The case in which A is *not B* has three subcases; one must make use of the fact that the inverse of c's inverse is c. The case in which A is *B and C* makes use of the fact that, if a formula X is of the form *A1 and A2 and . . . and Ak*, each Ai either unforced or *not B*, for some unforced B, then one fulfills the commitment associated with X iff one fulfills the commitment associated with each of X's conjuncts.

There is a natural way to introduce a notion of validity for the language. Let a model of the language be an assignment of claims to its unforced sentences, along with an assignment of truth-values to those claims assigned to atomic sentences. The truth-value of an unforced sentence in a model is determined by using the strong Kleene truth tables; the commitment assigned to a (forced or unforced) sentence in a model is determined using the definition above. We say that a model M validates a first-order commitment <s1, s2> when it makes each member of s1 true and no member of s2 so. M validates (the second-order commitment assigned to) a sentence A (in M) provided it validates one of the constituents of the SOC assigned to A (in M). Let S be a set of sentences of the language, A a single sentence. A is a c-consequence of S provided every model which validates all the members of S validates A as well; A is c-valid if validated in every model.

C-consequence can be thought of as a pragmatic counterpart to the ordinary notion of semantic consequence. To say that S c-entails A is, roughly, to say that anyone who seriously utters all of the members of S, thereby incurring the commitments associated with those sentences, incurs also the commitment associated with A. It is routine to verify that c-consequence has appropriate properties. For example: the c-consequences of a set are closed under c-entailment; if A is a semantic consequence of S (i.e. S ∪ {A} contains only unforced sentences and A is true in all models in which all of S is true), then A is a c-consequence of S; if A is a semantic consequence of the (finite) set S, then, where T is the conjunction of S's members, *not T* is a c-consequence of *not A*. These last two facts correspond to the claims that one is committed to asserting whatever is a logical consequence of what one asserts, and to denying anything from which that which one denies follows. Notice that since the notion of logical consequence is based on strong Kleene valuations of sentences, *A ∨ −A* is not a semantic consequence of *B*, as there are models in which *B* is true while *A* is without truth-value. Thus, *not B* is neither a c-consequence of *not (A ∨ −A)* nor of *not A and not −A*.

I suppose someone might object to the idea, that this language provides a partial representation of the linguistic activity of English speakers, that it commits us to the idea that there are an indefinite number of different types of speech acts which English speakers do, or at least could, perform. Indeed, the picture we are being invited to accept would have it that (exaggerating only slightly), with each increase in the logical complexity of a sentence, there comes (given that the sentence's operators are force indicators) a new speech act. But surely this is absurd.

In response: Consider the standard view of serious declarative utterance, on which such is always a matter of (an attempt at) asserting a proposition.[34] There

---

[34] Well, perhaps this isn't quite the standard view, since one normally wants to accommodate the possibility of sentences which are declarative in form, but are conventionally used for purposes

is *a* sense of the phrase 'type of speech act' on which this view is committed to there being an indefinitely large number of types of speech acts which English speakers do, or at least could, perform. There is asserting a proposition, asserting a proposition's negation, asserting a conjunction of two propositions, asserting the negation of a conjunction, . . . There is nothing particularly frightening about *this* infinitude of types, especially because they are all species of one primary type of speech act, assertion. Why should the infinity of types of speech acts in the current picture be any more frightening? We have one *primary* type of speech act, assuming a second-order commitment.[35] Since there are infinitely many kinds of SOCs, there are, in a perfectly benign sense, infinitely many kinds of speech acts we can perform: for each SOC c there's the act one performs when one assumes c. It would, of course, be unacceptable if there wasn't some way to systematically determine what speech act any sentence was fit to perform, working from some finite basis of information. But (so long as the number of atomic expressions of the language is finite), there is a way to do this—we just showed how it's done.

We should show that it is possible to extend the language to include the apparatus of quantification and identity, explaining, as we do this, what to make of sentences in which quantifiers and commitment operators occur ('All happy men are mortal or happy'). Suppose the language has been extended so that it includes the syntax of some standard version of first-order logic (FOL) with identity; ignore function symbols. Besides the truth-functional connectives and commitment operators, the language has the conventional quantifiers '∀' and '∃' and the 'commitment quantifiers' 'for some' and 'for any' with the syntax of the conventional quantifiers. Sentences are formed by generalizing the instructions given above: The sentences are the smallest set which closes the set of (open and closed) unforced sentences—i.e. the set of conventional wffs of FOL—under the application of force operators, including *for some v* and *for any v*, v any variable.

What *are* we supposed to make of something like the following?

(7) For any x: if having only x hairs is being bald, then having only x + 1 hairs is.

If we follow the pattern set above, (7) should have associated with it a second-order commitment. But exactly what commitment? Note that as things stand we cannot say something like: the commitment which is fulfilled iff, for each u, one asserts the proposition expressed by 'If having only x hairs is being bald, then

---

other than assertion or rejection. (e.g. one might say that 'One doesn't eat peas with one's spoon', while declarative in form, is used to prescribe, not assert.) This is orthogonal to the point I am trying to make, and so I propose to ignore it.

[35] We can identify assertion and denial with certain particularly simple sorts of second-order commitment.

having only x + 1 hairs is', when u is assigned to 'x'. The problem here is not with the idea that there are 'practically unfulfillable' commitments (unfulfillable because of the infinitude of acts needed to perform them). 'Fulfillment' is a technical term, introduced to facilitate statement of the individuation conditions of commitments; there is no censure to be attached to incurring such a commitment and failing to fulfill it in *this* sense. Rather, the problem is that, as things stand, we have not been associating *propositions* with molecular sentences such as 'Either having only 4,000 hairs is not being bald, or having 4,001 hairs is being bald'; we have been associating second-order *commitments* with such sentences. Since commitments are not propositions, there is not a simple, straightforward extension of what we have so far done which will achieve the result that (7) expresses a commitment to the assertability of some class of conditional propositions.

How, then, do we proceed? Take (7)'s interior,

(8) If having only x hairs is being bald, then having only x + 1 hairs is.

Let us pretend that antecedent and consequent here are atomic. We assume that when *Px* is atomic in the relevant sense we can speak of the proposition expressed by *Px*, relative to an assignment of an object u to 'x'. Thus, relative to such an assignment, (8) expresses a second-order commitment, one fulfilled by X iff X rejects the proposition that having only u hairs is being bald, or X accepts the proposition that having only u + 1 hairs is being bald. Thus, relative to a domain D of individuals, (8) determines a class of second-order commitments, one for each member of D. Thus, (speaking a bit loosely), given that (7) is to express a second-order commitment, its quantifier must be assigned a rule which maps classes of second-order commitments to second-order commitments.

It is not hard to see what this rule must be: It will map a class C of second-order commitments to a commitment c which is fulfilled just in case for each c' in C, c' is fulfilled. In the case at hand, this means that associated with (7) will be a commitment which is fulfilled iff, for each object u (over which the quantifier in (7) ranges), either the claim that having only u hairs is being bald, is rejected, or the claim that having only u + 1 hairs is being bald is asserted.[36] A

---

[36] And the asserted claims are not rejected, and the rejected ones not asserted. Henceforth I leave this rider tacit.

We defined second-order commitments as commitments to the appropriateness of at least one pattern of first-order commitment, the latter being what one incurs by asserting all the propositions in a set s1 and rejecting all those in a set s2. It should be clear that the commitment assigned to a universal quantification, relative to a domain D, *is* a SOC in this sense, since, relative to a fixed domain, a universal quantification is equivalent to (a possibly infinitary) conjunction.

The treatment being sketched here assigns distinct commitments to a universal quantification, relative to distinct domains. I am not sure that this is intrinsically undesirable. It does not seem to be the case that we must assign different propositions to unforced universal quantifications as the domain varies. I am not sure that one's intuitions that what one says in uttering 'All men are mortal' does not vary as the domain varies demand anything more than the latter.

definition which effects this can be straightforwardly obtained from the definition above: We assume that claims are assigned to atomic sentences relative to an assignment to the variables from a domain D. We relativize the assignment of commitments to sentences to assignments to the variables, making the obvious alterations in clauses A through D of our definition. We redefine *C is the conjunction of the class T of second-order commitments* so: C is the second-order commitment such that a set X of first-order commitments is in C iff there is a function g, whose domain is the class T, such that, for each t in T, g(t) is a member of t, and X is the union of g(t), for all t in T. We finally add to the definition of *the commitment associated with the sentence S*:

E. If S is $\forall \nu\, T$, then the commitment assigned to S relative to an assignment f is the conjunction of the set of those commitments c such that, for some u in D, c is the commitment assigned to T relative to an assignment just like f, save that it assigns u to ν.

2.5 (B)

This section gives a brief, non-technical summary of section 2.5(a); if you feel you've gotten 2.5(a)'s point, by all means go directly to Section 2.6.

Section 2.4 introduced the idea that assertion is but a special case of what happens when someone seriously and sincerely utters something which purports to 'describe how things are'. I suggested that when one 'states the facts', what one does is take on a commitment to the correctness of one among some set of assignments of truth-values to claims. Since one way to assign a truth-value to a claim is to *refuse* to assign any value, such commitments can't be explained simply in terms of assertion, as assertions are commitments to the *truth* of claims (and, when a negation is asserted, to the *falsity* of the negated claim). Such commitments can, however, be explained in terms of assertion *and* the *sui generis* speech act of denial, denial being the appropriate thing to do with a claim which is neither true nor false. Section 2.5(a) developed a simple language in which one can tell, just by looking at the form of a sentence, exactly what sort of commitment a serious utterance of it incurs. It showed that one could make sense of the idea that (use of) a sentence of the language might be a logical consequence of (uses of) other sentences of the language *without* supposing that (uses of) the sentences were even potentially bearers of truth-value.

The language is the result of adding to sentence logic—where sentence logic's vocabulary consists of the sentence letters 'A', 'B', 'C', etc. plus the truth-functions '-', 'v', '&', and so on—some 'commitment operators': 'not', 'or', 'and', and so forth. The familiar parts of the language work in the familiar way: sentence letters stand in for sentences which express claims; truth-functional connectives compound such claims to give truth-functions thereof. The commitment operators have the syntax of the truth-functional connectives: given a sentence S, there's a sentence *not* S; given sentences S and T, there are sentences *S or T, S and T*. When a truth-functional connective is the main connective of a sentence, the sentence is one whose 'job' is to be a vehicle of assertion. When a commitment operator is the main operator of a sentence, the sentence is a vehicle for some other sort of speech act—denial (such is the role of *not A*), commitment to the deniability of p or the assertability of q (this is the role of *(not p) or q)*), etc.[37]

One understands such a language only if one can tell, for any of its sentences, what sort of speech act it is a vehicle for—only if one knows, reverting to the jargon introduced in Section 2.4, what second-order commitment one incurs by uttering it. The central project of section 2.5(a) was to systematically explain this. This is straightforward for sentences without any commitment connectives. They are all vehicles of assertion. 'A' is a sentence used to assert—i.e. commit to the truth of—the claim that A; '−A v B' is a vehicle for asserting that either not A or B. What of the force operators? The word, 'and' 'adds up' commitments: if uttering *A* involves assuming a commitment c, uttering *B* assuming commitment c^*, then uttering *A and B* is the assumption of both c and c^*. The word, 'or' 'disjoins' commitments in the obvious way: if A, c, B, c^* are as before, uttering *A or B* is assuming a commitment apt just in case c or c^* is apt. Finally, 'not' 'reverses' commitments, in the sense that the commitment associated with *not A* is appropriate just in case the commitment associated with A isn't appropriate. For example:

Using atom 'A' commits one to A's assertability (i.e. truth); using *not A* commits one to the appropriateness of denying A (i.e. to A's being false or without truth-value).

Using *A and B* commits one to what using A and to what using B commits one to; using *not (A and B)* commits one to this not being appropriate—i.e. to either the commitment associated with A being inapt, or to that associated with B being inapt.

Using *not not A* commits one to the inappropriateness of the commitment associated with *not A*: since that is a commitment to the inappropriateness of the commitment associated with A, *not not A* commits one to just what A does.

An illustration might help here. Consider *(not A) or B*. Using 'A' commits one to A's being assertible, so using 'not A' commits one to its not being so—i.e. to its being deniable. Using 'B' commits one to B's being assertible, so using

---

[37] The truth-functional connectives can occur inside of the commitment connectives, but not vice versa. This is because a truth-functional connective sensibly applies only to something which is a potential vehicle of assertion. What one gets if one applies 'not', 'or', and 'and' to a sentence is something which is a vehicle for a sort of speech act other than assertion.

(not A) or B is assuming a commitment apt iff A is deniable or B is assertible. Likewise, *(not B) or A* voices commitment apt iff B is deniable or A is assertible. Think of 'commitment conditionals and biconditionals' as defined in the standard way: *if p then q* is short for *(not p) or q*; *p iff q* is short for *(if p then q) and (if q then p)*. This means, if you work through it, that the commitment one assumes if one utters

A iff B

is apt just in case

A is deniable or B is assertible; B is deniable or A is assertible.

Since nothing can be both deniable and assertible, this is just a complicated way of saying that the commitment is apt iff

A is deniable and B is deniable, or A is assertible and B is assertible.

Consider, now, a liar sentence, say

(9) −Sentence (9) is true

'−' here expressing truth-functional negation. We want to say that this sentence is true just in case things are as it says. We want, that is, to say

(10) '−Sentence (9) is true' is true iff −sentence (9) is true.

And if we understand the 'iff' here as a commitment connective, this is *exactly* the right thing to say. For, so understood, what (10) expresses is apt iff one of these is apt:

  (a) Assert both: '−Sentence (9) is true' is true; sentence (9) is true.
  (b) Deny both: '−Sentence (9) is true' is true; sentence (9) is true.

And indeed, we should do one of these—we should deny both of the claims, for they are not true. Quite generally, for *any* sentence S, the claim *'S' is true iff S* is the right thing to say, so long as 'iff' is understood as signaling a certain (non-assertoric) force.

    Section 2.5(a) concluded by pointing out that there is a perfectly good sense in which the language just sketched has a logic, but a logic which is *not* based on the idea that validity is the guarantee of preservation of truth. Sentences of the language are associated with various commitments, commitments which may be apt or inapt; validity is simply preservation of the aptness of commitment: that is, an argument is valid provided that whenever the commitments associated with all of its premises are appropriate, so is the commitment associated with its conclusion. We turn in the next sections to examples of how, by employing this notion of validity, we can respond to Frege's and Geach's complaints against the idea that some 'serious utterances'—utterances which make claims which are potentially premises or conclusions of arguments—are not assertions.

2.6

We can now respond to Frege's and Geach's points. To the charge that 'ambiguating' 'not' unnecessarily complicates logic, we have already responded: The 'complication' is motivated by facts surrounding truth-valueless but significant sentences such as the liar and applications of vague predicates to borderline cases. Section 2.5 responds to the valid point, that utterance of *If not A, then B* does not involve denial, even if unembedded utterance of *not A* invariably does. "Commitment connectives" have as their meanings functions from (tuples of) second-order commitments to second-order commitments. In the language just sketched, a sentence of the form *not A* has associated with it the second-order commitment which (roughly) is that which one incurs by denying the claim one asserts when one utters *A*.[38] The force connective *if. . . then . . .* in *If not A, then B* operates on the second-order commitments expressed by its operands to yield a new second-order commitment C appropriate just in case incurring the inverse of the commitment associated with 'A' or incurring the commitment associated with 'B' is appropriate. To incur this commitment need not involve denying anything.[39] Looked on this way, it is no more mysterious that uttering *not A* involves denial though uttering *If not A, then B* does not than it is 'mysterious' that uttering $-A$ involves asserting a negation while uttering $-A \rightarrow B$ does not.

It should be clear that all this explains how the denial of A (in our language, a sentence of the form *not A*) can be teamed up with something of the form *If not A, then B* to yield a formally valid argument. If we consider the English argument schema *If not A, then B; not A; thus, B*, we find in the language of Section 2.5 a number of possible regimentations, some valid, some not. The regimentations—labeled as valid or otherwise—follow, coupled with (representations of) the second-order commitments associated with premises and conclusion. (For simplicity, we assume that A and B are unforced.)[40]

$-A \rightarrow B;$	$-A;$	thus, B
$\{\{<-A \rightarrow B, \Phi>\}\}$	$\{\{<-A, \Phi>\}\}$	$\{\{<B, \Phi>\}\}$ Valid
$-A \rightarrow B;$	not A;	thus, B
$\{\{<-A \rightarrow B, \Phi>\}\}$	$\{\{<\Phi, A>\}\}$	$\{\{<B, \Phi>\}\}$ Valid

---

[38] This is rough because *A* itself may contain force operators; the claim is correct only for the case where *A* is unforced.

[39] In certain cases, the commitment associated with such a conditional does involve denial; *If A, then not A* is an example.

[40] Exercise: Take *If A, then B* as having been introduced as an abbreviation for *not A or B*. Validate that in each case second-order commitments are assigned correctly, using the semantics from the last section. Show that when an argument is valid, models validating the commitments associated with both premises validate those associated with the conclusion; find (possibly partial) distributions of truth-values which show the invalid arguments to be such.

If not A, then B;	−A;	thus, B
{{<A, Φ>}, {<B, Φ>}}	{{<−A, Φ>}}	{{<B, Φ>}} Valid

If not A, then B;	not A;	thus, B
{{<A, Φ>}, {<B, Φ>}}	{{<Φ, A>}}	{{<B, Φ>}} Valid

If −A, then B;	−A;	thus, B
{{<Φ, −A>}, {<B, Φ>}}	{{<−A, Φ>}}	{{<B, Φ>}} Valid

If −A, then B;	not A;	thus, B
{{<Φ, −A>}, {<B, Φ>}}	{{<Φ, A>}}	{{<B, Φ>}} INVALID

Note that whenever the regimentation is free of equivocation—that is, the premises do not mix *not A* with *−A*—the argument is valid.

One might, I suppose, object that the account being sketched has the consequence that it is possible to use the English schema *If not A, then B; not A; thus, B* to argue invalidly (since the schema has invalid regimentations), but surely it is not possible to do this. In response: Surely it *is* possible to so argue. Note, first off, that in saying that such an argument might be invalid, I'm not claiming that the premises can be *true* while the conclusion is *false*; the operative notion of validity here is what we called in section 2.5(a) c-validity. Secondly, consider the following use of the English schema, where 'she' refers to a borderline case for 'bald':

(a) If it's not true that she's bald, she's not bald.
(b) It's not true that she's bald.
So (c) she's not bald.

If the woman in question is a borderline case of baldness, there certainly is *a* sense in which the second premise is appropriate. And there certainly is *a* sense in which the first one is too, since it is a consequence of the appropriate

(d) It's not true that she's bald iff she's not bald.[41]

But if the woman is a borderline case for 'bald', the conclusion is not true, and thus (c) has an understanding—as the assertion of a negation—on which it is not appropriate.

So much for Frege and Geach on denial. Of course, Geach's main targets in 'Assertion' were not those who posit a *sui generis* speech act of denial, but those, like the naive emotivists, who say that some pieces of discourse—such as evaluations of acts and character—which we naturally use as premises or conclusions of arguments are not assertoric. One might think that the cases we have been considering—applications of vague predicates to their borderline

---

[41] Appendix I shows that once a (Kripkean) truth predicate is introduced, this sentence is c-valid.

instances, paradoxical sentences—are rather special, certainly quite different from (what the emotivist takes to be) expressions of approval or enthusiasm. The question thus arises, How much bearing does any of this have on views which see ranges of what appears to be discursive discourse to be in a business completely different from the business of 'stating the facts'?

The next chapter tries to answer this question.

3

What the Emotivists Should Have Said

Geach's main targets in 'Assertion' were not those who posit a *sui generis* speech act of denial, but those like the naive emotivists who say that sentences which function as premises or conclusions of arguments needn't be vehicles of assertion. One might think that the cases discussed in Chapter 2—applications of vague predicates to their borderline instances, paradoxical sentences—are rather special, and certainly quite different from (what the emotivist takes to be) expressions of approval or enthusiasm. The question thus arises, How much bearing does Chapter 2 have on views which see ranges of what appears to be discursive discourse to be in a business completely different from the business of 'stating the facts'?

The answer, I think, is 'Quite a lot'. In this chapter I discuss in a general way how Chapter 2's account of the particles 'not', 'if', and so forth generalizes to an account on which they are seen as devices for compounding sentences expressing a range of commitments—assertoric, evaluative, and otherwise. I argue that even the naive emotivists could have made use of something like the ideas of the last chapter to respond to Geach. I also discuss how one might make use of the machinery of Chapter 2 in the context of contemporary, 'expressivist' accounts of normative talk.

One might defend the emotivism of A. J. Ayer or Charles Stevenson. More cautiously, one might defend the somewhat more nuanced views of their modern heirs. Yet more cautiously, one might defend the coherence of such views against various objections. My project in this chapter is for the most part only this last, quite modest one. Even if the emotivists and expressivists are wrong about normative discourse, it seems to me worth defending the coherence of their views because there *are* ranges of talk—in particular, talk about 'matters of taste'—which are best thought of in a way kindred to the way in which the emotivists thought of moral talk: as talk whose function is to express various 'evaluative attitudes' which are not well understood in terms of truth and falsity. So, at least, I'll argue in Chapter 5.

3.1

The toy language of Chapter 2 has as its basis a collection of sentences (the 'unforced sentences') whose meaning makes them vehicles for assertion. The language was generated from this basis with the force indicators 'not', 'and', and so forth; when we apply a force indicator F to some sentences, the resulting sentence is a vehicle for performing a certain kind of speech act K, K being determined by the meaning of F and by the kinds of acts for which the sentences were vehicles.

Assertions have a distinguished axis of evaluation: they are evaluated as appropriate or otherwise, depending upon whether what is asserted is true. There is no reason to suppose a priori that every speech act that we have reason to evaluate as appropriate or otherwise is to be so evaluated on the basis of whether or not it is the production of something that's true. We might, for example, take an imperative to be appropriate if it is backed by 'the right kind of reasons', inappropriate otherwise.

Suppose that acts of type A are evaluated as appropriate or otherwise in terms other than truth. Depending on the nature of the appropriateness conditions, it might be that such acts stand in broadly logical relations, for the obtaining of the appropriateness condition for one act might require or prohibit that the appropriateness condition for some other acts obtain. An order to do A and B cannot, one thinks, be backed by the right kind of reasons unless imperatives to do A and to do B are.

Given that the unforced sentences of the last chapter's toy language were vehicles of assertion, those sentences had associated with them the appropriateness conditions of assertions. Once the appropriateness conditions for the simplest sentences of that language were in place, appropriateness conditions for all of the language's sentences were determined, as the appropriateness condition for the result of applying force indicator F to some sentences was systematically determined by the appropriateness conditions of the acts associated with the sentences and the meaning of F. But this didn't depend upon all of the simple sentences of the language being vehicles of assertion; it would be true even if other sorts of commitments were associated with those sentences, so long as those commitments could be evaluated as appropriate or otherwise.

To make this vivid, let us ask, When is it appropriate to perform the act associated with *not A*, A one of the language's simple sentences?[1] It is perfectly possible to answer this—at a certain level of generality—without knowing what a serious utterance of A does. Uttering A will be performing a particular instance k of a speech act of some kind K. Acts of kind K will be appropriate if conditions of some sort C obtain; so the particular act, k, performed in uttering A, will be appropriate just in case some particular condition c of sort C obtains. When is uttering *not A* appropriate? Well, when c does not obtain. Cognate tales can be told about *A and B*, *A or B*, and so on.[2] There is nothing about this story that

---

[1] I tend to concentrate on negation because its interpretation looms so large in the literature on expressivism.

[2] For example, uttering *A and B* would be appropriate iff assuming the commitments associated both with A and with B were appropriate.

requires any sentence to be a vehicle for assertion, and so no reason that it could not apply when K was something other than assertion, C something other than the condition of what is asserted being true.

We have a recipe for determining, once we know the conditions under which it is appropriate to do whatever it is that one does in uttering the sentence A, the conditions under which it's appropriate to do whatever it is that one does when one utters *not A, A or B*, and *A and B*. But that doesn't quite tell us how to get from a specification of what one does, in uttering A and uttering B, to a specification of what one *does* in uttering *not A, A or B*, or *A and B*. Can something informative be said about this?

In trying to answer this question, let's concentrate for the nonce on the case from Chapter 2. For an unforced sentence of that language, there are three possibilities: it's true, it's false, it's neither. The appropriateness of what is said by uttering a sentence of the language is determined by how these possibilities are realized by its atomic parts. If one knew, of every atomic, whether it was true, false, or neither, there would be no need—beyond our needs for economy of expression—to ever make use of the force indicators 'not' and so on. We could, instead, introduce an operator I (for 'indeterminate'), and then utter lists of atomic sentences and/or such sentences prefixed with the operator when we needed to convey some information.

Of course, we aren't omniscient, and so we need to be able to express commitments other than the specific commitments expressed by such things as 'A', '−B', and 'IC'. One might, for instance, not know the specifics about the truth-values of A and −B, while knowing that they were either both assertible or that neither was. In this case one has a—regional, as we might call it—commitment expressible by

−B iff A.

The commitment incurred by uttering ('$-B$ *iff A*') is quite different from that incurred by asserting the biconditional $-B \leftrightarrow A$. To make an assertion is always to incur a specific commitment, to the truth or falsity of a specific claim. This is not so with denial, (force) disjunction, (force) conjunction, or with the biconditional speech act above.[3] Denial and the rest are acts that work at a different level from assertion (and, I will suggest in a moment, other 'first-level' acts like that performed on an emotivist view by simple evaluations). To deny p is not to incur a specific commitment; it is rather to *disavow* (the appropriateness of) a commitment. Of course, *sometimes* disavowing a commitment is *ipso facto* incurring a specific commitment, as when I say that not not A. But these are special cases; in general, to disavow a commitment *can't* be to incur a specific commitment, because in general there will be more than one alternative to the

---

[3] This may not be obvious for force conjunction. But consider what I am committed to by saying *(not A) and (not B)*.

specific commitment disavowed (if p is not true, it might be false, it might be neither).

It is obviously necessary that we be able to make commitments beyond specific ones. It is obvious, too, I think, that in order to do this we want a device that allows us to disavow a commitment in the sense I have been outlining—that allows us, as it were, to point at a commitment and express 'the opposite commitment', where oppositeness is a matter of complementary appropriateness conditions. Likewise, it is obvious that we should have use for a device that would allow us to incur the sort of structural commitments we incur by using 'or' and 'and' in the way they are used in the language of Section 2.5. And it is just this sort of thing that a speaker of that language does with force negations, disjunctions, and conjunctions. I don't see that any deeper explanation of what one *does* in uttering a force negation (disjunction, conjunction) when speaking the language of Section 2.5 is possible, necessary, or desirable.

Exactly the same sort of thing will be true of a language in which the sorts of commitments one can incur with atomic sentences are expanded. One will still have reason to express and incur structural commitments. One will still, in particular, want to disavow, disjoin, and conjoin such commitments. The fact that the new commitments are not assertive—i.e. not commitments to the truth of anything—makes no difference at all. So long as the commitments have appropriateness conditions to begin with, it will make perfect sense not simply to incur them, but to disavow, disjoin, and conjoin them. Again, deeper explanation of what one *does* in uttering a force negation (disjunction, conjunction) when speaking the language is neither possible, necessary, nor desirable.[4]

I have a particular, not terribly complex, picture in mind in telling the story I just told, and perhaps it is worth briefly spelling it out. On this picture, we have commitments of various sorts. We are committed to the truth of claims or to their likelihood, certainty, or credibility. We have enthusiasms—commitments to doing, watching, hearing various things when time allows. We have evaluative stances—we approve or disapprove, in various ways, of various things and activities. The commitments we have may be thought of as drawn from a larger 'space of possible commitments', made up of the various beliefs, credences, enthusiasms, valuations, obligations, and so on which a person might have. When we speak or think we present ourselves as 'located in a particular place

---

[4] In Chapter 2 denial was characterized as the dual of assertion, with denial of p appropriate when and only when its assertion is not; 'not' was said to have two roles in English—to express denial in this sense and to express truth-functional negation. This was a simplification, harmless enough when we were concerned with a language the simple sentences of which are all conventional devices for making assertions. We are now entertaining the possibility that some of the simple declarative sentences of our language have non-assertoric work to perform, and have generalized our account of denial and 'not': If S is a declarative sentence which is a conventional vehicle for performing a speech act A appropriate just in case condition C obtains, *not* S is a conventional vehicle for performing an act appropriate when and only when A is not appropriate—when, that is, C does not obtain.

in the space of commitments' by expressing some of our commitments. If we (assertively) utter 'There is vodka in the fridge', we express a belief and present ourselves as being committed to the truth of the claim that there's vodka in the fridge. If the naive emotivist's story about evaluative language is correct, in saying 'Chastity is good' we express approval of chastity and present ourselves as committed to chastity being worthy of approval.

If to speak is to locate one's self somewhere in the 'space of commitments', we may expect that the sentence-compounding devices will have as their meanings rules that map a 'location in the space of commitments' to another location in that space.[5] And this is exactly how they function when they are to be interpreted as force indicators. Sentences without force indicators are typically used to locate oneself at a particular point in the space of commitments. One asserts *p*, expressing acceptance of p, and is thereby committed to *p*'s truth. One expresses evaluative enthusiasm or distaste for something ('That's cool', 'She's gorgeous', 'He's an ass'), and thereby presents oneself as evaluating in a certain way and thus committed to the appropriateness of so valuing. I called such commitments *specific*, as they are commitments to (the appropriateness of) being at specific points in what I called above the space of possible commitments.

One may commit not necessarily to a specific point in the space of commitments as being where one is (or ought to be) but to a particular *region*, or combination of regions, as being places in the space of commitments that are or are not appropriate places to be. So it goes, for example, when one utters *'S' is true if and only if S* using 'if and only if' as a force operator. One portrays the space of commitments as being so: either it is appropriate to assert both the claim that 'S' is true and the claim that S, or it is appropriate to deny both. So it goes, assuming that something like the naive-emotivist view is correct, when one says that if stealing from your parents is bad, so is stealing from your siblings: one commits not to disvaluing stealing from the parents nor to disvaluing stealing from the siblings, but to the appropriateness of either a lack of disvaluing of parental theft or a disvaluing of sibling theft. Such commitments are (simply a generalization of) what I called second-order commitments in Chapter 2, and I shall continue to call them such. Of course, whenever one incurs a specific commitment—whenever one places one's self at a particular point p in the space of commitments—one incurs a second-order commitment, to the region containing just point p being an appropriate one to occupy.

To assert p is not to assert that p is true, but it is to commit to its truth. Likewise, to utter 'Hurrah for honesty!' (or, if the naive emotivist is correct, 'Honesty is good') is not to *assert* that one is enthusiastic for honesty. It is not to *assert* that it is appropriate to be enthusiastic for honesty. Rather, it is to express that enthusiasm and to commit to that enthusiasm being appropriate. In the case

---

[5] One-place connectives would have such a meaning; n-place connectives would map n-tuples of locations to a location.

of utterances which involve us in specific commitments, we incur second-order commitments, though we do not *say* that we incur them: if I utter 'There's a spot on your tie', I commit myself to the truth of the claim, that there's a spot on your tie, but I do not *say* that I am so committed; I do not even *say* that the claim is true. The same applies to utterances which express second-order commitments without landing the utterer at a specific point in the space of commitments. When I say that it's true that Sam is bald iff Sam is bald (and am not to be interpreted as merely asserting a material biconditional), I do not assert or say that appropriate points in the space of commitments to occupy are either those at which one holds true *that it's true that Sam is bald* and *that Sam is bald*, or points at which one rejects both. I don't do this any more than when I say that Sam is bald I say that it's true that he's bald.

I go on about this because I expect the reader to be tempted to 'assertize' utterances which involve assuming second-order commitments (but don't involve incurring specific commitments). For I expect the reader to reason as follows: If uttering

If stealing from your parents is bad, stealing from your siblings is worse.

has appropriateness conditions and uttering it is committing to those conditions being in place—to their *obtaining*—why not just look upon such utterance as an assertion, either that these conditions obtain, or at least as an assertion of something that is true iff such conditions obtain? The advantage, it will be thought, is that we achieve a uniform story about (more) utterances, taking (more of) them to be assertions, and thus not needing (quite such) a novel, complicated story involving armies of novel speech acts.

But we already know that this line of thought can't be correct. I can't be *asserting* of the claims made by the sentences flanking the 'if and only if' in

'Jo is bald' is true if and only if Jo is bald.

(Jo is a borderline case of baldness) that they are either both assertible (and thus true) or are both not ('not' here truth-functional) assertible. At least I can't be asserting this and saying something it's right to say. There's nothing I might *assert* with this biconditional that's true. To commit to things being a certain way, to display one's self as having a certain kind of commitment and to that being appropriate, is *sometimes* to make an assertion. But *very often* it is not. I take it that because the story I've told about the liar, vagueness, and denial is so satisfying—it is *so obviously* correct—we *know* this to be so.

3.2

Suppose that there is a distinctive sort of 'moral approval' of acts, character traits, and states of affairs, *m-approval*, that typically accompanies sincere utterances of the sentence form *X is (morally) good*; assume that m-approval is mirrored by a distinct sort of moral disapproval, *m-disapproval*, that accompanies sincere utterances of *X is (morally) bad*. Let's suppose, as emotivists like Ayer seemed to, that sincere utterance of something of the form *To V is (morally) good* is no more and no less than a conventional device for expressing m-approval for V-ing; analogously for *To V is (morally) bad* and m-disapproval. Just as we represented the F(irst) O(rder) C(ommitment) associated with 'Snow is wet' <assertion, that snow is wet>, we may represent the FOC associated with a normal use of 'Promise keeping is good' with <m-approval, promise keeping>, the FOC associated with 'lying is bad' with <m-disapproval, lying>, thereby modeling what emotivists said about the simplest evaluative sentences.[6]

Emotivists had nothing (at least nothing coherent) to say about more complex sentences in which evaluations are combined with 'not', 'if', and other sentence-compounding devices. But, given what we have said about denial and 'not', it is not hard to see what sort of a story they *ought* to have told. What someone like Ayer *should* have said is that 'Promise keeping is not good' is a conventional device for performing an act appropriate just in case the FOC <m-approval, promise keeping> is not apt. That commitment is not apt just in case it is appropriate to lack m-approval for promise keeping, which is the case iff the appropriate attitude towards promise keeping is not m-approval, but is instead either m-disapproval or the sort of moral neutrality one has towards an activity when one neither m-approves nor m-disapproves of it.

What, it will be asked, *are* the commitments associated with 'Promise keeping is good' or 'Lying is bad' supposed to be? What is it for them to be appropriate or otherwise? Isn't the idea that moral approval or disapproval can be *appropriate* or *inappropriate* one that is *completely* foreign to the emotivist way of thinking of normative language? To claim that the judgment that lying is bad has appropriateness conditions presupposes that there is some distinguished dimension of evaluation for normative utterances (or for the sorts of act performed by them). It is to suppose that there is something that stands to the utterance (or the act it performs) of 'That is good' as truth/the absence thereof stands to utterances which perform assertions, denials of assertions, and the rest of the hierarchy discussed in the last chapter. But surely the point of anything that deserves to be called 'emotivism' is that this is exactly what is *missing* from normative discourse. After all, to think that there is a distinguished dimension along which normative discourse can be assessed as appropriate/inappropriate, correct/incorrect, or apt/inapt is to think that we can give reasons for and against normative judgments. For if the judgment that lying is bad is apt, then it is a

---

[6] If we were to keep representations completely parallel, we would need to introduce terminology for the acts of expressing moral approval ('positively m-valuing'?) and expressing moral disapproval and then represent the commitments as pairs of these acts with their objects. Keeping the representations perfectly parallel doesn't seem worth another layer of novel jargon.

judgment one ought (if the question of the moral status of lying should arise) to make. And if the judgment is apt, then the conditions under which it is apt, call them C, obtain. So there is a reason one can provide for making the judgment; namely, (i) that C obtains, and (ii) that if C obtains, then lying is bad. But to think this is surely to part company completely with the emotivists: where we have reason and argument, we have cognition; the hallmark of emotivism is its insistence that normative talk is non-cognitive.

In response: The emotivist view was that simple normative sentences such as 'Contributing to charities is good' and 'Lying is bad' express *attitudes* of approval and disapproval. And attitudes are of course complex standing states with both affective and cognitive components. To approve of giving alms is not *simply* to have a warm feeling when one sees someone put a coin in a cup; someone who could only complete the sentence 'Giving alms is good because . . .' with the likes of 'Uh, uh, well it makes *me* feel good' doesn't count as having an *attitude* of approval towards the practice.[7] The sophisticated emotivist view—the sort of view found in Stevenson's *Ethics and Language*, for example—is one on which normative talk involves both descriptive and affective elements;[8] an attitude of approval towards alms giving involves having a positive reaction towards alms giving *because* it has such and such properties. Reading an emotivist like Stevenson as holding that we do not typically have reasons for our normative opinions is reading him shallowly indeed[9].

Consider a view that holds that certain affective reactions are ones for which we can have reasons either good or bad; in virtue of this, such reactions may be appropriate or otherwise; but that is not to say that such reactions have properties that are very much (or even remotely) like truth and falsity. Must such a view be incoherent? Surely not. This, after all, is the way that we normally think of reactions such as pride, shame, embarrassment, and guilt. We classify these as appropriate or otherwise; we don't classify them as true or false.[10] And we see people as having reasons for having, or not having, such feelings, and think that some such reasons are good, others not so good.

---

[7] Compare the extended discussion of the attitude of approval in Urmson (1968: ch. 4).

[8] Consider, for example, Stevenson's idea that normative talk has various 'patterns of analysis'—that such talk is vague and involves both a descriptive element (saying that something is good implies or says something about the qualities it has in virtue of which it is deserving of approval) and a normative one (saying that something is good is a conventional means of expressing a positive affective reaction). An informative critical exposition of Stevenson's views is given in Urmson (1968).

[9] More likely, it is not reading him at all and relying on dim memories of glib lectures from graduate school.

[10] Some say that pride and so forth are a marriage of a belief and an affective response; my pride in robbing the bank in under five minutes, on this view, involves something like a belief that I robbed the bank in under five minutes, a positive attitude towards efficient bank robbing, and a positive attitude towards myself that is the result of the belief and the positive evaluation of the activity. Note that even if we agreed with this account of pride, we would not (obviously want to) assimilate appropriateness to truth. Suppose that I did indeed rob the bank in three minutes flat. My pride in the example is inappropriate, but not because my belief that I robbed the bank in under five minutes is false.

What the emotivists should have said to critics like Geach is that the fact that the judgment that lying is bad is ('merely') an expression of a certain kind of attitude towards lying in no way implies that the judgment isn't one for which reasons can be given. It in no way implies that the judgment cannot serve as a reason for other judgments, even 'purely factual' judgments. It doesn't mean that we cannot have evidence for them or that they cannot give reasons for other judgments. It doesn't mean that we cannot theorize about them, committing ourselves to having them should certain situations arise—i.e. incurring the sort of second-order commitments expressed by sentences such as 'If Smith will die if he does not steal the apple, then it is not the case that Smith's stealing the apple is bad'. We can reason with and about such commitments, adopting them when they seem to us apt, discarding them when they seem inapt: the sort of (affective) approval that is expressed by 'That's [morally] good', after all, is to a good extent under our control; we can bring ourselves to feel it or to extinguish it by reason and reflection.

What the emotivists should have said is that the judgments—that one sort of act is (m-)good, that another kind of act is (m-)bad—have one foot in our affect, one foot in the sort of deliberation and reasoning we engage in when we ask what to believe or to do. To think that lying is bad is (roughly) to have a stable disposition to have a certain kind of affective reaction to (what one takes to be) instances of lying, the sort of reaction we called above m-disapproval, *and* for that disposition to be based upon and connected to beliefs and evaluations in such a way that we have a story to tell about why (we think that) lying is bad, so that we have *reasons* for the moral opinion. The affective reaction we evince when we say that something is bad is one that is under rational control—we can cultivate it in certain cases, try to extinguish it in others, commit to having or lacking it in various situations.

What the emotivists should have said is that it is because (a) these judgments are expressions of *affective* attitudes, and (b) there is no *particular* collection of (substantive) reasons that one needs to associate with one's moral evaluations—there is no analytic connection between something's being (morally) good and its (say) promoting pleasure, or being such that any reasonable person would approve of it—that the judgments aren't to be evaluated in terms of truth and falsity.[11] The natural thing for an emotivist to say about moral judgments—a thing which may not be right but is perfectly coherent—is that whether it is apt to feel m-approval or disapproval towards something rests on nothing more than what, after we have sufficiently reflected on and reasoned about matters, we judge we

[11] There are of course things that might be said in response to an emotivist (or 'expressivist') who says these sorts of things. For example, one might say the sort of thing the 'Cornell moral realists' say—that (a) and (b) do not entail that the judgments in question aren't truth-apt, as they are consistent with a sort of 'natural-kind semantics' for 'good'. I don't propose to here retrace the recent history of metaethics, as my current project is only to convince you that Geach-style objections to emotivism are completely and profoundly without merit.

should and should not feel m-approval towards.[12] That is, the appropriateness of our feelings of m-approval and disapproval rests on nothing more (or less) than how, on (sustained) reflection, we tend to react with m-approval and disapproval. What, after all, could one say to someone whose affective reactions were different enough from our own that, even after carefully considering our evaluations of action and character and our reasons for them—after trying to understand our moral attitudes and our reasons for them—he was simply unmoved by some large segment of our evaluations? One could say 'You are very different from us', of course. But would saying 'You are making a mistake' be anything more than a rhetorical way of pointing out this difference?

If the emotivists had said this, and said (as they seemed prepared to) that a judgment's being true or false is a matter of its purport or purpose being to represent something 'outside of' or beyond the practice of making it—if they had said this, their view that moral judgments are not to be appraised in terms of truth and falsity, but are instead expressions of a certain kind of attitude, would have been perfectly comprehensible, certainly coherent. Perhaps such a view is inferior to other views. But it is not absurd. Nor, so far as I can see, is it seriously out of whack with obvious data about the possibility of reasoning about normative matters.

3.3

The emotivist and his contemporary heir, the 'expressivist', say the primary function of the simplest normative sentences is to express attitudes of approval or disapproval, not to describe the world. The emotivists concluded that such sentences don't put forward a claim that is to be evaluated as true or false. The canny expressivist may hedge this last claim, especially if he takes a deflationary attitude towards truth, thinking that to say something's true is do little more than to assent to it.

On either view, normative talk is 'expressive of our attitudes', not (at least not in any heavy-duty sense) representational. Many—including, one sometimes suspects, some of the expressivists—take this to imply that on an emotivist or expressivist view any sentence in which normative vocabulary occurs has as its function the expression of a ('non-cognitive') attitude. And from this it is often

---

[12] My goal in this chapter is to defend the coherence of a broadly emotivist position which allows for—indeed, insists upon—the possibility of (good and bad) normative arguments. It is not to defend *tout court* such a view. That said, I can't keep myself from observing that an emotivist who says something like this can make sense of the idea that we can reflect upon and correct our normative beliefs: it can seem to us that we have reflected long enough to know that no matter how long we reflect on the war in Iraq we will think it a good thing (and thus think ourselves justified in thinking that it is a good thing), while we are in fact wrong about how a longer meditation on the war would in fact go.

inferred that an 'emotivist semantics' for normative language would be centered upon a systematic mapping of sentences, simple and complex, to types of attitudes. This generates worries about the coherence of emotivism and expressivism, since they now seem committed to the existence for each (normative) attitude A of an attitude which is the 'negation of A', an attitude which an emotivist semantics associates with the negation of a sentence which expresses A. And thus is born an industry whose laborers construct and deconstruct attempts to map the language of evaluation onto the minds and moods of evaluators.[13]

This isn't a particularly fruitful way of thinking about emotivism or expressivism. As I see it, what we should conclude from the emotivist's idea—simple normative sentences are vehicles of expression, not assertion—is simply that the sort of commitment expressed by normative sentences is different from that expressed by vehicles of assertion. It is reasonable to infer from this that the 'semantic values'—the things a systematic account of meaning and significance associates with sentences and their parts—of sentences in which normative vocabulary occurs will be different in some interesting way from the semantic values of other sentences. Does it follow from this that a sentence such as 'Same-sex dancing is not a bad thing' expresses a distinctive kind of attitude that is 'the negation' of the attitude conventionally associated with 'Same-sex dancing is a bad thing'? *Perhaps* it does if we have a *very* permissive story to tell about what counts as a mental attitude. But there is no reason to think that someone who is interested in what the semantics for normative language is like, if something like emotivism is correct, needs to invoke such an attitude. *Certainly* one needn't appeal to it while doing semantics. One would have occasion to appeal to the attitude expressed by sentences of the form *To V is bad*, for the appropriateness of this attitude (and some other things) would determine appropriateness conditions for (particular uses of) the sentence. But once they are in place, systematic semantics takes over, as I stressed in Section 3.1. *Perhaps* there is a distinctive attitude that is 'the negation' of disapproval. I doubt it. But even if there is, it is *completely irrelevant* to the sort of program that the emotivists and expressivists are engaged in.

This bears on certain criticisms of expressivism. Consider, for example (the trenchant development of some points in Unwin (2001) and Dreier (2006).

An expressivist says that sentences of the form *It ought to be that A* express a particular attitude towards the state of affairs that A. Let us call the attitude *requirement*. The expressivist will say that sentences of the form *It is permissible that A* express another attitude, *toleration*. According to Dreier, the expressivist needs to say more than this, for there is a *logical* connection between claims about obligation and claims about permission; (deontic) logic tells us that

---

[13] The best-known expressivist accounts of normative language are due to Simon Blackburn (1984, 1993, 1998) and Alan Gibbard (1990, 1993, 2003*b*). Among the more interesting discussions of this work are Hale (1986), Unwin (1999, 2001), and Dreier (1995, 1999, 2006).

(D) It's obligatory that A if and only if it's not permissible that −A.

It's permissible that A if and only if it's not obligatory that −A.

If we simply say that 'ought' expresses requirement, 'may' expresses permission, we leave it 'mysterious why the two attitudes . . . are related to one another logically. Why is there any incoherence in tolerating something and also requiring its contradictory?'[14] According to Dreier, the underlying problem is that the expressivist cannot give a 'coherent semantics for negation': what is needed is an explanation of how an attitude can be negated.[15]

If one thinks that an expressivist semantics associates states of mind with normative sentences and mappings from states to states with the connectives, this is exactly what the expressivist needs to give us, if we think that sentences in (D) are logically true. But an expressivist *needn't* think of her enterprise in this way. She can, if she likes, accede to the idea that the mental states expressed by uses of *It ought to be that A* and *It's OK that A* are 'logically related'. But she should insist that when mental states are 'logically related' to one another, the explanation lies not (so much) in the attitudes themselves, but in the commitments those attitudes involve. To respond to Dreier what needs to be done is to say enough about the commitments incurred in thinking that something is obligatory or permissible so that we can see what it would be for such *commitments* to be consistent or inconsistent.

There is a more or less standard, more or less obvious *kind* of story to be told here, one that has been discussed and developed by Allan Gibbard.[16] On this story there is some sort of thing—systems of norms, or of plans, or something of these sorts—to which actors can be related and which dictates that certain things must be done, certain states of affairs must be realized. Norms and plans likewise require that certain things must not be done, certain states of affairs may not be realized; and they permit that certain things be done, certain states obtain. Such a story explains tolerance and the like in terms of 'accepting' norms or plans. To bear the mental attitude of requirement towards an act is to accept norms or plans which dictate performing the act; to tolerate it is to accept a norm or plan that allows it and no norms or plans that rule it out. Likewise, I have a particular attitude—rejection, we could call it—towards the acts forbidden by the norms/plans I accept.

A norm or a plan requires that certain states of affairs obtain; it permits certain others. To accept a norm or plan is, *inter alia*, to endorse it, and thus to endorse the vision of how things ought, may, cannot be that is embodied therein. And thus to accept a norm or plan is to be committed to certain states of affairs being realized, certain other states of affairs not being realized, and to certain states of affairs not being required: If I accept a plan or norm, and it can be carried out or adhered to only if the world is a certain way, I am committed, by my

---

[14] Dreier (2006; 219).   [15] Ibid.   [16] Particularly in Gibbard (1990) and (2003*b*).

acceptance of the norm or plan, to the world being the relevant way. It is this sort of commitment that I express when I say that it ought to be the case that A—a particular sort of commitment that one has in virtue of accepting a norm or plan that requires that A obtain. Likewise, suppose that I accept a plan or norm, and it allows me, in carrying it out or adhering to it, to let it be the case that A. Then, so long as I accept no plan or norm that conflicts with this one as far as A is concerned—that requires that A not obtain—I am committed, by my acceptance, to tolerating A. It is this sort of commitment that I express when I say that it may be the case that A; it is the sort of commitment one has in virtue of accepting a plan that tolerates A and accepting no plan that overrides or conflicts with this plan so far as A is concerned.

There is nothing mysterious about when such commitments conflict. Someone who has the commitment expressed by *It ought to be the case that* ϕ is committed to there being no satisfactory situation in which ϕ obtains; someone who has the commitment expressed by *It may be the case that* $-\phi$ is committed to there being some satisfactory situation in which $-\phi$ obtains. No matter what counts as a satisfactory situation, both of these commitments can't be on the mark. All that is needed in an 'expressivist account of negation' is contained in these observations; no account over and above this, of when one attitude 'negates another attitude' is necessary.

3.4

So should the emotivist respond to Geach-style objections. I will end this chapter with a sketch of how one might implement the ideas discussed in the previous sections. Nothing crucial to later discussion occurs in this section; those uninterested in this sort of thing are welcome to skim or skip it.

Plans and norms prescribe, proscribe, and permit situations. Situations stand in logical relations of compatibility and incompatibility; thus, so do plans and norms. Given that the commitments of those who accept norms and make plans are to be characterized in terms of the situations the norms and plans rule in, rule out, and permit, the states of mind of plan making and norm accepting stand in logical relations, even given that those states of mind are not truth-evaluable.

Like quotidian beliefs, plans and norms can suffer from indeterminacy. Sometimes this is a result of non-normative indeterminacy: it may be indeterminate whether vervet monkeys can plan for the future; thus, a norm that enjoins objectifying something iff it is capable of future plans suffers from indeterminacy. Sometimes the indeterminacy a plan is subject to is not reducible to 'factual indeterminacy'. Bob may value both public welfare and individual freedom but be clueless as to how to resolve certain conflicts between them. Norms that reflect his values will also be clueless about this, and thus will leave it indeterminate whether certain acts and situations are permissible.

There is a difference between its being permissible that A and permissible that B (where A and B are incompatible), and its being indeterminate which of A and B (if either) is permissible. It may not be altogether clear how in the context of a story like the one just sketched this distinction is to be drawn.[17] This complication makes it worth constructing an extension of the toy language of Section 2.5 which embeds an emotivist/expressivist treatment of claims about permission and obligation.

Add operators, *O* ('It's obligatory that') and *P* ('It's permissible that'), to the language L of Section 2.6. How should these operators relate, in terms of embedability, to the truth-functional operators and the force functors?

Plans and norms are plans that something should/should not/may/may not obtain; a plan or a norm is a plan concerning some state of affairs, some claim which (vagueness ignored) is true or false. Utterances that give voice to one's allegiance to a plan or norm, on the sort of view currently under discussion, are not themselves truth-apt, but rather utterances that give voice to (something like) one's commitment to follow or support the dictates of a plan or norm. This much suggests the beginnings of a hierarchy. The deontic operators ought to be able to embed the truth-functional operators, since a plan might (for example) require that either Vernon eat lunch or he eat dinner. The truth-functional operators ought not to be able to embed the deontic operators, since saying that something must or may be is not saying something that could determine a truth-value. And, while the force operators can embed both the deontic and the truth-functional operators, there does not seem to be any reason to think that deontic operators embed force functors. For what may or must be the case are things that a norm or plan might enjoin or forbid, and these are things that may be true or false. Thus, there is no need to decide whether, for example, the claim *It ought to be the case that if A, then B* is apt or otherwise, save when both *A* and *B* are themselves truth-apt. There is no need to interpret a conditional embedded under a deontic operator as anything other than a truth-functional operator. This leaves open whether the deontic operators can self-embed; let us finesse the issue of how to understand embeddings of 'ought' and 'may' within 'ought' and 'may' by simply barring them. This determines the syntax of the language.[18]

---

[17] Dreier (2006) suggests that Gibbard will have difficulty drawing this distinction. Dreier may be correct that it is difficult to draw the distinction using the apparatus in Gibbard (2003*b*), in which (simplifying in inessential ways) plans are assumed to dictate what is to be done in any possible situation. But this aspect of Gibbard's account can be understood as just an expository simplification.

[18] So the syntactic rules of the language, which sort the language's sentences into four types—forced, unforced, normative, non-normative—are as follows:

1. Atomic sentences and truth-functional combinations of them are unforced, non-normative sentences.
2. If *A* is non-normative and unforced, then *OA* and *PA* are normative, unforced sentences.

Think of a norm as something which classifies states of affairs/propositions as obligatory or not obligatory, as permitted or not permitted. A norm may simply fail to make a classification in some cases, leaving the deontic status of the case indeterminate. Because there are broadly logical relations between the classifications *obligatory* and *permissible*, norms can only make these classifications in certain ways. Continuing to think of propositions as primitive (i.e. not thinking of them as sets of worlds), we assume an entailment relation between (sets of) propositions to be given.[19] We then think of a norm as a pair $< o, p >$ of partial functions from propositions to $\{0,1\}$. Here, o+ (the claims o maps to 1) are the propositions the norm classifies as obligatory, o− (the claims o maps to 0) are those the norm classifies as not obligatory; analogously for p+ and p−. As o+ and o− need not exhaust the class of propositions, this allows for indeterminacy in obligation; likewise for permission.[20] We assume that for any norm $n = < o, p >$: o+ is consistent (it doesn't entail a set which contains a proposition and its negation); o+ is a subset of p+, and is closed under entailment; o+ remains consistent when any member of p+ is added to it (so that no one thing that is permitted is inconsistent with the sum of what's obligatory); members of p− are not in o+ (if p is not permitted, it's not required); the negation of a claim is not in o+ if the claim is in p+ (−p isn't required if p is permitted).[21]

A model is a triple $< V, w, n >$ where: V is a function which assigns truth-apt claims to unforced non-normative sentences, doing so in such a way that (for example) if p is assigned to atomic A and q is assigned to atomic B, then the conjunction of p and q is assigned to *A & B*; w (is a representative of a possible

3. If *A* and *B* are wffs, then *not A, A and B, A or B* are forced wffs, normative if either A or B is. (Conditionals and biconditionals may be thought of as introduced by the usual definitions.)
4. Something is a wff just in case its being so follows from (1) through (3).

I acknowledge the terminological oddness of clause (2), given that the expressivist's view might well be said to be that what is distinctive about claims about obligation and permission is that they involve a distinctive, non-assertoric force.

[19] When A and B are sets, A entails B just in case the joint truth of all of A insures the joint truth of all of B.

[20] Thinking of norms in this way, it would be in principle possible to represent the idea that obligations can conflict, with both *OA* and $O − A$ apt in a model. The easiest way to do this, I think, is to allow norms to assign more than one value to a proposition, so that a claim might be assigned the following: o; o and p; p; nothing. We would probably wish to impose various global constraints on norms, depending on what relations we think should hold between claims of obligation and claims of permission.

Since this issue is orthogonal to our current concerns, let us ignore this possibility.

[21] The standard representation of a normative system is as a set of worlds, with the system requiring what obtains in every world in the representation, permitting what is true in some. It would be interesting if some variant of this representation could be used in the present case. What occurs to one is to replace worlds with partial functions from propositions to truth-values which are closed in the obvious sense under entailment (e.g. if w(p) = 1 and p entails q, then w(p) is 1 as well). I have not been able to find a way of duplicating the above representation of a norm in this format, but it seems as if it ought to be possible.

world and) determines a partial assignment of truth-values to the field of V; n a norm in the sense just characterized.[22] We assume that w's assignment of values from $\{t, f\}$ respects the strong Kleene tables.

F(irst) O(rder) C(ommitment)s for the language of Section 2.5 were pairs $< a, b >$, a and b sets of truth-apt claims; such a commitment was one to the truth of all of a, the truth of none of b. We generalize this for the current language, so that a first-order commitment involves this sort of commitment along with a commitment to all of some set o of (truth-apt) claims being obligatory, none of a set o''s being so, and to all of some set p of such claims being permissible, none of a set p''s being so. We represent such a commitment as a triple $<< a, b >, < o, o' >, < p, p' >>$. SOCs are sets of FOCs.

We generalize as well the definitions of the operations DISJ, CONJ, and INV (which map SOCs to SOCs) from Section 2.5.[23] If a is the n-tuple $< a1, a2, \ldots an >$ and b is the n-tuple $< b1, b2, \ldots bn >$ with the ai's and bi's sets, then, $a + b$ is $< a1 \cup b1, \ldots an \cup bn >$; if the ai's and bi's are themselves m-tuples of sets, then $a + b$ is $< a1 + b1, \ldots an + bn >$; if a is an n-tuple and C is a collection of n-tuples $\{b1, \ldots bk\}$ (a and the bi's all sets or all m-tuples), then $a + C$ is $\{a + b1, \ldots a + bk\}$.

DIS is the operation of union on SOCs. CONJ is a binary operation on SOCs defined so:

$$CONJ \, (\{c\}, C) = c + C$$
$$CONJ \, (C' \cup \{a\}, C) = a + CONJ \, (C' \; C).$$

INV is the unary function on SOCs such that

$INV(\{<< a, b >, < o, o' >, < p, p' >>\}) =$ the set of trios $<< A, B >,$ $< O, O' >, < P, P' >>$ such that either:
A is $\{q\}$ for some q in b, and the rest (i.e. B, O, O', P, P') are null; *or*
B is $\{q\}$ for some q in a, and the rest are null; *or*
O is $\{q\}$ for some q in o', and the rest are null; *or*
O' is $\{q\}$ for some q in o, and the rest are null; *or*

---

[22] Standard model theory treats atomic sentences in a Wittgensteinian way, so that any assignment of truth-values to atoms is possible—and thus whatever propositions we think of atoms as expressing, any distribution of truth-values to them is possible. In the framework in which we are working, propositions are supposed to be assigned to sentences, thereby inducing an assignment of truth-values to the sentences. Because the language of Chapter 2 contains no operators with a modal dimension, any incompatibility among the propositions assigned to atoms was irrelevant.

In the current application of Chapter 2's framework we ought, strictly speaking, be concerned about this—and thus the model theory ought to stipulate that whatever the field of the function V below is, any distribution of truth-values to its members is possible. Since this too represents an orthogonal complication, it seems best to confine its mention to this note.

[23] The definitions being generalized here are in Ch. 2 n. 29.

P is {q} for some q in p′, and the rest are null; *or*
P′ is {q} for some q in p, and the rest are null.
INV ({c1, . . . cn}) = CONJ (INV(c1), . . . INV(ck)).

We now assign SOCs to sentences of the language relative to a model: To an unforced non-normative sentence A we assign $\{<< V(A), \Lambda>, <\Lambda, \Lambda>, <\Lambda, \Lambda>>\}$; to *OA* we assign $\{<<\Lambda, \Lambda>, <V(A), \Lambda>, <\Lambda, \Lambda>>\}$; to *PA* we assign $\{<<\Lambda, \Lambda>, <\Lambda, \Lambda>, <V(A), \Lambda>>\}$. Force conjunctions (disjunctions, and negations) are assigned the result of applying CONJ (DISJ, INV) to the operands of *and* (*or*, *not*). Appropriateness in a model is defined as before, save with the addition of clauses that make the commitment assigned to *OA* appropriate in $M = <V, w, n>$ iff n $(V(A)) = 1$; analogously for *PA*. Validity is defined as in Section 2.5.

4

What's the Matter with Relativism?

The last three chapters defended the idea that not all of what we believe, of what we argue about, of what we use as evidence is properly evaluated in terms of truth. This chapter takes up a somewhat different issue: whether truth is absolute or relative to human interests.

Two sorts of views could be called relativist. Consider

(W)   It's wrong to cheat.

One might say that a use of (W) says that cheating is wrong *relative to* something determined by human interests—the speaker's standards, a moral code, a society's view, etc. On this view (W) involves ellipsis, or a place holder for something indicating a set of standards, a code, whatever; what (W)'s use says depends on what has been elided or what is being substituted for or assigned to the place holder. On this view there need be no inconsistency between what the principal says in uttering the sentence (as she says something like *According to the standards I enforce, cheating is wrong*) and what the student says in uttering it in denial (as she says something like *According to my standards, cheating is not wrong*). Since what's expressed by (W) is being relativized, I'll call this view *expressive relativism*.

A second view is that (W) is not elliptical, is not in need of supplementation before it expresses a thought. On this view different uses of the sentence (matters of tense to the side) say the same thing. However, this thing the sentence says is not true or false absolutely, but only relative to something determined by human interests—a moral code, a society, a set of standards, etc. On this view there is a genuine inconsistency between what the principal says when she utters (W) and what the student says when she utters 'There's nothing wrong with cheating', for the student denies the very thing the principal says. Since on this view it is not what is being said but the truth-value of what's said that is held to be relative, I'll call this sort of view *truth relativism*.[1]

---

[1] Expressive relativisms are thus views about the relation of sentence types to claims—an expressive relativist holds that there is systematic variation across uses or contexts in what certain sentences say, a variation that is not associated with something in the sentence which is 'visible to the naked eye' (or ear). Truth relativism is a view about 'the nature of truth', the truth relativist holding that the truth of certain claims must be assessed relative to more than just a world (or world at a time).

Relativists are relativists *about particular discourses*. One can be a relativist about (say) some of normative discourse without being a relativist about all of it; one might hold that the claims of science are only relatively true, but not so the claims of mathematics. Of course relativism will be more plausible for some domains than for others. Many—perhaps most—people accept something like expressive relativism about discourse about height. For, typically, when we say that someone is tall or short or of average height, what we mean—indeed, what we 'strictly and literally say'—is that they are tall, short, or average for an F, F a property determined by the interests or intentions of the speaker.

It might seem that truth and expressive relativism come to pretty much the same thing. Return to our initial example. Suppose that the relevant moral code for the principal is C, for the student C*. Suppose C forbids cheating, C* allows it. The expressive relativist tells us that the principal says that according to C, cheating is wrong (and so speaks truly), while the student says that according to C*, cheating isn't wrong (and so speaks truly). We seem to get the same distribution of truth-values to utterances with truth relativism: though truth relativism has the two saying the same thing, it holds that we have to specify a moral code relative to which an utterance or claim is to be assessed for truth. If we specify these in the natural way, assessing the principal's utterance relative to her code, the student's relative to hers, what each says comes out true. The same sort of thing holds for any 'ground-level' normative claim, that a particular act or character trait is good or bad: if the expressive relativist and the truth relativist use the same code for relativizing a particular sentence use, they will assign it the same truth-value.[2]

But there are genuine differences between the two views. For one thing, truth relativism, but not expressive relativism, challenges the orthodox view that truth is in an important sense absolute. Orthodoxy tells us that it makes no sense to suppose that the things we say and think might be true in one place or culture while false elsewhere, as the truth relativist insists. The expressive relativist has

---

One can be both an expressive relativist and a truth relativist about a discourse. One might hold that sentences in which an adjective like 'tall' occurs need supplementation before they express something evaluable for truth: to say that someone is tall is to say he is tall for an F, for some particular F. To hold this is to be an expressive relativist about talk about height. One might go on to say that even once we have fixed a reference class or property, a claim about height is only relatively true. For whether someone is tall for (say) a twentieth-century American chess player depends in part on how one 'draws the line' demarcating where the tall begin within the class—and this is something that can and does vary with the interests of a speaker. I will in the course of the chapter defend the view that discourse about height (wealth, redness, and so on) is relative in both of these ways.

[2] In these informal, introductory remarks, I do not make heavy weather about the difference for the truth relativist between saying that something is true *simpliciter* and saying that it is true relative to a context (or relative to whatever parameter to which truth is relativized). The savvy reader will recognize that some of this paragraph threatens contradiction. (How can it be true that cheating is wrong and true that it's not?) I ask the savvy reader to read on to sections 4.4 through 4.6, where these sorts of worries are discussed.

no commitment to *this* sort of relativism. An expressive relativist who claims that the principal's use of (W) says that according to the principal's code cheating is wrong will take this claim to be absolutely true or false: if it is 'true for somebody' that according to the principal's code cheating is wrong, it is 'true for everybody' that according to *that* code the act is wrong.

On the other hand, expressive relativism, but not truth relativism, makes our practices of diagnosing and ascribing agreement and disagreement hard to understand. We think the student *contradicts* the principal when she utters 'Cheating is not bad'. But what the expressive relativist has the principal and the student saying (cheating is bad according the principal's code; cheating's not bad according to the student's) is not inconsistent.

Expressive relativism also sits poorly with received wisdom about ascription of belief and other propositional attitudes. The standard picture of thought, assertion, and their ascription is this: saying and thinking involve being related to the sort of thing expressed by a sentence, a proposition. If you believe or assert proposition p, then for me to correctly say that you say or think p I need (and only need) to find a sentence which, when I use it, expresses p. Provided S is such a sentence, I can then ascribe your belief or assertion to you by uttering *You think/said that S*.

Expressive relativism must either reject this picture or say that we are very confused about the status of our attitude ascriptions. If the principal utters (W), the student will report to her friends

(T) The principal thinks that it's wrong to cheat.

According to the expressive relativist, 'It's wrong to cheat', in the student's mouth, says that according to the student's moral code it's wrong to cheat. So, given the standard picture, when the student utters (T), he says that the principal thinks that according to the student's moral code cheating is wrong. But of course that's *not* what the principal thinks; this is not what (T) says.[3]

---

[3] An expressive relativist might try telling a non-standard story about sentences such as (T). Perhaps he will say that my use of a sentence of the form

(F) X believes that y is wrong.

is to be understood as saying that X believes *what X would say* by uttering '*y is wrong*'. Among the problems with this is that it doesn't make sense of the pretty much universal intuition that if I say 'The principal thinks that cheating is wrong, but the student doesn't [think it is wrong]', I report them as having inconsistent beliefs.

The problems with this sort of proposal about (F) are very similar to the problems traditional Fregeanism has, once it acknowledges that different people may associate very different senses with names that refer to the same thing. I have discussed these problems in some detail in chapter 2 of Richard (1990). Most of the criticisms made there of Fregean views seem to apply to natural elaborations of expressive relativism about discourse which, like much normative discourse, does not seem to be elliptical or to involve implicit reference to some relativizing element.

The point of the last few paragraphs in the text has been to show how expressive and truth relativism differ by concentrating on *particular* versions of each view. My point is *not* that any

I distinguish expressive and truth relativism so that I can push expressive relativism to the side. My primary interest in this chapter is whether truth relativism is a plausible view to take about *any* discourse. I think it is. Indeed, I think it is probably the correct view of a great deal of rather banal discourse. I thus think truth relativism a coherent, defensible view. My reasons for thinking this, as well as a sketch of how I think relativism fits into an account of natural-language semantics, occupies Sections 4.1 through 4.3.

Many, perhaps most, philosophers think that relativism is *obviously* wrong. I should stress at the outset that I am not attempting a blanket defense of relativism. Many relativist views are just nuts, and the relativism I defend here is tempered—I do not, for example, think that *all* truth is relative. Even against a 'modest' relativism (henceforth 'relativism' means 'truth relativism') the list of complaints is a lengthy one. A relativist about a particular discourse, it is said, is committed to the absurdities that: whatever opinions someone has in the discourse are correct (that is, there's no interesting difference between thinking p and being right in so thinking); the world is populated with contradictions (since if something is 'true for me' I can correctly say that it's true, and if something is 'false for you', you can correctly say that it's not true); we should not impose our beliefs on others because their dissenting beliefs are true. I take up what seem important, or at least very common, objections to relativism in Section 4.4. Section 4.5 attempts to connect my discussion to broader issues about agreement, disagreement, and rational change of view. Much more needs to be said about these last matters than I have been able to say here.[4]

4.1

The semantic properties of many expressions depend on the situation in which they are used. Indexicals and demonstratives—'I', 'you', 'he', 'she', 'this', 'those', and so on—are the most obvious examples. A moment's reflection suggests that the same is true of pretty much every gradable adjective—every adjective that, like 'rich', 'round', and 'ribald', has comparative and superlative forms. We can't say who's rich and who's not until we have determined what counts as a luxury and what a necessity; what so counts varies across class, culture, and current focus. Who counts as tall varies with the reference class we measure against; whether

version of expressive relativism whatsoever will have a hard time accounting for our intuitions about disagreement and what is said. Someone who holds that a use of 'Mary is tall' is invariably elliptical for something of the form 'Mary is tall for an F' is 'an expressive relativist about discourse about height'. But such a view doesn't (for example) mispredict our intuitions about whether Naomi's utterance of 'Mary isn't tall' contradicts Didi's utterance of 'Mary is tall' when the first compares Mary to sportswomen, while the second compares her to high-school sophomores.

[4] I should note up front that this chapter doesn't discuss relativism and normative talk. I hope to discuss this elsewhere, elsewhen.

'square' applies to a thing apparently depends upon the operative 'standards of precision'. And so on. Context provides parameters necessary for such adjectives to determine even a vague extension. I use the term *contextualist* for views that hold that the application conditions of an adjective, noun, or verb vary with something which differs across contexts, where the something is at least in part determined by the interests, opinions, or other intentional states of conversants.

Contextualism about the gradable adjectives might seem to imply that sentences in which such adjectives occur say different things in different contexts. After all, one might reason, if 'rich' used in one situation is true of Mary, false of her when used in another, then, absent a change in Mary, 'rich' must be expressing different properties in the different situations. So use of 'Mary is rich' in the first situation ascribes one property to Mary, use in the other another. But then the uses of the sentences say different things.

It isn't at all clear that a contextualist ought to say this. If he does, he'll have to say that many cases we automatically take to involve disagreement over who is rich (or what is puzzling or dangerous or . . .) turn out to be cases in which there is no disagreement. Suppose, to take an example, that Mary wins a million-dollar lottery. Didi is impressed, and remarks to a friend 'Mary's rich'. Naomi, for whom a million dollars is not really all that much, remarks in a conversation disjoint from Didi's, 'Mary is not rich at all'. Suppose the salient comparison class is the same in both cases (it is, say, New Yorkers) and that there is no difference between the two conversations so far as the point of assessing people as rich or otherwise goes—each conversation began with the observation that some wealthy person doesn't deserve to be rich, and each of the women is now assessing people as rich or otherwise, and then assessing whether the rich ones deserve their wealth.

It seems to most of us that Naomi is contradicting Didi. But, especially if each remark is part of a longer conversation (with Naomi assessing various people she and her friend know for wealth, Didi doing the same), it is very plausible that the truth of their claims about wealth turns on whatever standards prevail within their conversations. This is, in any case, part and parcel of standard contextualist views of the semantics of 'rich'.[5] But if each woman speaks the truth, then it seems that Namoi and Didi *don't* disagree, in the sense that one asserts something which is inconsistent with what the other asserts.

So we have a puzzle. Let's focus on two questions. (1) Suppose that I am privy to both Didi's and Naomi's conversations, and say to myself 'They disagree: one thinks Mary's rich; the other does not'. Call my so reporting the content of Didi's and Naomi's separate conversations *The Report*. It strains credulity to think that I am just wrong to say that the two disagree. What we might call *the semantic question* is: What disagreement is reported in The Report? (2) We can ask more

---

[5] Perhaps the canonical contextualist account of these matters is that in Lewis (1979). That account is discussed in Section 4.3.

simply, What substantive disagreement would the two be having if they were to overhear one another and turn to argue about whether a person with a million dollars is in fact rich? Call this case, in which the two turn from their respective conversations to an argument with each other over Mary's status, *The Argument*. *The substantive question* is, What disagreement are Naomi and Didi having in The Argument?

There seem to be three standard responses to these questions.

Response 1. In The Argument, Naomi is actually talking about the word 'rich' (or the sentence 'Mary is rich'); in The Report I am reporting a difference concerning the sentence 'Mary is rich'. The dispute in The Argument is over the criteria to be associated in the conversation with 'rich'. Sometimes negation is used not to deny content but to comment in one way or another on a word or sentence's interpretation; a standard example is 'She's not rich; she's filthy rich'. The current response has it that Naomi's use of 'not' is such a use of 'not'—she is in effect rejecting (Didi's use of) the sentence 'Mary is rich'. When I utter 'Naomi says that Mary's not rich' in The Report, I am reporting Naomi's negative attitude towards 'Mary is rich'. In The Argument, what is at issue is how the word 'rich' is to be used; the content of the dispute is something like whether 'rich' should be applied to million-dollar-lottery winners.

Observations. One problem with this proposal is that it doesn't seem to help with cases parallel to The Argument. Change the example, so that the women are looking at shirts and evaluating whether they are dirty. (Perhaps the issue is which shirts should go to the dry cleaners.) They always evaluate them as 'clean' or 'dirty'; ironing is not an issue. One would report them to disagree if Didi calls a shirt clean and Naomi calls it dirty; they would take themselves, in a variant of The Argument, to disagree about the shirt. But there is no negation involved in the report 'One thinks the shirt clean, the other thinks it's dirty'; neither is negation involved when one says 'It's clean', the other 'It's dirty'.[6]

In my opinion it is just not very plausible that *Naomi* is using 'not' metalinguistically: she's made a comment about Mary, not a comment about the sentence 'Mary's rich'. A worry about the idea that *I* am using 'not' metalinguistically in The Report is that it prima facie overgeneralizes. If I can use 'not' metalinguistically to report Naomi's assertive use of 'She's not rich', it is because it is sometimes open to us to so use negation in attitude reports to report attitudes which are not expressed by using metalinguistic negation. For in The Report I am reporting Naomi's passing comment that Mary is not rich.

But then under what conditions can I use metalinguistic negation in an ascription of attitude? The simplest answer—whenever I am reporting a saying

---

[6] Another problem is that it isn't altogether obvious that on response 1 Didi *contradicts* Naomi. Surely Didi says nothing about the word 'rich' or the sentence 'Mary is rich'. Given the other problems this response has, it's not really worth exploring this.

that involves negation—is obviously wrong. Save in exceptional circumstances, it would be incorrect to report Naomi's contribution to any of the following

(1) (a) Didi: Mary gave me the flu.
    (b) Naomi: Mary didn't give me the flu.
(2) (a) Didi (in England): The wine Bob drank last night is domestic.
    (b) Naomi (in France): The wine Bob drank last night is not domestic.
(3) (a) Didi (comparing Bob to chess players): Bob is tall.
    (b) Naomi (comparing Bob to soccer players): Bob is not tall.

by simply uttering 'Naomi said that' and then echoing Naomi's utterance. But if we could freely use metalinguistic negation in a report of a negated utterance, such a report would be acceptable. So what are the constraints on the use of metalinguistic negation in attitude reports? We must, if the response is acceptable, be able to use it in cases in which we are not reporting a metalinguistic attitude. Until we have an account of this, we really don't have a response to the semantic question.

What of the idea that the substantive disagreement between Didi and Naomi is over the criteria that ought be used with the word 'rich'? Well, they do disagree about that. But this is a consequence of a more basic disagreement, which is over what it is for someone to be rich. If you doubt this, ask yourself: Do they disagree as to whether 'rich' applies to Mary because they disagree about what it is to be rich, or do they disagree about what it is to be rich because they disagree as to whether 'rich' applies to Mary? Surely the answer to the first question is affirmative, the answer to the second negative. But if they disagree over criteria because they disagree over the nature of wealth, then it is a difference over what it is to be rich which is at the root of their differences. And if so, then the right answer to the question *What is their substantive disagreement?* is surely one in which the word 'rich' is used, and not just mentioned.

Response 2. The substantive dispute is over how to sharpen the vague concept of being rich. The concept the word 'rich' expresses is vague. Vague concepts may be made precise for conversational purposes so long as those in the conversation can agree on how to do so. If conversants can't agree, the concepts retain their vagueness. In The Argument we may assume that Didi's and Naomi's use of 'rich' are acceptable. That is: in some contexts, the concept's extension is in accord with Didi's usage; in others, it's in accord with Naomi's. But since the two do not agree on how to apply the term to Mary, she remains a borderline case for the concept in the conversational context. The substantive dispute in The Argument is thus whether for Didi's and Naomi's purposes the best way of sharpening the concept *rich* involves putting Mary in its extension. They also disagree about the indeterminate claim that Mary is rich. Since this is so, we can take my utterance in The Report to report Didi and Naomi's differing attitudes towards this indeterminate claim.

Observations. First of all, this does not seem to solve the problem posed by The Report. There, Didi and Naomi are not arguing with each other. Each is engaged in her own conversation; within the confines of each conversation, the application of the concept *rich* and the predicate 'rich' is not under dispute. We recognize each use as a perfectly acceptable way to use the predicate 'rich'. Certainly the spirit of contextualism about 'rich' would have us grant that each application of 'rich' in the conversations reported on in The Report is correct. And nothing in the current response suggests a way of reconciling contextualism with the idea that one or both of these applications are incorrect.

So how can the account this response gives of The Report be correct? On the current response I am supposed to be reporting that the two differ about something whose truth-value is indeterminate. But if my use of 'Mary is rich' expresses something without truth-value and Didi's use expresses something true, then reporting Didi as asserting what my use says is incorrect. At least it is on standard, non-relativist views, on which a difference in the truth of what sentences say requires that the sentences say different things.

A second problem with this response is phenomenological. In examples like The Report and The Argument speakers do not feel that they are sharpening a vague concept in applying it. Indeed, they would challenge the claim that they are sharpening indeterminate usage. Suppose someone happened upon The Argument and suggested that it is indeterminate whether Mary is rich, but that the best way to sharpen the notion of being rich would make Mary non-rich. We would expect *both* Didi and Naomi to object to this suggestion.

Finally, this response has an odd consequence concerning identity of what is said. Didi's standards of wealth presumably do not change, when she turns from the conversation in The Report to the conversation with Naomi in The Argument. One has a fairly strong intuition that in The Argument Didi would be asserting and defending the truth of what she says in The Report. But this cannot be on the current response, since what she says in The Report is true, and what she says in The Argument is without truth-value. At least, this cannot be unless the truth of what she says is relativized, so that it may be true-in-The-Report, not-true-in-The-Argument.

Response 3. Once we recognize that we are often ignorant about the application criteria for our terms, both the semantic and the substantive questions can be answered rather simply: Didi claims that Mary is rich for a New Yorker; Naomi denies it. In The Report, I report this disagreement; in The Argument, the women differ over whether Mary is rich for a New Yorker. Consider Didi's and Naomi's uses of 'rich' in The Argument, uses which we are assuming are each elliptical for 'rich for a New Yorker'. Whether these uses of 'rich' apply to the same things depends on whether those uses have the same criteria of application. According to contextualism, the criteria for applying 'rich (for a New Yorker)' are determined, in part anyway, by the standards of wealth of the user. It seems as if the women are applying different standards, simply because it seems obvious to Didi that a million dollars makes one rich for a New Yorker, obvious to Naomi that it doesn't. But this could well be chalked up to the non-transparency of their standards for wealth. After all, one or both of them may be deferential so far as standards for wealth are concerned. Obviously, if the opinions of others contribute to determining the application of one's terms, one may be wrong about what those criteria entail. Even if Didi and Naomi defer to no one, each may have a lot to learn about what her standards for wealth require. What is a necessity, what a luxury, depend on facts about human nature and needs; if Didi is ignorant of the relevant facts (or does not realize that a fact is relevant), she will need more information before she knows what her standards for wealth demand.

Once we grant this, we must grant that in The Argument Didi and Naomi may have a straightforward, substantive disagreement over whether Mary is rich for a New Yorker. For their context may supply a single standard for wealth (for a New Yorker) which determines the application of both of their uses of 'rich'. Their disagreement is then simply over whether Mary satisfies this standard for wealth; at least one of them is mistaken about what this standard requires. In fact, the response goes, we must understand The Argument in this way. In a normal conversation speakers are committed to using terms in the same way: otherwise, they just talk past each other. This commitment ensures that in a normal conversation uses of 'rich' by various conversants have the same extensions and content.[7] The upshot is that there will be genuine conflict between Didi and Naomi—one contradicts the other; at most one can be correct.

Observations. Let us grant that the criteria associated with our terms are often not transparent to us. Let us grant that often enough in conversation when there is disagreement about how to apply a vague term such as 'rich' to borderline cases, those cases remain borderline cases for the purposes of the conversation. We may thus grant that in many situations which look like the situation in The Argument there will be a simple, substantive disagreement between Didi and Naomi as to whether Mary is rich according to the standards of wealth governing the conversation.

Even granting this, the response doesn't speak to the semantic problem raised by The Report. If we accept contextualism about 'rich', there is every reason to think that different standards for application govern 'rich' in the two conversations in The Report. Didi (along with her friends) and Naomi (along with hers) have different considered opinions about what is a necessity, what is a luxury. They have (we may suppose) different considered opinions about what counts as *significantly* more than the average level of wealth in New York. Each group's considered opinions and standards may constitute perfectly reasonable, perfectly normal ways of using the term 'rich' when the comparison class for the use is the class of New Yorkers. The point of a contextualist

---

[7] Thus, in The Argument it will be simply indeterminate whether Mary is in the extension of 'rich', unless one of the women can convince the other that her usage ought to be accepted.

account of 'rich', in part, is to acknowledge that agreement among conversants on reasonable standards for applying the term has a semantic effect. If Mary meets the standards Didi and her friends are using in applying 'rich', then their application is correct; ditto for Naomi. But we report the two as disagreeing in The Report. It's not clear what the current response has to say about this sort of case. Is the report correct? If not, why not? If so, are we supposed to think that at most one of the two speaks correctly? If so, contextualism about 'rich' seems to have been rejected; if not, one needs an explanation of how one can be correct that Mary's rich and the other correct that she's not. This the response doesn't provide.

Furthermore, the response doesn't even speak to the issue The Argument raises. In that case, Didi and Naomi each begin (before they confront each other) by saying something true. They then confront each other, each intending to defend the truth of what each uttered before the confrontation. It is not easy to believe that they can't do this. After all, couldn't they just refer to what they said in the previous conversations? Didi might say, for instance, 'What I said about Mary is right—think of all the things she can do with a million dollars'. But if Didi is defending the truth of what she said before her confrontation with Naomi, she is defending the truth of something true; likewise for Naomi.

We have been trying to square contextualism about 'rich' with our intuitions about disagreement. We could, of course, give up or hedge one or the other of these. Holding onto contextualism, we might say that our reporting practices—and the intuitions underlying them—are sloppy and inaccurate: Didi and Naomi do not really disagree, and we report them as doing so simply because we don't have a convenient way to capture the sense of 'rich' as each uses it. Holding onto the way we interpret one another, we might say that the contextual shiftiness of 'rich' is limited to ellipsis of what is not contextually shifty. On this view (a) we can use 'Mary is rich' to say that Mary is rich for a twenty-first-century middle-class American, or for a worker at MacDonald's, or enough to take a vacation, or . . . But (b) there is no contextual variation in the extension of phrases such as 'rich for a twenty-first-century American' or 'rich enough to afford a Lexus'. So if Didi's and Naomi's uses of 'Mary is rich' are each elliptical for the same more complex phrase—Didi, say, means to say that Mary is rich for a twenty-first-century middle-class American, and Naomi means to deny this—then they really do disagree. But at most one can be correct, as 'rich for a twenty-first-century middle-class American' does not shift extension across contexts.

Neither of these options is particularly satisfying. Against the first we might observe that we *do* have a way to relativize Didi's and Naomi's uses of 'rich'. We can say, for example, that Mary is rich on Didi's view, or according to Didi's conception of being rich. We employ such devices when we don't sense a genuine disagreement. But we do sense a real disagreement in The Report, and we don't relativize.

One worries about the second option. Competent users of phrases such as 'rich for a twenty-first-century American' or 'rich enough to buy a Lexus' can and do differ about what it is to be rich for an American, rich enough to buy a Lexus. They may take somewhat different cases as paradigmatic for being rich; they may generalize from paradigms in somewhat different ways; they may bring somewhat different 'theoretical' commitments to the assessment of wealth. We do not find that such differences make speakers mean different things by the phrase, even if those differences play out so that one speaker finds Mary rich for a twenty-first-century American while another does not. We will assess the different uses of such speakers as acceptable uses of the phrase. Within a conversation in which the speaker's use of 'rich for an American' is accommodated by other speakers, we naturally use the terms 'correct' and 'true' in assessing applications of the term which accord with the speaker's settled dispositions for using the term and which don't involve factual mistakes. The fact is that we don't think that there is only one correct way to use a vague phrase like 'rich for a twenty-first-century American'. The second option, unless it has an account of how an application of 'rich' can be correct though not true of that to which it is applied, seems bound to deny this.

What are we to say, then, about gradable adjectives such as 'rich'? Well, we could take appearances at face value. In The Report, Didi and Naomi disagree. So there is something that Didi says and Naomi denies. Within the confines of each woman's conversation, each use of 'is rich' is correct. So Didi says something true in her context when she utters 'Mary is rich', Naomi something true in hers when she utters the sentence's denial. This is consistent with the two disagreeing over the truth of a single claim, if the truth of the claim may be relative, so that it may be 'true for Didi, but not for Naomi'. We can make sense of both contextualism and The Report, that is, if we relativize not what is said by sentences such as 'Mary is rich', but the truth of what is said. And if we do this, we solve the substantive problem: the women's substantive disagreement is simply one as to whether Mary is rich.

4.2

Why would one want to speak or think the thoughts expressible in a language for which truth is relative? The short answer is that we need, and will always need, to work out the details of our concepts while we are using them.

The extension of 'rich' varies across contexts as a result of how individuals within the context use the expression. It is subject to what David Lewis has called *accommodation*—roughly put, its extension shifts to make sentences in which it is used true, provided no one objects to the use in question.[8] Correlatively, 'rich'

---

[8] Lewis (1979).

is subject to 'contextual negotiation': when speakers differ over how it is to be applied to cases, they can and often do attempt to reach a consensus as to how it is to be applied, via examples, argument, mutually agreeable stipulation, and so on.[9] It is this—that 'rich' is subject to the processes of accommodation and negotiation (A & N, for short)—which explains why 'Mary is rich' expresses a claim whose truth is relative.

How so? Because 'rich' is subject to accommodation, speakers in different conversations (or thinkers who use the expression to frame their thoughts to themselves) are able to impose different extensions (and thus intensions) on 'rich'; the result is that different speakers' uses of 'Mary is rich' can have different truth-values. Put otherwise: Because of accommodation, the sentence 'Mary is rich' can in one context say something true, while in some other (simultaneous) context it will say something false. But now consider the speakers in two such contexts, contexts relative to which 'Mary is rich' differs in truth-value. Suppose, as may be the case, that the comparison classes each uses to assess Mary for wealth are the same, and their interests in judging wealth are the same as well. These speakers still disagree, and may well reasonably disagree, as to whether Mary is rich. Such speakers (or thinkers) can in principle subject their uses of 'Mary is rich' to negotiation. Such negotiation is not (merely) metalinguistic: Should Naomi choose to argue with Didi, she does not (merely) argue with her about whether 'rich' applies to Mary; she argues with her about whether Mary is rich. Accommodation and negotiation are not (simply) metalinguistic, but substantive; in particular, when Naomi refuses to accommodate Didi's claim that Mary is rich, they differ as to whether *the claim*, that Mary is rich, is true. Put otherwise: Because negotiation is substantive, speakers like Naomi and Didi must be negotiating about what it is to be wealthy, and so are disputing about whether Mary is rich. If the expression e is subject to A & N, then uses by different speakers of the sentence . . . *e* . . . (so long as it is free of conventional demonstratives and indexicals such as 'that' and 'I') say the same thing. Otherwise, the agreement and disagreement involved in A & N are not substantive in the way we just noted they are.

When a predicate is open to A & N, it is context-sensitive, as what it is true of varies across contexts.[10] But the context-sensitivity of 'rich' is of a different sort than that of the much-studied demonstratives ('this', 'that', etc.) and indexicals ('I', 'here', 'now', and so on). Part of the difference is that variation in the semantic properties of demonstratives and indexicals isn't 'up for negotiation' in the way the variation in the semantics of 'rich' is. The audience just doesn't have a say in deciding who the speaker's use of 'I', 'you', 'this' or 'she' refers to—there is no such thing as accommodating (or failing to accommodate) the use of a demonstrative or indexical.

---

[9] This idea is developed in Moravscik (1990).

[10] Dotting 'i's: across simultaneous contexts in the same world. Let this be understood henceforth.

This difference is accompanied by a difference in the relation of what varies contextually (in the semantic properties of an expression) to what is said (by sentences in which the expression occurs). As we observed two paragraphs back, the variation in the semantics of 'rich' that's caused by contextual accommodation doesn't affect what is said. What is said by 'Mary is rich' remains the same even as the extension of 'rich' shifts with the context's 'standards of wealth'. Conversely, when a semantic feature is *not* up for contextual negotiation, fixing that feature *does* have an effect on what is said: as the reference of 'I' ('you', 'she', etc.) varies across contexts, so does what is said by a sentence in which the expression occurs.

Call a claim that could be relatively true—true when made by one person, not true when made by another (in the same world)—an r-claim. What I've said suggests that when a sentence can be used to express an r-claim, that is to be explained by finding an expression in it which is subject to the processes of accommodation and negotiation—and, conversely, that when such an expression occurs in a sentence, it can be used to express an r-claim.[11] I would think that every vague expression is subject to accommodation and negotiation. If so, then the range of r-claims is at least as large as the range of sentences that contain vague expressions—on most accounts, a very large range indeed. Should we be frightened by this rampant relativism? I don't see why. Vague expressions are vague within a certain range; accommodation and negotiation presumably take place only within that range. That we can within limits adjust the extension of 'flat' to include short stretches of the interstate does not mean that we can say that the earth is flat and, if no one challenges us, thereby make it true that the earth is flat.[12]

We do not always take speakers to disagree when they differ on the application of an expression subject to A & N. We do not feel that Didi's use of 'Mary is tall' at graduation ceremonies need contradict Naomi's use of 'Mary isn't tall' at basketball games. Why doesn't this count against the proposal that sentences containing expressions subject to A & N express r-claims?

Gradable adjectives like 'tall' and 'rich' enjoy at least two sorts of context-sensitivity. Associated with such an adjective is a measure or scale: with 'tall', a measure of height; with 'rich', of wealth.[13] In context, we can adjust to what we apply the measure, as well as adjusting how the measure will apply. That is to say: for such adjectives, there are shifts across context as to what is the relevant reference class (shifts in what), and there are shifts across contexts as to the point

---

[11] This claim is subject to a caveat which is developed in the next chapter. It would, I think, simply confuse matters to discuss it here.

[12] Note that insofar as relative truth is only a result of meaning being subject to A & N, there is no reason to think that all truth is relative. And insofar as there are—as there obviously are—limits as to what is 'up for negotiation' in the meanings of our words, there are limits to the relativity of truth. See the discussion in Section 4.4.

[13] This idea is interestingly developed in Kennedy (1999).

on the adjective's scale which is the cut-off for the adjective's application (shifts in how).[14]

The fact that 'tall' requires a reference class does not in and of itself make it subject to A & N. The word is subject to A & N because even after we fix a reference class for it we can adjust the point on the scale of height at which the cut-off for being tall lies. To see this, note that there are two ways in which we can object to the claim that Michael is tall (for a skier). We can object because he's not very tall relative to the skiers; we can also object to the claim because it's irrelevant—when, for example, we have been discussing basketball. The first sort of objection involves disagreement with what the speaker said: it's a refusal to accommodate the speaker's proposal about where to draw the line for tallness among the skiers. The second objection involves a sort of disagreement, but not with what the speaker said. What is at issue is not what the speaker said, but its relevance. If the speaker concedes the first sort of objection, she makes a concession about the extension of her use of 'tall'. If the speaker concedes the second sort of objection, she is not making such a concession; she is conceding irrelevance. It is a fact about how we talk that to what a gradable adjectives is applied—that is, the reference class for application—is up to the speaker. A speaker's selection of a reference class (or of a property determining such) can't be challenged as wrong, but simply as irrelevant or misguided. Since this is so, what reference class is relevant to a use of 'tall' is not open to A & N.

We saw above that when variation in an expression's semantics was not open to contextual negotiation, that variation affected what is said. So we should expect that the reference class associated with a use of 'tall' invariably helps 'determine the content of what is said'. Didi's graduation use of 'Mary is tall' is a claim that Mary is tall for a graduating senior; Naomi's sporting use of 'Mary is not tall' makes the claim that Mary is not tall for a basketball player. This explains why we see no disagreement between Didi and Naomi in this case. None of this implies that Didi and Naomi don't make r-claims when they utter 'Mary is/is not tall'. As noted above, even if the reference class of 'tall' is fixed by speaker's intentions alone, the cut-off point on the measure associated with the adjective is subject to A & N. This fact is obscured in the example of Didi, Naomi, and Mary's height, for we are focused on a shift in reference class. The upshot is that the fact that we don't see any sort of conflict between the utterances in question

---

[14] I characterize 'shifts in what' as shifts in a reference class. It would be better to say that what shifts in these cases is a *notion* which, relative to a context, determines a property and thereby a class for comparison. (The idea of a notion is discussed in the next section.)

The remarks in the text are idealized. The measure associated with many adjectives will induce at best a partial ordering, since there may be many factors relevant to the adjective's application, with the balance among them itself being subject to A & N. And there are probably terms subject to A & N which do not have scales associated with them. If the application of a term depends on such factors, it may make little sense to think that a scale or measure is associated with the term, even if each of the factors is scalar.

casts no doubt at all on the hypothesis, that a sentence's expressing an r-claim is explained by its containing an expression open to A & N.

4.3

What does 'true for Naomi' mean, if we cannot go reliably from *It's true for Naomi that p* to *p*? How can it be that the r-claims—that Mary is rich, that she is not rich—are inconsistent, if the first can be true (for Didi) while the second is true (for Naomi)?

The contextualist about 'rich' should hold that

(a) 'rich' expresses different properties in different contexts;
(b) for any individual x, there is an r-claim that x is rich, and an r-claim that x is not rich. Whether such a claim is true relative to a context or conversation depends on whether x has the property expressed by 'rich' in the context or conversation.[15]

Let us introduce *t-claim* to contrast with *r-claim*, so that t-claims are ones which cannot, within a single world, differ in truth-value across conversations. Let us assume that for any r-claim p and context c there is at most one t-claim q which is the 'completion' of p in c. In the case of the r-claim that Mary is rich, its completion in my context is the proposition that Mary has P, where P is the property 'is rich' expresses when I use it; I hope the way I intend to generalize the notion of the completion of an r-claim is clear enough. Use 'completion' in such a way that for any context c and t-claim p, p is the completion of p in c. Inconsistency of claims may now be characterized in terms of completion: p and q are inconsistent provided for any context c the completions of p and q are incompatible (i.e. there is no world in which both completions are true).[16]

---

[15] It should be clear from the way in which we introduced the notion of an r-claim in the last section that such claims are true or false relative to a possible world and (the standards determined by) a context or conversation. What plays the role of 'circumstances of evaluation' for the relativist—that is, the role of that relative to which we can intelligibly ask whether a claim is true or false—is a *pairing* of a possible world and a set of standards.

I take a context (as well as a conversation) to be an abstraction from an actual or possible speech situation. As such, a context (a conversation) is something 'located' at a particular possible world. Talk of a claim being true relative to a context (conversation) is thus elliptical for talk of the claim being true relative to (the standards provided by) a context (conversation) *and* the world which the context/conversation provides.

[16] 'i'-dotting: claims are inconsistent provided their completions in any context in which both have such cannot both be true. The text makes use of the notion of a claim p being true *simpliciter* in a world. If we take worlds to be, or to determine, sets of t-claims, this notion can be identified with a world (or the set of t-claims it determines) containing p. This means that r-claims are not true *simpliciter* at worlds. Since their truth is relative, not just to a world, but to something like a conversational context, this hardly seems a drawback.

If Mary is rich, then it is true that Mary is rich. And vice versa. The contextualist about 'rich' says that it need not be 'absolutely true or false' that Mary is rich; it may be true relative to Didi's context that she is, false relative to Naomi's. But then what goes for the claim that Mary is rich also goes for the claim that it's true that Mary is rich—'true' patterns with 'rich':

(c) 'true' expresses different properties in different contexts;
(d) for any r-claim p, there is an r-claim that p is true, and an r-claim that p is not true. Whether such a claim is true relative to a context or conversation depends on whether p has the property expressed by 'true' in the context or conversation.

Given that the claim that p and the claim that p is true will always agree in truth (in a context), (d) tells us what it is for a claim to be relatively true.

'Rich', 'true', and the rest express different properties in different contexts. But there is something common to different uses of 'rich' that entitles us to say that the word means the same on its different uses. Let us call this something a *notion*. A notion could be partially represented as a rule that takes a context as input and yields a property as output. On such a representation the notion expressed by 'rich'—the notion of wealth—gets represented as the rule that maps

my context to the property I would express with 'rich';
your context to the property you would express with 'rich';
The Donald's context to the property His Trumpness would express with 'rich'; etc.

It's not exactly an informative representation, but for formal purposes such representations can be useful.[17]

A more adequate representation of notions, incorporating more of what is common to different uses, would involve something like a functional or conceptual role (perhaps along with a core extension and a prototype structure, depending upon the concept). What unites our different uses of 'rich'—what makes it the case that we express a common notion with the word—is roughly that we take being rich as being a matter of being able to afford to indulge oneself in luxuries beyond what is necessary for a comfortable life. This manifests itself in our being disposed (for example) to infer such as things as that Smith can afford food from the claim that Smith is rich. What is common to different uses of 'true' is (something like) accepting the claims that it is true that snow is white iff snow is white, that it is true that Larry is a fusspot iff Larry is a fusspot, and so on. The association of these beliefs with the notion of

---

17 In the framework for thinking about context-sensitivity popularized by David Kaplan's work on demonstratives (see Kaplan 1989*a*, 1989*b*), what is being done here is to represent notions as what Kaplan calls *characters*. Characters are Kaplan's candidates for (the formal representations of) meanings, and so it's not all that surprising that they function as representations of notions.

truth manifests itself in the competent speaker's being disposed (for example) to infer that Larry is a fusspot from the claim that it is true that Larry is a fusspot.

Actually, different 'developments of the notion of truth'—that is, different ways of getting from the notion of truth to a property which that notion can determine—will have more in common than just this. To see why, let us suppose that it is 'part of our notion of wealth' that a person who has only a penny is not rich. If so, then no way of 'developing' the notion of being rich is one on which a person with only a penny counts as rich. So the r-claim, that Jason is rich only if he has more than a penny, will be true no matter how we 'develop' the notion of truth. So any two 'developments' of the notion of truth will have in common that they apply to the r-claim, that Jason is rich only if he has more than a penny. More generally: if a notion N is such that any way of fleshing it out is one on which it applies to x, then any way of fleshing out the notion of truth is one on which it applies to the claim that x is N.[18]

We explicate the idea of a claim's being true in a context c thus:

(e) To say that claim p is true in context c is to say something that is true iff the completion of p in c has the property 'true' expresses in c.

Here 'is true' is to be understood as expressing the notion of truth, not the property of being true in Mark Richard's current context.[19] This ties the notion of being-true-in-c, which we are trying to understand, to the notion of something having a property, a notion we presumably already understand: p is true relative to c iff a certain claim, determined by p and c, has a certain property, determined by c and our notion of truth.

The story I've told about the relations between *It's true that p* and *It's true for Naomi that p* implies that while the claims made by p and *It's true that p* may be only relatively true, the claim made by P *is true for Naomi* will be absolutely true or false. So the story I've told has the result that, for example, it may be

---

[18] What follows is meant to explain how I see notions as being related to claims and propositions—that is, to what is said by a sentence's use.

I am working with a picture of claims and propositions on which they are structured entities, along the lines of Russellian propositions. My picture is one on which r-claims are like traditional propositions, save that they have notions at one or more loci where the traditional propositions have properties or relations. On this picture, the characterization of r-claims in the text is slightly misleading. There, I characterize an r-claim as one which may have different truth-values relative to different contexts in a single world. That's not quite right, as there will be, for example, an r-claim which results from replacing the occurrences of the property of being an adult, in the proposition that either Matty is an adult or she isn't, with the notion of being an adult; if bivalence reigns, these r-claim will be true relative to any context at any world. It seemed best to keep the text free of technicalities such as this, which are orthogonal to the current discussion.

In the text when I say that having the notion of truth involves accepting that snow is white iff it is true that snow is white, I mean that having the notion involves believing (for example) the r-claim expressed by this sentence which involves the notions of truth, snow, and whiteness.

There is some further discussion of the idea of a notion in the next section.

[19] So what I say with (e) is what you would say with it.

true for Naomi that Mary is rich, though Mary isn't rich—though, that is, it's not true that Mary is rich. Of course, from Naomi's perspective, things will look otherwise: She will say *It's true for MR that Mary isn't rich, but (it's true that) Mary is rich.* And what she says will be true—for her.

4.4

There are an awful lot of objections to relativism. This section sorts through some of them.

(i) There is a kind of relativism—*jejune relativism*, we might call it—which holds that 'everything is relative': that for any consistent claim there is or could (actually) be a perspective or context in which it's true. I hope it is obvious that the view I am developing here isn't *that* view. I cannot see how it could (in fact) be true (from some actual perspective) that the earth is flat, for example. I can see how someone might mean something a bit *like* what we mean by 'flat' and 'the earth' and be able to say correctly 'The earth is flat'. But that doesn't mean that it's true from some perspective that the earth is flat. Likewise, I can't see how it could be true for Naomi that Mary is rich, and true for Didi that it's not true for Naomi that Mary is rich. That is, I can't see how truth from a perspective itself might be perspectival.

This is relevant to common one-line refutations of relativism—that the doctrine itself is either only relatively true (in which case, while it might be 'true for its propounder', it's not true for us—i.e. not true—and so it may be ignored) or it's not relatively true (in which case it's just false, as not everything is relative). Whatever the merits of this as a response to jejune relativism, it just doesn't apply to the view I'm developing here, on which some, but not all, truth is relative.

(ii) A standard worry about relativism is that it must be incoherent, since it holds that people can contradict one another and both speak truly, and thus is committed to the idea that there are true contradictions. But what exactly is the worry?

Well, relativism, as I have developed, is a kind of contextualism. And for the contextualist the truth of a use of 'Mary is rich' is determined by the standards for wealth operative when the sentence is used. Consider the example we've been calling The Report. In it, Didi uses 'rich' with low standards, low enough, we may suppose, so that Mary qualifies as rich according to those standards. Naomi uses it with high standards, high enough, we may suppose, so that Mary does not qualify as rich according to those standards. So it would seem that given contextualism, Didi and Naomi each speaks truly in the example. In the example Didi says that Mary is rich, Naomi says that she is not rich. Since each speaks truly, it follows that Mary is rich and she's not rich. Contradiction. Thus, we must reject contextualism.[20]

The objection misrepresents what any sensible relativist holds; it poses no problem for the contextualist who clear-headedly embraces relativism. The core of the relativist and of the contextualist view of 'rich' is that whether a use of the term applies to someone depends upon the standards of wealth associated with the use. So if different standards govern Didi's and Naomi's uses of 'rich', at least one of those standards will be different from the standards governing *our* use of 'rich'. Given the banality on which the puzzle rests—that (ignoring issues about tense) whenever someone assertively utters the English 'Mary is rich' they say that Mary is rich—neither the relativist nor the contextualist should allow that we can report both Didi and Naomi as having spoken the truth.[21] In our context we can evaluate sentences such as 'Mary is rich', 'It is true that Mary is rich', or 'What Didi said is true' for truth. In doing this we use the standards of *our* context to determine who is rich and what is true. No matter what those standards might be, they won't make Mary rich and not rich; nor will they make the claim that Mary is rich true and not true.

It is a mistake to formulate contextualism so that it implies that what Didi says with a sentence such as 'Mary is rich' is true just in case Mary meets Didi's standards of wealth.[22] What Didi says with 'Mary is rich' is true—i.e. has the property I ascribe (here and now) with 'true'—just in case Mary is rich—i.e. has the property I ascribe (here and now) with 'rich'. Once the contextualist accepts the banality that whoever utters 'Mary is rich' says that Mary is rich, he must use a relativized notion of truth to formulate contextualism. Contextualism about 'rich' must be formulated as the view that whether a use of 'Mary is rich' is valid—i.e. is true relative to the conversational context in which it occurs—turns upon the standards of wealth supplied by that context.

Once contextualism is so formulated, the puzzle two paragraphs back disappears. If we begin with the premise

The contextualist holds that the validity of a use of a sentence such as 'Mary is rich' is sensitive to the standards for wealth operative when the sentence is used.

we can infer that each of Didi and Naomi speaks validly in The Report. But we can't infer from

---

[20] This is a version of an objection to contextualism about the word 'knows' by John Hawthorne; see Hawthorne (2004: ch. 1). Contextualism about knowledge is discussed in Appendix II.

[21] Actually, things are slightly more complicated, as we need to allow that the speaker may intend to use 'is rich' to ascribe being rich for an F, for some F.

[22] Contextualists about the word 'know' make a cognate mistake. Contextualism about 'knows' is often formulated so that it implies that when X's 'standards for knowledge' are permissive—so that X can correctly say 'I know that I have hands'—then it is true (i.e. true when the contextualist himself says it) that X knows that X has hands. Such formulations of epistemic contextualism are vulnerable to the sort of objection we are currently considering. Again, see Appendix II.

Didi spoke validly (i.e. said something true in the confines of her conversation) when she said that Mary was rich.

that Didi spoke truly. Neither contextualism nor the relativism to which (as I see it) the contextualist is committed has any truck with 'true contradictions'.

I have exaggerated. There's nothing wrong with formulating contextualism—or the relativism that underlies it—as the view that whether a use of 'Mary is rich' is true depends on the standards of wealth associated with the use. Outside of philosophy the word 'true' pretty obviously leads a rich double life. Sometimes when a speaker says that something is true, she means to be endorsing it as true according to the standards of truth operative in her conversation or thought. Such uses are (for the speaker) straightforwardly disquotational. That is to say: when we use 'true' in this way, we can reliably infer S from *It's true that S*.

But, as anyone who's taught an introductory philosophy class knows, there's another deeply entrenched use of 'true' which relativizes truth ('It was true when the Greeks said it that the earth was flat') and which is *not* disquotational. On this use, to say that an utterance or thought is true is to say that it is valid—true in the utterer's or thinker's context. Philosophical resistance to this use is as deeply entrenched as the use itself. But that doesn't mean that the non-disquotational use of 'true' doesn't exist. It clearly does. If we use 'true' in this way, then we can indeed formulate contextualism about 'rich' as the view that whether a use of 'Mary is rich' is true (i.e. whether it is true in its context of use or thought) depends on the standards of wealth associated with the use.

(iii) One might worry that someone who adopts the sort of view I've been sketching won't be able to make sense of the propositional attitudes. Consider the simplest of claims we think and make, those made when we single out an object and ascribe it a property, as when we say that Mary is rich. A property is a characteristic of an object; either the object has the property or it doesn't. Whatever is going on when something whose truth is relative is asserted, it can't be the ascription of a property to an object—otherwise, it wouldn't make sense to think that what is said is relatively true. But then what *is* going on when we think or assert the claim that Mary is rich?

In responding, begin by observing that in the cases we've been discussing there is a sense—on everybody's view—on which Didi and Naomi mean the same thing with the word 'rich'. In what sense do they mean the same thing? Well, on natural fleshings out of the cases, all the following would be true. (a) The inferential role of the term 'rich' would be quite similar for the two. Each would take inferences such as *x is rich; so x can afford to buy food for herself and her family* to be obviously reliable; neither would be inclined to infer *x is rich* from *x can't afford to buy an SUV*. Both can be expected to endorse as obvious truths pretty much the same principles about comparative wealth—e.g. if x is rich and y has almost as much money as x, then, *ceteris paribus*, y is rich. (b) There would be a fair amount of overlap between the two, regarding what they do or would consider paradigmatic cases of people being rich or otherwise. Both would take it as obvious that Donald Trump and John Kerry are rich, that a migrant worker is not. (c) Each would recognize (most of) their differences, about who was and who was not rich, as differences which are not thought unusual or outlandish, relative to their culture and situation.

Points (a) through (c) underwrite our willingness to say that the women mean the same thing by 'rich', that they have the same concept (in one sense of 'concept') of wealth. Since the words 'meaning' and 'concept' are invested with so many prior associations, I use the term 'notion' here, and say that these sorts of facts make it the case that the women have the same *notion* of being rich. On the picture I am sketching, the basic concept of (the simplest sorts of) belief(s)—that is, the concept that normally figures in our judgments as to whether two people share a (simple) belief or have a disagreement—is the concept of subsuming individuals under notions. The objects of assertion, belief, and the other attitudes are (in at least some instances) cobbled out of notions—to assert that Mary is rich is to apply the notion of wealth to Mary.[23]

A property divides a range of objects into two camps, those that have it and those that don't. A notion isn't a property. But it is something which is, so to speak, on its way to being a property. If (a) through (c) above are typical ingredients of a notion, then when we have a notion we have something for which: there are *some* fixed points of application (there are some objects to which the notion obviously applies, and some to which it obviously doesn't); there are rules which partially constrain how one can go about extending the notion's application (given by inferential role); there are (somewhat vague) parameters as to what would and what would not be an acceptable way of applying the notion. When we combine a notion with the interests, assumptions, and so forth of an individual or of conversants, these will tend to flesh the notion out, so that what we have will be a lot more like a property, thought of as a partition on a domain of individuals.[24] And thus, when we apply notion to object, our situation—our interests, conversational and social relations, and so forth—tend to 'fill in' the notion, so that *in context* bringing someone under a notion is (something reasonably idealized as) ascribing a property to them. So the traditional picture of (the simplest) beliefs and assertions, as involving the ascription of a property or relation to an object or objects, doesn't misdescribe what's going on when someone has a belief. What it does is *under*describe what's going on.

(iv) Here is another worry about relativism and assertion. (a) To make an assertion, it is often said, is to select a set of worlds—those worlds in which the

---

[23] This is further spelled out in n. 18.
[24] We can think of a property as a special case of a notion—as a notion which has no room for contextual filling out, as its application conditions are already perfectly determinate.

claim made is true—and 'locate' one's self and one's audience as inhabiting one of them. To make a claim is also, of course, to invite one's audience to accept that claim as correct. Since the claim one makes is correct just in case the world one inhabits is one of the worlds in which the claim made is correct, to make a claim is to invite one's audience to 'locate' itself within the set of worlds in which that claim is true. But now (b) such an invitation makes sense only if the truth-conditions of a claim when I make it are the same as they are when you accept it. For suppose that when I claim p I make a claim true iff the actual world is in set W, but when you accept p you accept something as true iff the actual world is in W', W and W' distinct. What is to keep the actual world from being in W but not in W'? Nothing, it would seem. So why should I expect you to accept my claim? If I think you rational, I should expect you, as I expect myself, to strive to accept p only if p represents the way things are—only if p 'contains' the actual world. However, (c) if the truth of a claim is relative, then its truth-conditions must vary across individuals: if the claim is true for me, it will contain ('for me') the actual world; if it is false for you, it won't contain ('for you') the actual world. So (d) the practice of assertion seems incomprehensible on a relativist view, as there seems no reason in general for me to expect you to accept what I say when I make an assertion.

One problem with this objection is that the picture of assertion that undergirds it is at best incomplete. Suppose that I assertively utter 'Mary is rich', when it is not antecedently settled for conversational purposes whether Mary is in the term's extension. My statement that Mary is rich is as much an invitation to look at things in a certain way as it is a representation of how things are. In saying that Mary is rich, I am inviting you to think of being rich in such a way that Mary counts as rich. If you accept my invitation—that is, if you don't demur, and carry on the conversation—that sets the standards for wealth, for the purposes of the conversation, so as to make what I say true.[25]

It is this idea—that an assertion can be as much an invitation to conceptualize things in a certain way as a representation of how things are—that is missing from the picture of assertion on which the above worry rests. As I see it, there is a single notion of being rich which can be 'fleshed out'—i.e. whose extension can be determined—in various ways. Sometimes when I assert that Mary is rich I am simultaneously presenting Mary as rich—fleshing out the notion of wealth and placing her in its extension—and inviting you to go along with me. Whether you accept my invitation or not doesn't affect what claim I make. After all, if you accept what I've said, well, then you've accepted *what I said*; and if you reject what I've said, well, then you've rejected *what I've said*. But whether you accept what I've said does affect whether the claim is true within the confines of the

---

[25] Those familiar with David Lewis (1979) should, I think, recognize this picture of assertion as implicit in his views.

conversation. For 'rich''s application may be affected by the twists and turns of conversational use.

Where precisely does the current objection go wrong? Well, its first premise presupposes a picture of truth-conditions on which they are (adequately represented as) sets of worlds. But this isn't the relativist picture. If I say that Mary is rich, I am proposing that we should think of things in such a way as to think of Mary as rich. This is apt provided there is a(n acceptable) way of thinking of wealth on which Mary turns out rich. The (relative) truth or falsity of what I say is determined by pairing a possible world traditionally conceived with a perspective—a set of standards that flesh out our notions. It is sets of these sorts of things against which an assertion is to be evaluated—that play the role of truth-conditions for the relativist—not sets of traditional possible worlds.

So the first premise of the argument rests, as I see it, on a mistaken picture of assertion. And its third premise is flat-out wrong: to say that claim p is true (at world w) for someone A with standards s is to say that p's truth-conditions contain $<w, s>$; to say that p is not true (at w) for someone B with standards s' is to say that p's truth-conditions exclude $<w, s'>$. But this is consistent with p's having the same truth-conditions for A and B. And indeed, the truth-conditions of p, thought of as a collection of world/standard pairs, do not vary across individuals or contexts.

(v) Suppose that p is relatively true—it is true for me but false for you. Suppose furthermore that I know that p's truth is relative in this way. (a) Wouldn't it be irrational for me to believe p, instead of the 'absolutely true' claim that p is true for me but false for you? Shouldn't a rational person resist believing things whose truth he knows is only relative? (b) Wouldn't it be disingenuous of me to try to convince you of p? After all, my view is 'only true from my perspective'; I know that your view is true from yours. Either our perspectives are equally good perspectives on p or they aren't. If they are equally good, then surely it *is* disingenuous of me to try to convince you that p, as (our perspectives being equally good) I must admit that there's no reason for you to abandon your view and adopt mine. If our perspectives *aren't* equally good, then why should I think that p's truth-value varies across our perspectives? Surely its (absolute) truth-value is whatever truth-value it has in 'the best perspective'.[26]

I don't see all that much force in worry (a). Suppose that I know what criteria for wealth are operative in my conversation and know that Mary satisfies them. Then I know that Mary is rich. Suppose I know that you and your friends use different criteria, and that Mary satisfies them, and thus know that it is true, using your criteria for wealth, that she is rich. Why *must* I feel an inclination, if I

---

[26] Worry (a) is raised in Zimmermann (2007). Versions of worry (b) abound in the literature on moral relativism. A version of it occurs in Postow (1979); a nuanced discussion of a variant of such an objection, from which I have learned a great deal, is Scanlon (1995).

am rational, to abandon my belief that Mary is rich? Presumably I think that my criteria for wealth are the appropriate criteria to adopt; I think that the way we *ought* to think about wealth is the way that I do. So I think that I am right about the matter—Mary *is* rich—and you are wrong to think that she isn't. There's nothing irrational in thinking: your thought that Mary isn't rich is true given the way you think about wealth, but since your way of thinking of wealth is a bad way to think of it, we shouldn't agree with you. If anything is irrational in this sort of case, it seems to be my *abandoning* my belief that Mary is rich.

Let us turn to worry (b). As I see it, in the sort of situation involved in this objection, there is nothing disingenuous in my asking you to examine your values and priorities or in my trying to change them. And often enough my urging you to abandon a view that is 'true for you' in favor of one that is (currently) 'false for you' comes to nothing more or less than my trying to get you to change your priorities and values.

In slightly more detail: (1) How we shape the boundaries of our concepts is in part determined by our interests and values. Therefore, differences in the truth-value of a claim will often reflect differences in interests and values. (2) You and I may rationally differ on the relative importance we place on competing considerations—in particular, we may each have good reasons for ordering those considerations in ways that are incompatible with the way the other does—without there being any 'perspective-independent' way of choosing one ordering as better than the other. (1) and (2) suggest that claims like the claims that Mary is rich or that the field is flat may be true for me, false for you without there being any 'perspective-independent' considerations which can be offered for choosing one of our perspectives as better than the other. (3) In a situation like (2) there is nothing disingenuous in my trying to convince you to adopt my view of how the relevant considerations ought to be ordered, and thus nothing disingenuous in my trying to convince you to change your mind about a claim that is true for you.

Expanding on all this, suppose that our soccer team wants to practice and needs to find a flat field. The two fields close by aren't all that flat; a very flat field is a healthy drive away. I don't want to drive a half hour given the small amount of time we have and am willing to practice on a bumpy field; you would prefer not to practice on a bumpy field and are willing to curtail the length of the practice. I judge that the flatter nearby field (Flanders Field), as well as the faraway field, is flat enough for us to practice soccer on; you judge that only the faraway field is flat enough for this.

Suppose there are six of us involved in the coming practice, and that I and two like-minded players agree in conversation that Flanders Field is flat enough; you and two like-minded players agree in conversation that it is not. Each of our uses of 'is flat enough for the team to practice on' gets accommodated, and so each of us makes a claim true relative to his own conversation. This much is, I take it, an example of the phenomenon labeled '(1)' two paragraphs back.

In (a fleshing out of) this situation, you and I have common interests and aims—in particular, we want to practice soccer, to maximize the length of our practice, to avoid a long drive, to practice on something whose topography is close to that of a regulation soccer field. Our judgments about Flanders Field reflect a difference in the way in which we order the importance of these interests and aims. *Must* there be something about the situation, our interests and aims, and our judgments that would bring 'any rational person' after sufficient reflection and consideration to pronounce me correct about the field and you wrong, or vice versa? Surely not. We each want non-bumpiness and ease of access to the practice field; we are inclined towards different trade-offs in satisfying these desires. Perhaps the difference between my ordering and yours reflects differences in our long-term aims, personalities, and the like. Why on earth *must* there be something about (say) my preference ordering, or my preference ordering and the underlying long-term aims and personality traits that my ordering reflects, which is 'intrinsically' or 'rationally' preferable to your ordering/your ordering plus your aims and traits? Surely there is no reason that either my ordering has to be intrinsically better than yours or vice versa. So there need be no 'perspective-independent' consideration that shows that one of our ways of ordering preferences is superior to the other's. But if there is no perspective-independent consideration that shows your take on matters better than mine or vice versa, then we have a case in which (2) above obtains: there is a claim—that Flanders Field is flat enough for practice—whose truth varies across two perspectives, neither of which is in some 'objective' (i.e. perspective-independent) sense superior to the other.

Why would it be disingenuous in this sort of situation for one of us to try to change the other's mind about whether the field is flat enough for a practice? I suppose that the charge of disingenuity arises so: It would be disingenuous for me to say that you ought to believe p when I know, or should know, that you have no reason to believe p. But whether you have a reason to believe that the field is flat enough for a practice turns on whether your interests, desires, and such dictate, along with 'interest-independent facts', that the field is flat enough. In the envisioned situation they do not, and I may be assumed to know this. So if I attempt to get you to believe that the field is flat enough, I can't be giving you something that you can see to be a *reason* to change your mind. So my attempt to change your mind is nothing more than a move in a power struggle in which I attempt to force you to accede to my interest.

To see that this is wrong, think about a first-person attempt to decide whether the field is flat enough. Even if at the moment I have a fairly strong inclination towards one way of ordering preferences—I'm pretty strongly disinclined to drive a long way, and so I'm willing to use a bumpy field—there is nothing irrational in reviewing opposing ways of thinking about matters. Sometimes when I do this I find that my preferences change—not necessarily because I become aware of some interest-independent fact that I have ignored, but because the process of reviewing opposing considerations itself sometimes brings me to weigh things differently. Often the way in which I weigh different interests is not something that I am deeply committed to, but rather is something I am open to reconsidering. If this is so, then when I reconsider from occasion to occasion how strongly I weigh various factors, my weighing sometimes changes. I may notice that a consideration that once weighed heavily now seems not so important; a change of the weight of one consideration may prompt me to weigh kindred ones heavily. Of course changes in preferences that are prompted by this sort of process are very often ones I believe after the fact to have been for the best.

The process I am describing is one in which I take a new way of thinking about a matter seriously in deliberation and as a result alter my preferences and desires. There is nothing irrational about this. We all recognize that this sort of thing is on occasion important, is something that rationality on occasion demands. But then why should it be thought intrinsically disingenuous for someone with particular interests and views of how they should be weighed to present as strong a case for thinking of things that way as she can? Someone who sincerely advocates an alternative way of weighing considerations, who offers their own way of looking at matters as a model for us to consider, who offers to thoughtfully respond to the worries and objections we might have about her way of valuing things while we puzzle over how we are to value them—surely such a person needn't be held to be *disingenuous*. They are, if anything, doing us a genuine favor.

4.5

The relativism I have sketched is motivated by a desire to reconcile the license we allow ourselves in conversation—to shape the contours of our concepts to fit the needs of the moment—with the way we interpret one another as disagreeing. One might wonder whether I have actually achieved reconciliation, for one might wonder whether on my account cases like The Argument involve an interesting or genuine disagreement.

A merely verbal disagreement isn't much of a disagreement. I insist that in cases like The Argument the disagreement is substantive because there is a concept the disputants share about the application of which they disagree. It is not merely a verbal matter, if you and I agree about what it is to be rich (we agree that it is to have significantly more money than one's social peers, enough to acquire and maintain luxuries) but disagree about how to flesh out the details—about whether, for example, someone who can draw on a saved million dollars to supplement their 60k of yearly income should be taken to be rich—and thus disagree on the concept's application.

One might say that the disagreement here is awfully close to a verbal one. As I have sketched the case, it seems that Didi and Naomi's disagreement (or the disagreement over the soccer field) may rest on little more than the fact that disputants 'draw the line' for wealth (adequate flatness) at different places. And this, one might say, is not a very interesting disagreement. It is not very interesting, if it is merely a matter of how the two draw the line, because there is nothing but fiat or capitulation that could resolve it. There is nothing Didi and Naomi could learn about being rich that would resolve the disagreement—the dispute is not one about 'the facts', but about how to apply the label 'rich'. But if we would learn nothing in resolving a disagreement, if no uncovering of a fact could resolve it—well, then it's not very interesting.[27]

There are several ideas lurking here. The first is that the sort of dispute involved in The Argument is for all intents and purposes of no more interest than a dispute about how we should label things—and such disputes are just not interesting. The second idea is that there's no dispute 'about the facts' in this case because one can't resolve it by teaching one of Didi and Naomi something they don't already know. And the third is that if there's no dispute about the facts, the dispute isn't one which is going to be solved by rational means—if it's resolved, it will be resolved by fiat or capitulation.

I disagree with all these ideas. Let's begin with the first. I suspect that anyone who responds in this way to our examples reasons so: In the case of vocabulary that's not context-sensitive—'plant', 'bird', 'number', 'narcissistic', and so on—whether a dispute over how to apply a term is a verbal dispute turns on whether the disputants use the term to pick out the same property, where a property is (or determines) something which exhaustively partitions objects into two sets. If the disputants associate the same property with the term, the dispute is substantive; otherwise not. Extending this to the case of expressions such as 'rich' and 'flat enough for soccer practice', we will say that whether a dispute involving the expression's application is verbal also turns on whether, on the particular uses in the dispute, the expression determines the same property. But in the cases we're discussing the disputants' uses determine distinct properties. So the disputes are merely verbal.

Are disputes expressed using a word like 'plant', 'bird', 'number', 'narcissistic', and so on substantive only if disputants express the same property with the word? Well, if a property is something that effects a *complete* partition of its domain into exclusive sets, one wonders why, if this is necessary for a dispute to be substantive, we should think that *any* dispute expressed with these words is substantive. Surely Wittgenstein was on to something when he remarked that 'the extension of the concept [of a game, of a plant, or of a number] is not closed by a frontier'.[28] Surely Mark Wilson is on to something when he observes that current practice (and any other semantically relevant facts) may not settle

---

[27] A disagreement might be practically important, even if not interesting in the sense that it could be resolved by the parties to the dispute learning something. Sometimes we have to draw a distinction for practical reasons when it is perfectly arbitrary where, within some range, we draw it.
[28] Wittgenstein (1958: sect. 66).

whether a word like 'bird' as used by a particular group does or does not apply to some large class of objects—airplanes, missiles, or the like.[29] The way our notions apply to the world is surely not something fixed in advance of our using those notions. What a concept or notion is a concept or notion *of* gets worked out over time via something like a process of cultural accommodation and negotiation—different uses of a notion are disputed, speakers argue, make discoveries, people contract or correct some parts of how the notions get applied, plain old happy happenstance extends and entrenches a novel way of applying the notion. The relatively fixed point in such a process is not a more or less complete set of semantic links of word to objects, but a shared word or notion whose interpretation our ongoing discussions, arguments, and so forth establish and extend.[30]

What does this tell us about disagreement, be the disagreement one expressed by (relatively) context-insensitive vocabulary like 'bird' and 'plant' or by (more obviously) contextually sensitive vocabulary such as 'rich' and 'round'? Well, it tells us that there are a number of different things that might be at stake when I say *a is F* and you say *a is not F*. (a) We might not even associate the same or kindred notions with *F*, in which case the dispute *is* merely verbal. Or (b) we may associate the same notion with the term but 'elaborate' the disputed notion in different ways, as each of us gives different accounts ('definitions') of 'subnotions' of the disputed notion. (For example, we might agree that what it is to be rich is to be able to afford luxuries after having been able to provide for the necessities of a decent life, but disagree about what is essential for a decent life.) Or (c) we might, because of differences in interest or values, 'draw the line' for various components of our shared notion differently. (I might, for example, blanch at the idea that someone who made merely 150 per cent of the national average income was rich while you do not). Or we might, because of differences in interest or inclination, weigh different components in a notion differently in deciding whether it applies. Or (d) it might be that the referential properties

[29] Wilson (1982); repr. in Richard (2003). The example to which the text alludes is one in which a tribe uses 'ave' to apply to ambient birds and has never seen an airplane, dirigible, etc. As Wilson aptly observes, quite contingent facts—who sees it, under what conditions, whether the first observers have a hangover, etc.—which seem to have little bearing on the meaning or semantics of 'ave', may determine whether the term is seen by its users to 'naturally' apply to airplanes and the like.

[30] What about natural-kind terms?

Well, what are natural kinds? I take it they are supposed to be something like observer-independent properties fit to play an important explanatory role. I'm willing to concede for the sake of argument that there are natural kinds and that some of our terms—in particular, some of the terms of some relatively mature sciences—have as extensions the extensions of such kinds. But conceding this is not conceding anything that makes it at all plausible that the extensions of most of our predicates are fixed in advance of their use. Everyday predicates which express categories determined by our contingent interests and values will rarely correspond to such kinds.

Wilson (2006) has an extensive discussion of how the interpretation of words and concepts, including many that purport to be natural-kind terms, changes over time.

of the components of our shared notion are exactly the same, and we simply disagree as to whether a certain individual falls under the notion.

Why should only the last option mark a 'substantive' (or, for that matter, an 'empirical') disagreement? In cases (b) and (c) our dispute can generally be understood as one about how best to make sense of the world, about what similarities, contrasts, and degrees 'go together' to make up the properties and relations we see. We will, in interesting cases, point to facts on which we agree, similarities we do and don't see between the case at hand and cases already decided, etc., in the attempt to justify our position—just as we do in what are by all accounts 'substantive, empirical' differences. An argument about what it is to have a certain empirically manifest property, one which proceeds by adducing empirical evidence, noting similarities and differences between objects, among properties and relations—this certainly sounds like a substantive, empirical dispute.

He who wants to say that such a dispute is not substantive is presumably disquieted by the fact that there is a sort of indeterminacy in how the dispute is to be resolved. Each of us can after all hold onto our position and be right—that is, each of us can hold onto our position secure in the knowledge that our position is true for us. But why should this mark our dispute as non-substantive (or non-empirical)? Perhaps the idea is that if there is this sort of slack, then it can't really make any difference how the dispute is resolved, and so the dispute is without substance.

But surely this is not so. First of all, the fact that each of our views is true relative to our own context does *not* imply that our views are equally good. Suppose you in your context say 'France is hexagonal' and are accommodated; I in my context say 'France is not hexagonal' and am accommodated. Each of us says something valid. Suppose that in each context our interest in the shapes of countries turns on their suitability for teaching the children elementary geometry. It might well be better, given such an interest and the way the children learn, to not let France count as hexagonal. But this does not override the fact that you were accommodated and so what you say was valid.[31]

---

[31] This point cannot be stressed too much. Although the two seem to be associated in the current academic imagination (thanks in good part to Richard Rorty), there is no reason whatsoever to suppose that a relativistic outlook on truth goes hand in hand with a crude (or a refined) pragmatist picture of truth, on which there is an intimate relation between the truth of a claim and the usefulness, relative to our interests (actual or refined), in believing the claim.

Whether the claim that (say) Mary is rich is true (i.e. true relative to my context) does indeed turn on certain of my interests, insofar as (1) the truth of the claim is a matter of whether Mary falls in the extension of the notion *rich*, and (2) the extension of that notion (relative to my context) turns on certain facts involving my interests. For example, I and my cohort may value creature comfort so highly that we steadfastly deny that a tolerably high level of such comfort is a luxury; this in turn may 'draw the line' for wealth amongst my cohort and me at a level higher than it's drawn for you. Since valuing something is a kind of interest, certain of my interests bear on whether the claim that Mary is rich is true relative to my perspective.

Secondly, it is worth pointing out that we all take disputes of the sort under discussion to be both substantive and (often) of great moment. Take a term that is (arguably) subject to Lewisian accommodation and whose application *matters*—'obese', 'anorexic', 'obsessive compulsive', 'paranoid', 'sadistic', 'narcissistic' are examples of the sort of word I have in mind. Imagine a dispute between A and B about how to shape the boundaries of the concept—to make it vivid, imagine that the concept at issue is the concept of narcissism, and (no offense) which way the dispute goes makes a difference to you, as if A prevails you won't be classified narcissistic, but if B does you will. There need not be any 'inconsistency of total world-views' between those who want to apply the adjective to you and those who deny that the application is correct.[32] There may just be some slack in the concept's application, different ways of fleshing out the common core of the notion which are possible, so that there is no linguistic mistake made by either party when they come to categorize your self-absorption.

You sincerely don't think you're narcissistic. Your so thinking need not be unreasonable—after all, it requires a certain amount of negotiation for the application of the term 'narcissistic' to you to go through. Your friends, we may imagine, agree with you, sincerely and reasonably, that you are not narcissistic. Do you seriously want to say you are willing to shrug off what B says because . . . well, what he says is valid? Because . . . well, after all, the way B used the term is a way it is used, and those in his conversation reasonably and with awareness allowed him to talk that way?

But it is a far cry from this to the idea that there is *any* interesting relationship between the extensions of our notions (and, therefore, between the truth of our claims) and our interests *in the normal sense of 'interest'* in whether or not a claim is true. It might be in our interest for any number of reasons either for Mary to be rich or for us to believe this to be so; this, in and of itself, is completely irrelevant to whether it is true that she is.

Truth and other semantic properties are 'interest-relative' in a focused way: it is not the case that *any* interest we might have that would be affected by the truth or falsity of p is relevant to whether p is true. It is, as I see it anyway, a relatively narrow collection of propensities, interests, and other intentional states that have an effect on the application conditions of one's use of 'rich'. Because of this, when inconsistent views p and q are each valid—i.e. when each is true relative to some context—one of the views may be clearly superior, all things told, to the other. This is because when one weighs all considerations it may be more sensible for both the partisan of p and the partisan of q to adopt the view that p than to adopt the view that q.

I think that the possibility of saying this sort of thing allows us to hold that it is a relative matter whether p is true, *though* one of the views—*p, not-p*—is objectively superior to the other. I hope to pursue these ideas at greater length elsewhere.

[32] Here is what I mean by this. Suppose that we identify the truth-conditions of relatively true claims with sets of pairs <w, s>, w a possible world, s a set of standards; to make everything uniform, non-relatively true claims can be taken to have such sets as truth-conditions too, their non-relativity witnessed by the fact that if <w, s> is one of the truth-conditions of a non-relatively true claim, so is <w, s'> for any set of standards s'. If we assume that each person (or her context) determines a single set of standards, we can then say that X's total world-view is the set of those worlds w such that for any p which X believes, <w, s> (s the standards X determines) is in p. That is, put otherwise: X's total world-view is the set of worlds in which the completions in X's context of everything X believes are true.

Of course not. You would insist that you are *not* narcissistic; you would resent and be upset about someone's 'making you so'. Even if the context of the other is described in enough detail so that you can see that no one meant to be mean, spiteful, or malicious in accommodating the application of the term to you, and you recognize that it is within the bounds of usage to apply the term as it was applied, you will blanch—you'll grant that yes, you could think of others a little bit more and go more with the flow—but you are *not* narcissistic. You will, in fact, say—and say correctly—that you *know* that you are not *and* that this other person is just wrong. You will point to all the good reasons you have for denying your narcissism.

Even though argument about you can go either way, one can give evidence for and against the claim that you are narcissistic. You and an adversary can argue rationally about this—one of you may even persuade the other to come around, for one of you may be able to give the other good reason to think that one way of shaping the concept makes more sense, given the interests and purposes the concept serves. This seems to be good evidence that we feel that in such cases there is a substantive, genuine, important disagreement, even when we will acknowledge that there is slack in the concept's application in the case under dispute.

I have been responding to the first of the three ideas mentioned above—that in cases like The Argument, the dispute is 'merely verbal', and without substance. Let us turn to the second idea, that in such cases there is 'no dispute about the facts'. It is not too hard to see why someone might think this. A person X's beliefs, it will be said, determine a set of possible worlds, those worlds in which all of those beliefs (their completions in X's context, in the case of beliefs only relatively true) are true. There is a factual disagreement between two people only if the sets of worlds their beliefs determine—their total world-views, if you will—are disjoint, so that it's impossible for both of their total world-views to be true. But Didi and Naomi's total world-views needn't be inconsistent—they could, for all that, be identical! After all, they may be assumed to agree about all the facts: about Mary's income, hair color, age, and so on. Naomi believes the completion-in-Naomi's-context of the r-claim that Mary is not rich—that is, the claim that Mary is not rich-according-to-Naomi's-standards-of-wealth; Didi (presumably) believes this too. And both of them believe the completion of the r-claim relative to Didi's context—viz. that Mary is rich-according-to-Didi's-standards-of-wealth. And this means that there need be *no* fact on which the two disagree, and so no factual disagreement between them.

I think this account of what it is to have a factual disagreement is just wrong. It is certainly wrong if what I said above is on track. The account of 'factuality' contained in the definition of factual dispute (factual disputes involve inconsistent total world-views) takes the facts to be exhausted by those truths that are non-relative. But what is non-relatively true often does not suffice to determine all the facts. You and I, on considering it, agree that you are not narcissistic. We can point to various non-relatively true claims (about how you have treated other people, who comes first for you, etc.) and on their basis say—correctly—that you are not narcissistic. Since we speak truly, in a perfectly good sense—perhaps the only good sense—we state a fact. But to get to the fact we stated, we had to add something to what is non-relatively true; after all, the person who validly applied 'narcissistic' to you started with the same set of non-relative truths, but ended up at a different place.

In an important sense, I may have to *decide* whether you are (to be judged) narcissistic, if you have the marks—self-absorption, a tendency to see everything as reflecting on you, etc.—of narcissism. This is part of what it is for a concept to be subject to such processes as accommodation and negotiation. As I see it, there is a perfectly good sense in which when we argue about the application of concepts, about their boundaries and borders, we are not arguing about what possible world we *are* in, but about what possible world we *are to be* in. When I utter *p*, the act I perform is often best glossed

Here is how we ought to think of things: p.

Does this mean that our argument is 'non-factual'? Surely not. If I'm right, when I say that you aren't narcissistic, that's a fact, and if the way we ought to think of things is so—you're not narcissistic—then it's a fact that you're not. Those who disagree with this disagree about the facts.

That said, I should acknowledge that on the view I am sketching there is a real and important sense in which we 'construct' our world. We manufacture what I have been calling notions and we decide—via discussions, cultural pressures, argument and intimidation, etc.—what does and does not fall under these notions. As I noted above, to say this is not to say, that we are free to tailor the facts to suit our desires.[33]

One might object that the sorts of disputes we are discussing aren't 'factual'—or at least aren't about anything objective—because they are 'really' disputes about (the relative importance of) values and interests. Return to the dispute over whether Flanders Field is flat enough for a soccer practice. Whether a field is flat enough for some activity turns in part on the interests of those who are to perform the activity. Given one way of balancing interests, the field

---

[33] Of course the picture of facts and worlds these last sentences presuppose is one on which some facts are relative and some worlds differ (only) in the relative facts they contain. It is, in my opinion, a shortcoming of the standard way of thinking about facts and 'the world' in analytic philosophy (on which the world must in some sense be exhausted by some set of facts which supervene on the facts of physics, biology, and so on) that this sort of 'construction of the world' is very hard to describe within it.

Anyone who is familiar with it will hear echoes here of the work of Ian Hacking and Arnold Davidson—work that, in my opinion, ought to be taken more seriously by analytic philosophy than it seems to be. A nice introduction to Hacking on these matters is Hacking (1999); some of Davidson's papers are collected in Davidson (2001).

is flat enough; given others it's not. How these factors are weighed varies across individuals: I weigh them one way (W1), you weigh them in a different way (W2). So, the objection runs, it may well be that each of us is correct, when I say the field's flat enough and you deny it; but since the matter turns on interests and values, the difference isn't factual.[34]

I agree that the answer to the question, Is the field is flat enough for a practice? turns on our interests and values. (Indeed, the answer to the question, Is the field flat, period? turns on our interests and values.) How does it follow that the question isn't a factual one? Is it simply because the dispute involves a concept whose extension is shaped by the interests and values of those involved in the dispute? Then almost every dispute threatens to become 'non-factual'. Whether

---

[34] Does saying that our claims about the field are each true because each of us has different interests (or each of us weighs our interests differently) mean that we don't contradict one another when I say the field is flat enough and you deny it?

Suppose, contrary to the view I am defending, that we do not contradict each other. I say to my comrades

(S) Flanders Field is flat enough for practice.

You say to your comrades

(S') Flanders Field is not flat enough for practice.

What exactly is each one of us saying?

The only answer I can see is something like this: Each of our utterances is elliptical (or contains some variable-like entity that needs an assignment; I concentrate on the first option here). My use of 'is flat enough for practice' is elliptical for (something like) 'is flat enough relative to [or presupposing] an ordering of preferences on which length of practice and ease of transportation are more important than resemblance to a regulation field'; your use of 'is not flat enough' is elliptical for something like 'is not flat enough relative to [or presupposing] an ordering of preferences on which resemblance to a regulation field is more important than length of practice or ease of transportation'. On this view, my use of 'is flat enough' ascribes a property (being flat enough relative to way W1 of ordering preferences) which something can have while also having the property (not being flat enough relative to way W2 of ordering preferences) ascribed by your use of the other predicate.

The problem with the story about (S) and (S') is that it simply doesn't square with the way speakers interpret their components. Suppose you overhear me and feel compelled to object. You will not say

(O) (Because I don't value length of practice and ease of transportation more than resemblance to a regulation field) I deny what you say; that is, I deny that f is flat enough relative to an ordering of preferences which makes length of practice and ease of transportation more important than resemblance to a regulation field.

After all, presumably you *don't* deny that relative to an ordering of preferences like mine, the field is flat enough. What you deny—and what you take me to be saying when I draw the conclusion in (S)—is that the field is flat enough for a practice, period. You wouldn't use something like (O) to disagree with me; you'd use something like

(O') (Because I don't value length of practice and ease of transportation more than resemblance to a regulation field) I deny what you say; that is, I deny that f is flat enough.

The fact that we would use (O') but not (O) to object to the conclusion in (S) is good evidence against the claim that 'is flat enough' is elliptical in (S) for a predicate relativized to a particular preference ordering. For the only difference between (O) and (O') is that the material that is putatively elided has been inserted. If that material really was elided and (O') is acceptable—as indeed it is—(O) ought to be as well.

something or someone is correctly classified as a chair or a cheapskate, a melody, modern, morose, or misanthropic depends in any number of ways on our interests and values. Surely this is obvious for categories whose extensions vary across contexts due to Lewisian accommodation and negotiation. A good part of the *point* of having expressions that are open to contextual accommodation is to be able to adjust the boundaries of our concepts on the fly, as our interests and their weighting vary.

Perhaps she who lodges this objection will retrench, dropping complaints about 'factuality' and insisting that because the dispute arises from differences in personal preferences, it is not about anything objective. What to make of this depends, of course, on what's meant by saying that a claim isn't objective. If what's meant is simply that whether the claim is correct or not depends upon the interests and values of the person making it, then of course I concede that this is so. The question is why this should be thought to be *an objection* to the view I am limning.

One might worry that if the sorts of disputes I am discussing aren't objective in this sense, then they aren't capable of rational resolution—they can only be resolved by one party capitulating to the other or by one of them undergoing a sort of conversion experience to the other's point of view. This was the last of the three worries mentioned at the beginning of this section. I think it's mistaken; indeed, I think it's downright bizarre.

Certainly it's possible to offer someone a reason for changing their preferences. You might, for example, point out to me that even though I dislike car rides and want a long practice, I might find the trade-off in this case worth the effort because the car ride isn't all that long. In doing this, you needn't be offering a piece of information of which I was ignorant—I may be well aware of how long it takes to get to each field. You may be—well, asking me to adopt a different weighing of my interests and pointing out a justification for doing so. And in this case, as in ever so many cases, my preferences need not be etched in stone: I may indeed at the moment prefer longer practice on the close field to shorter practice on the better field, while acknowledging that there is a case to be made for the other side. If I decide to change my preferences in part because I accept your argument, why is my change of mind irrational, or capitulating to you?

The points made at the end of the last section are of course relevant here, so let me, in ending this section, repeat them. Think about a first-person attempt to decide whether the field is flat enough. Even if at the moment I have a fairly strong inclination towards one way of ordering preferences—I'm pretty strongly disinclined to drive a long way, and so I'm willing to use a bumpy field—there is nothing irrational in reviewing opposing ways of thinking about matters. Indeed, it seems the height of rationality to do so, especially if the issue is of real importance to me and I think that I *might* not have ordered my preferences optimally. Now sometimes when I reconsider my preference ordering in this way

I find that my preferences change—not necessarily because I become aware of some interest-independent fact that I have ignored, but because the process of reviewing opposing considerations itself sometimes brings me to weigh things differently. I may, for example, notice that a consideration that once weighed heavily now seems not so important; a change of the weight of one consideration may prompt me to weigh kindred ones heavily.

There is nothing irrational about taking a new way of thinking about a matter seriously in deliberation and, as a result of this, altering my preferences and desires. It is a perfectly normal part of rational deliberation. If it is a kind of 'conversion', then 'conversion' is part of rational deliberation. Whatever we choose to call the process, we all recognize that this sort of thing, at least on occasion, is important, and something that rationality demands. But if my going through this process is part of rational deliberation, how can it be suggested that if I take seriously your sincerely offered defense of a weighing of preferences opposed to my own and, finding it cogent, alter my own preferences, I am 'capitulating' to you or 'undergoing a conversion experience in some sense that makes our dialogue something outside the pale of the rational?

4.6

If what's come before in this chapter is anywhere near on target, there is quite a bit more to say about the nature of disagreement. In fact, all the hard work is yet to come. For insofar as we can't explain what is going on when there is disagreement and rational argument using the notion of absolute truth, we don't really have a handle on what it would be for one side or the other in a dispute to be the side whose view ought to prevail.

Of course one story one could tell is that if a difference of opinion is not a difference in which someone's opinion is absolutely true, there is nothing to be said as to whose opinion ought to prevail. We may feel solidarity with one side or the other, and want that side to prevail—we will, presumably, feel this way about our own view if we are party to the dispute. But those on the other side will have the same sort of feelings about their own views, and how, it might be asked, is one to arbitrate such a dispute, save from some particular perspective which might be called into question by some other one?[35]

I cannot bring myself to believe that this sort of reaction is correct, as should be obvious from the remarks above about the nature of disagreement and its rational resolution. Indeed, I cannot bring myself to believe that there isn't *something* of a general sort—the sort of thing which is not specific to a particular dispute, or to the disputes in some (more or less) narrowly circumscribed area

[35] I am, of course, alluding to views of Richard Rorty here. See, for example, the first few essays in Rorty (1998).

of discourse—to be said about how one perspective or opinion might be better or preferable to some other, even if a traditional notion of truth is not the appropriate way to explain its superiority. But it would take another book to lay out what this—objectivity without absolute truth—might come to. The job of this chapter was to make a case for the view that, since a great deal of truth is, indeed, relative or perspectival, we need to take this question seriously.

5

Matters of Taste

Talk about the rich, the round, or the recondite isn't the most likely place to go looking for relative truth. Most would look for it in 'matters of taste'—what activities or artists are cool, who is and isn't sexy, what are and are not, as Philippa Foot once put it, 'the good-looking, the good tasting, the good combinations of colors'.[1] If Arroyo consistently strikes you as good-looking, that is all that's needed to certify your utterance of 'Arroyo is good-looking'; if he consistently strikes your neighbor as plain and gaunt, that is all that's needed to certify his utterance of 'Arroyo isn't good-looking'. Here we have genuine relativity of some sort, for it seems that both you and your neighbor speak correctly, but you seem to disagree.

Are matters of taste a locus of the sort of relativity discussed in Chapter 4? You and your neighbor do disagree. You believe something—that Arroyo is attractive; he believes its denial. But many of us would say that neither you nor he, at least when you are talking to each other, should assess these beliefs in terms of truth and falsity. For, though you disagree, neither of you need think that the other is making a mistake. But when divergent, inconsistent opinions can both be correct, we are not in the realm of truth and falsity, but somewhere else.

If we accept this line of argument, we will say that matters of taste, not being a locus of truth, aren't a locus of relative truth. But there is, of course, an apparent problem with endorsing the argument. For though you and your neighbor will each sometimes deny that the other is making some sort of mistake, sometimes each of you will insist that the other *is* mistaken.[2] If the ground for saying that matters of taste are not a locus of truth is the absence of a sense of contrary opinions being mistaken, the ground is pretty shaky.

As I see it, when we disagree about matters of taste, it is often correct to say that though we disagree neither of us is making an error. From this it follows that our beliefs are not even relatively true or false. But it is also the case that people

---

[1] Foot (1979: 23). See also Foot (1970). I stumbled upon Foot's articles only as a first draft of this chapter was nearing completion. There is overlap between the position I reach in this chapter and that which Foot explores in these two papers.

[2] The greater the normal overlap in your judgments about looks is (and the greater the normal overlap in your explanations and justifications of such judgments), the more likely it is that neither of you will tolerate the other's opinion.

may disagree about a matter of taste—they may have the same disagreement as we have—and one of them may validly judge that the other is mistaken, where to say that a judgment is valid is to ascribe it relative truth in the sense explained in the last chapter. And from this it follows that the disputed claim enjoys at least a relative truth.

That last paragraph might sound a tad inconsistent. It holds out the possibility of there being a claim (over which you and I disagree) that isn't (even) relatively true or false, although it is identical with a claim (over which some other people disagree) that is relatively true or false. But there's no inconsistency here, given that not only may the assignment of a truth-value to a claim be 'perspective-relative', but that whether a claim is truth-apt may also be 'perspective-relative'. And, as we'll see, the right thing to say about matters of taste seems to be that not only is it a matter of taste whether duck-liver mousse is delicious, it is (so to speak) a matter of taste whether the claim that it's delicious is true or false. So, at any rate, I'll argue in this chapter.

5.1

What am I doing when I spontaneously and sincerely say 'Cool!' in response to something salient—someone motoring along on a Segway, leopard-skin pants, a shin-length red-leather cape? First and foremost, one might say, I am expressing a particular kind of appreciation for the object in question, and thus expressing a kind of valuing of the object. The object or activity grabs me in a way that makes me admire it or the person who has or does it; my admiration is, furthermore, based upon the object of admiration seeming different, striking, edgy, unconventional, and worth admiration for that.[3]

What am I doing when I spontaneously and sincerely say 'That's cool' in response to something salient—someone motoring along on a Segway, leopard-skin pants, a shin-length red-leather cape? First and foremost, one might say, I am expressing a belief about the object in question. That the state expressed is a belief is made plausible by various humdrum facts—one appeals to it to explain or justify behavior in the way one appeals to other beliefs, one will produce evidence for it if challenged, or challenge it if one disagrees, etc., etc.[4]

---

[3] 'Cool' has, of course, any number of uses, and the uses different people put it to are often different enough that we would not say that the word's meaning was the same across different uses. Still, some people do use the word in recognizably the same way, although they and we take them to disagree about what is and what is not cool in that realm. In what follows, I suppose that we have focused upon some such set of uses.

[4] In some sense, there is not a great deal of difference in saying (to vary the example) 'Yuck!' and saying 'That is yucky'—i.e. saying 'That is disgusting'. There is not a lot of difference because *the point* of saying that something is disgusting is typically to express the feeling of disgust. But that doesn't mean that there aren't differences as well. 'Yuck!', one might say, *directly expresses* one's

There are of course connections between the state of appreciation expressed by 'Cool!' and the belief expressed by 'That is cool', when both are directed towards the same object. (Likewise, of course, for the states expressed by 'What a hottie!', 'Yum yum!', 'Oh, yuck!' and 'He's hot', 'That's tasty', or 'Ça c'est tout à fait dégueulasse'.) One place we might look, if we want to explicate these connections, is in the evaluation of the states. We can say, of an enthusiasm, a valuing, a belief, a wish, some anger, and so on that it is or is not apt in various ways. It is tempting—I know *I* am tempted—to suppose that if a mental state can be sensibly evaluated as apt or otherwise to begin with, then some dimensions of evaluation of the state are in some important sense primary or central. Surely this is the case for states—like those expressed by 'Cool!' and 'That's cool'—where one way to evaluate them is by (doing something which looks for all the world like) agreeing or disagreeing with them.

It is not easy to say what makes the valuation (and the state of valuing) expressed by 'Cool!' (or 'What a hottie!' or 'Yum yum!' or 'Oh, yuck!') appropriate or otherwise. Our immediate and our considered reactions to the object which elicits the response have a great deal to do with it. Obviously, though, those reactions are not the only measure of appropriateness. We typically have *reasons* for thinking that something is or isn't cool. I think the red cape cool in part (only) *because* I think it's leather. If it's not, my appreciation is inappropriate. Evaluation of something may not cohere with one's desires, projects, and other commitments, as when the addict's sincere valuing of the object of his addiction conflicts with his other commitments. This sort of inconsistency can also render a state of valuing in some important sense inapt. And we can come over time to reject our valuing of something we once valued as tasty, disgusting, or cool, as our desires, plans, and tastes mature; often in such cases we evaluate our earlier evaluations as inappropriate.

We also sometimes evaluate something as cool (tasty, etc.) in cases in which we do not personally find it so, but know that those whose tastes are considered normal, or those to whom we defer about what 'one ought' to find tasty, etc., judge the person or thing to be cool (tasty, etc.). I acknowledge that there is such a deferential use of predicates of taste; for most of what follows (save in the digression at the end of Section 5.2) I will ignore this somewhat disjunctive aspect of our use of predicates of taste.[5]

Suppose we agree that when *I* value something as cool (or judge it to not be cool, and thereby value it in the way in which one values that to which one says

disgust, insofar as its (one and only) linguistic job is to give vent to the feeling of disgust. 'That is yucky/disgusting!' *indirectly expresses* one's disgust: its linguistic job is to ascribe the property of deserving (or at least eliciting) the feeling of disgust. At the least, this is a very plausible tale to tell about 'Yuck!' and 'yucky'.

[5] Disjunctive because it makes an application of a predicate of taste apt iff (roughly) one's considered judgment is that it applies or one is willing to defer to common opinion and common opinion is that it applies or one is willing to defer to 'experts' and their opinion is that it applies.

'No thanks'), *I* may evaluate that valuing as appropriate if (very, very roughly) my considered reaction to the object, when not based on mistaken beliefs about it or induced by states that I am committed to disowning, would be to so value it.[6] Let us suppose this quite generally so: X is entitled to evaluate his valuing something as cool as appropriate when X's considered reaction to the object of evaluation, when not based on mistaken beliefs about the object or induced by states X is committed to disowning, would be to so value the object. It will be useful to have a concise way of expressing this; let us thus say that X's valuing x as cool is something X is entitled to evaluate as appropriate iff from X's perspective x appears cool.[7]

Agreeing to this much is not agreeing to anything which tells us, for example, under what conditions *I* may evaluate *your* valuing something as cool as appropriate, or when *you* may so evaluate *my* so valuing. What shall we say about this?[8] One might think that here our second-order judgments track our first-order ones: if it is appropriate (inappropriate) for me to judge x cool, it is appropriate (inappropriate) for me to judge your evaluation, that x is cool, as appropriate (not appropriate). But surely this is not so.

It is obvious that x may appear cool (handsome, sexy) from my perspective while x appears not to be from yours, for our informed, considered reactions to x may just be different. But though our perspectives differ, I *may* acknowledge

The account I am giving of predicates of taste takes it as a datum that when I say 'Piaf is cool' and you say 'Piaf is not cool' we contradict each other. In the digression in the next section I will consider (and argue against) an alternative view.

[6] This is meant as a first approximation, and surely needs fine-tuning. Perhaps, for example, this characterization should incorporate something that ensures my evaluation would be stable as I gained more and more information and reflected upon it. Mark Johnston (1989, 1993) makes such a suggestion about the concept of a state of affairs being valuable. (But see n. 13 below for a significant difference between the story I am telling about matters of taste and the sort of story Johnston tells about value.)

[7] My talk of entitlement here—of someone's being entitled to take a certain evaluative attitude towards one of their states—suggests that there might be a gap between being entitled to a certain opinion about the attitude and being *right* to take that attitude. Certainly if the sort of entitlement here is like that we have when we have warrant for one of our opinions, that should be so—I can be warranted in thinking that it's about to rain but still be wrong.

I do not (quite) intend such a gap, as will become apparent below: normally, if I am entitled to think that my valuing x as cool is appropriate, then my belief that my so valuing is appropriate will be correct—in whatever sense such beliefs can be correct to begin with.

I admit that the text does not quite answer the question that needs answering. One wants an account of appropriateness of judgments of taste that would allow us to classify *potential* judgments—including judgments of objects that one will never see or otherwise think about—as appropriate or otherwise. The above most obviously applies only to judgments that one has made. The obvious way to extend it is to invoke dispositions to judge or one another collection of counterfactuals. This sort of extension, while of course needed in order to judge the overall adequacy of the story I am telling, I am going to forego. I see the (difficult) issues it would raise as by and large orthogonal to the concerns of this chapter. I hope to address these issues elsewhere.

[8] Of course, if your valuing something is based upon false beliefs about the object, or your valuing the object conflicts with other of your commitments, there is something inapt about your valuing of the object. Let us set this sort of case to the side to keep things simple. Let us also assume that I know all the relevant facts about your reasons for valuing things as you do.

your perspective as one way to think about what is cool (handsome, . . .). After all, tastes *do* differ, and my attitude towards your attitude towards, say, bungee jumping might be: Well, it's not for me, but if you like it, more power to you. Of course, there are limits to this sort of thing. I may not just fail to find something you do cool; I may find your *perspective* on what's cool unacceptable. To Bill's smoking the occasional joint I may say *Not for me, but if he finds it cool, so be it*, but to George's ongoing flirtation with junk I say *This is just not a way anyone should live; I can't accept a view that thinks that's cool*. When perspectives disagree about matters of taste, the occupant of one perspective may, as I will put it, *acknowledge* the other perspective as a possible, an acceptable way of thinking about the matter, as I accept Bill's. Or the occupant of one perspective may be *intolerant* of the other perspective, as I am of George's.[9]

If I'm intolerant of a perspective, I take some of its judgments to be mistaken; if I acknowledge it, I do not. But even when I acknowledge a perspective, I may be critical of it. You might, after all, be doing something in an acceptable but not in the best possible way; when this is so, I might think that while you aren't (exactly) making a mistake, you could do what you are doing better. And so, I think, even given that I find no mistake in your evaluations, there are two attitudes I might have towards them.

Suppose, to make things concrete, that I think film noir worthwhile but you do not; suppose that I acknowledge your perspective, as I don't think that someone whose tastes in film exclude film noir is making a mistake. We can distinguish two ways in which my attitude might be fleshed out. I might, first of all, see no reason for you to change your tastes. In this case I (presumably) have reasons for liking the genre, but I don't think that they ought to move you. But I might think that there is a reason for you to change your tastes: there is, I think, some virtue in (good) film noir that any film buff like yourself ought to appreciate; or I think that if you gave it a chance you would come to appreciate the melancholy cynicism of the genre. I may think this without thinking that someone who doesn't like the genre is simply making a mistake, has a perspective on film that must be rejected. If this is right, there are two ways in which one might acknowledge a contrary evaluation: one could *accept*

---

[9] How shall we cash out the current talk about perspectives? For present purposes we can identify a perspective with a (partial) 'assignment of values', something that's given by a set of claims of the forms *Fs are(not) cool, Ging is (not) cool, Hs are (not) tasty, a is (not) sexy/tasty/handsome*, and so on.

I do not assume that one can straightforwardly read someone's evaluative perspective off of their actual reactions to objects, properties, events, and the like. An evaluative perspective, as I intend the notion, is an idealization of a person's evaluative dispositions. As an idealization, it should have a minimal coherence—if, for example, it contains *Fs are tasty* and *Gs are not tasty*, it must be possible for there to be some Fs, some Gs, and no F which is a G. There is no reason I can see to suppose that our evaluations are always this coherent. Our evaluations may also suffer various kinds of 'empirical incoherence', as when I believe that all amusement-park rides are fun—and so 'value *de dicto*' all such rides as fun—but have a visceral negative reaction to a particular ride—it's *not* fun—without knowing that it is an amusement-park ride. It is not clear (to me, at any rate) what to say about such cases.

it as one among a number of ways of valuing things, a way of valuing one has no reason to oppose. Or, while acknowledging it, one could still think it inferior to some alternative evaluation; one could, as I will put it, acknowledge it but find it *deficient*, thinking that there are reasons for preferring a contrary evaluation.

Summarizing: There are two ways in which I could find your valuing x as cool or otherwise to be appropriate. First of all, our perspectives could simply agree on x—we both, say, think x is cool. Or it could be that while we value x differently I acknowledge your perspective as one way to think, a way of valuing I have no reason to oppose that I think you ought to accept. I acknowledge that your attitude towards x is perfectly appropriate—I just don't share it. I will call these attitudes towards your valuing x as cool (or not cool, or handsome, or not sexy, or . . .) *agreement* and *acceptance* respectively. There are also two ways in which I could find your valuing x in a certain way inappropriate. First of all, even if I acknowledge your perspective and thus don't find your evaluation in error, I may differ with you over whether there is a reason to find x is cool you ought accept. If I do, I find your valuing x liable to reproach; I, as I shall put it, find valuing x as you do *deficient*. In this case I may while acknowledging that yours is one acceptable way to go through life, try to convince you that there is a better way. Secondly, I may not just find your valuation of x deficient; I may think your perspective intolerable, one which does not constitute an acceptable way of looking at things. I may, that is, be *intolerant* of your judgment, insofar as it is a manifestation of a perspective on the matter at hand which I find unacceptable.

Returning to the question posed above: under what conditions may I evaluate your valuing something as cool as appropriate? For the most part this, like my first-order judgments of what is cool, turns on my considered, stable opinion—*not* as to whether the object of your judgment is cool or otherwise, but as to whether your opinion on the matter is (one with which I agree or is) acceptable or not. We have the same sort of caveats as before—that my judgment about your judgment is apt only if it is not based on misinformation and only if it is not in conflict with other commitments I have.

I take myself to have expounded quotidian common sense about matters of taste. Perhaps I cleaned up a few rough edges, sharpened a few common-sense distinctions, introduced some terminology. But I doubt an ordinary Joe or Jane—your run-of-the-mill lawyer or car mechanic or Nobel winner in physics—would find anything very remarkable in what I just said. All pretty obvious stuff. Even querulous philosophers may be inclined to accept what I've said. After all, it amounts to little more than a pedantic gloss on the ideas that there are lots of different perspectives from which people carve out a life of likes and dislikes, passions positive and negative; that we sometimes value things differently; that on some such matters there's no ruling one way right, another wrong (which is not to say that *any* opinion on such matters is acceptable).

Now there is presumably a tight connection between the evaluative state expressed by 'Cool!' ('What a hottie!', etc.) being appropriate and the *belief* that the relevant thing is cool (etc.) being appropriate. On a first pass, one wants to say, the evaluation is appropriate iff the belief is. But if this is right, it looks like we may not want to invariably evaluate such beliefs as true or false. For suppose that I take your perspective on what's cool in contemporary music to be acceptable, but we differ on cases: I think Sleater-Kinney is a terrific band, you find their music at best a cunning refinement on the sound of fingernails scraped upon slate. When we explore our differences, I find that my reasons for liking them—the dissonance of minor keys married to Carrie Brownstein's vocals speaks to me of barely suppressed rage—just don't move you. You find the way the band conveys anger irritating. I can see why someone would feel that way. I don't think you're making a mistake in not being moved as I am; I acknowledge your attitude, though I don't agree with it.

While I am committed to my judgment that Sleater-Kinney is cool, I am also committed to its not being the case that you are making a mistake when you judge otherwise. But these judgments are *contradictory*—so, at any rate, do we proceed. You and I—if we are not *too* disparate in our tastes and musical ear—can and will argue about what is and is not cool. We have reasons for our evaluations which we offer to each other. We proceed, that is, as if there is disagreement over whether a particular band—Sleater-Kinney—has a particular attribute—being cool.[10]

Often when I say that something is cool and you deny it we see ourselves as disagreeing but are disinclined to say that one of us must be right. The sort of valuing associated with 'cool' is optional: different people can do it in different ways, and can acknowledge that there is no one 'right' way to do it. The appropriateness—the 'rightness'—of the belief that a thing is cool is tied closely indeed to the appropriateness of valuing it as cool. But this makes it look like truth—even relative truth—is the wrong dimension of evaluation for talk about what is cool and what is not. There are different, incompatible yet acceptable, answers to the question, What is hip? When multiple, incompatible answers are acceptable, we are not in the neighborhood of truth and falsity. If those who give the different answers are prepared to acknowledge the acceptability of answers inconsistent with their own, they cannot ascribe even relative truth to their own answers.[11]

---

[10] It will be said, perhaps, that while we proceed this way, that can't really be what is going on. The argument would be this. If there really are equally good ways of reacting to objects as cool or not, there can't be a single property, of being cool, that people who value things differently are ascribing to objects when they value them differently. For if there *were* such a property, there couldn't be multiple valid ways of valuing things as cool. After all, it's valid to value something as (having the property of) being cool just in case the thing *is* cool.

Part of the burden of the next sections is to address this sort of worry.

[11] I should observe that one can accept the conclusion here—that one can sensibly disagree with someone without holding that they are mistaken—without accepting the idea put forward

Some will disagree. Why, it will be asked, should we think that when the truth of a claim p is a relative matter it *must* be that when you and I disagree about p one of us is making a mistake? If my belief that p is valid (p is true from my perspective) and your belief that not p is valid (true, that is, from your perspective), why must there be a mistake? After all, my evidence may justify my judgment, so that I have justified true(-for-me) belief; analogously for you. Surely in a case like this no one is at fault. But if this is so, why not say this sort of thing about matters of taste? My judgment that Reblochon is tastier than Gruyère may be relatively true while yours that nothing is better than Gruyère is relatively true as well. No one is at fault or mistaken. End of story.

This view can't be sustained, simply because when one is willing to ascribe truth or falsity to a particular claim p, one treats p and the claim that p is true as equivalent: *within* a perspective, truth is 'disquotational'. Suppose I think that Beaufort is a better cheese than Tome, and you think the reverse. Suppose (for *reductio*) that each of our thoughts is valid—mine is true from my perspective, yours is from yours. Then not only can I (validly) say that Beaufort is better than Tome, I can (validly) say that it's true that Beaufort is better than Tome. And of course if you think Tome is better than Beaufort and not vice versa I can also (validly) say that you think that it's not the case that Beaufort is better than Tome. So I can (validly) say that it's true that Beaufort is better than Tome though you think Beaufort isn't better than Tome. From which it surely follows that you're mistaken—after all, if you have a false belief, you are mistaken about something. This line of reasoning is sound no matter what the object of dispute. So it is just wrong to think that if my view is valid—true relative to my perspective—and your contradictory view is valid—true, that is, relative to yours—then our disagreement is 'faultless'. Faultless disagreement is possible—but such disagreement is not one to be evaluated in terms of truth.

5.2

Judgments about what is cool and other matters of taste enjoy a double relativity. Such judgments are, I have suggested, made from a particular perspective, and this is one dimension of their relativity. And they are *evaluated* from a particular perspective. If we ask ourselves what to think about Cindy's judgment that

above, that one can sensibly hold that there is a reason someone ought to accept for thinking that p, though they make no mistake in not accepting the reason and thinking that p isn't so. I recognize that some find this last view odd. The example of Johnny Depp and Ethan Hawke in Section 5.3 is in part intended as an example of a case in which someone has a reason to think p (that Hawke is attractive, because Depp is and they resemble each other in relevant ways), but in which no mistake is made in disbelieving p (because someone who stably finds Hawke unattractive voices no mistake when he says that he is not attractive).

Metallica is cooler than Motorhead, we must pick some perspective(s) on coolness relative to which to evaluate it. We may evaluate Cindy's judgment by reference only to our own standards of cool. Or we may reckon Cindy's standards no worse but no better than our own, and thus measure the judgment against both. Or we may be willing to consider some wider set of standards as apt for evaluating her judgment.

This means that whether we find a judgment that x is cool to be true, false, or not even truth-apt may vary with our own evaluative perspective. Sometimes I ignore the very possibility of another way of thinking about the cool, the tasty, or the sexy. When I do and I judge Sleater-Kinney to be cool, I take what I say to be true. When I acknowledge the possibility of other perspectives, other choices of what to listen to, I still judge the band cool, but I acknowledge that you need not be making a mistake, if you disagree with me.[12]

My picture is this. A perspective is a particular individual's perspective. From individual M's perspective, a judgment that a particular thing is cool will be *appropriate* or otherwise, depending upon the properties and relations of the object of the judgment, the reactions, considered and otherwise, of M to the object, and so on. A perspective will, as we might say, *acknowledge* (itself and) some other perspectives as *acceptable*, so far as judgments concerning (certain) matters of taste are concerned. When M turns to evaluate judgments on matters of taste made from other perspectives, even those judgments with which M disagrees, they will be acceptable to M—he will or should be willing to acknowledge that they involve no mistake—provided there is some perspective P which M's perspective acknowledges as acceptable from which the judgment is appropriate. When M('s perspective) acknowledges as acceptable perspectives which diverge on some matter of taste—whether x is cool, y is sexy, or z disgusting—there is from M's perspective no ascribing truth or falsity to opinions on the matter. M will endorse a particular opinion, but (should) refrain from ascribing to that opinion properties whose possession entails that contrary opinions are mistaken. If every perspective M acknowledges agrees on the matter, M can ascribe truth to his opinion. But if M is reasonably tolerant concerning the matter at hand truth and falsity will often not get a hold.

Telegraphing what I have said: Some of our opinions matter, matter quite a lot. A life without likes and dislikes, enthusiasm and abhorrence, love and hate isn't worth much; to have a good life requires opinions about what is likeable, lovely, loathsome. But while it matters that we have such opinions,

---

[12] Foot (1979) makes a kindred observation, though she does not quite endorse the idea that there is a double relativity in the relevant judgments.

Someone might suggest that this means that we don't have to say that judgments about the cool are sometimes neither true nor false. After all, if we confine ourselves to a single perspective—our own—we will always be able to assign a truth-value to such judgments, at least until we run up against the bounds of vagueness in our own standards.

To this, I can only say: indeed. Intolerance is, alas, always an option.

it doesn't matter so much whether they are true or false. Indeed, such truth (or falsity) as such opinions have is often a product of narrowness of vision or intolerance.

That there is a double relativity involved in judgments about matters of taste explains why we are able to waffle on whether such judgments are truth-valued or are not sensibly thought of as bearers of truth. This double relativity is also relevant to explaining and justifying what must seem to the reader an incoherence in the view I have been sketching.

The putative incoherence is this. I seem to be committed to the idea that we might want to say *both* that Stanley Steamy is (say) sexy, *and* that someone who denies his sexiness makes no error. How can that *possibly* be? Think of the problem as one, so to speak, in metaphysics. We have an object, Mr Steamy. If we do an inventory of its properties, we will put sexiness on the list. But if that's on the list, mustn't we say that anyone who denies Mr Steamy's sexiness is making a mistake? Indeed, if that's on the list of his properties—and so it's *a fact* that he's sexy—how can it not be true that he is sexy?

I insist that there is no incoherence here. Consider what it is to be sexy. It is (roughly, and to a first approximation) to be a person who, behaving as they normally behave, is attractive in a way that is sexually arousing. In slightly different words: to be sexy is to be someone who plays a certain role, that of being attractive in a way that is sexually arousing when one behaves as one normally does. To have this property is to play a role insofar as one has or lacks the property only in, only relative to, a social context, relative to the perspective of another person or group. (After all, you can't play the role of a sexy person—you can't be sexy—without some people around to whom you are (potentially) sexy.[13]) Suppose we say, as is usually said, that property possession is something which is relative to a 'possible world' or (as I would prefer to say) a situation—relative because 'within a world' (situation) one either has the property or one doesn't, though 'across worlds' (situations) whether one has the property may vary. Then we must say that the 'worlds' (situations) in which properties like being sexy are had are partially constituted by (the people who are the possessors of) perspectives. If we think of matters this way, then of course it's possible that among the properties that Mr Steamy has is being sexy, though you make no mistake when you say that Mr Steamy isn't sexy. For the situation from which

---

[13] A ripe tomato could be red even if there were no animals about to appreciate its redness. Redness is *roughly* coextensive—roughly necessarily coextensive—with the disposition to cause the sort of reaction red objects in fact cause in those who have the sensory dispositions had by those who are in fact normal color perceivers. But, as I see it, sexiness, being tasty, and others matters of taste are tied more closely to the reactions of their world mates than are the colors. In a world where no one finds (someone who looks like the actual) Johnny Depp in the least attractive, that person is not attractive; a world where the (actual) taste of crème caramel causes universal disgust is a world in which the actual taste of crème caramel is not tasty. I think I differ here from some advocates—for example, Mark Johnston—of response-dependent accounts of predicates of taste (see Johnston 1989, 1993).

I speak, when I say that Steamy is sexy, is different from that from which you speak, when you say that he is not.[14]

A person's reactions and standards, her notions fleshed out as she fleshes them out (one thing we might mean by speaking of a thinker's perspective or context) play several different roles. They help supply something relative to which an individual can have a property like being sexy, or rich, or cool: My reactions to X, given various other facts about me and X, provide the ground against which X's sexiness is visible, for they provide something necessary for X to have the property, for X to *be* sexy to begin with. A distinct role of a perspective is normative: a thinker recognizes certain perspectives—certain sets of reactions, rules, standards and so forth—as being acceptable, and thus as having normative force for thought and talk, as determining when thought and talk can be said to be true or false. A truth is what any acceptable perspective would have to grant, if it is not to be convicted of error. Recognition that a perspective is acceptable may be more or less deferential, as when I defer to the doctor about what arthritis is. Such recognition may be piecemeal, as when I am prepared to defer to the chemist about hydrocarbons but not about whether Coca-Cola is water. Such recognition may also be negative, in that it consists in a refusal to recognize any among some collection of perspectives as having a privileged position as to when a thought is right, when it is wrong.[15]

These two roles for what a thinker's perspective provides often go together, for one tends to assume (when it comes to matters of taste) that one's perspective is *the* measure of whether one's thought and talk is true. But they can come apart, and so there is a distance between X's being sexy and it's being true that X is

[14] Terminology is bound to get in the way here. For the purposes of this note (and for the purposes of the technical digression at the end of this section) let us pretend that metaphysicians who speak of possible worlds all have the same sort of thing in mind; let us use 'possible world' to pick that sort of thing out. I want to take this notion as a primitive. I assume that a possible world in this sense is something that determines 'all the natural facts', where the natural facts are those facts that supervene on the physical, chemical, biological—on the natural—structure of the world. Unlike your typical naturalist, I do not want to assume that *every* fact is determined by a possible world in this sense, since I am suggesting that matters of taste—such as that Tome is tasty but not as tasty as a good chèvre—are facts that are determined only relative to a possible world *and* a perspective. In the text, when I speak of situations what I have in mind is *not* what situation semantics (the view developed in, for example, Barwise and Perry 1983) means by 'situation' (roughly, a collection of objects with some, but not necessarily all, of their properties and relations); rather, I intend a pairing of a possible world with a perspective. That is to say: on the picture I am sketching, only some properties are possessed relative to a (traditional) possible world; other properties are only possessed relative to a situation—i.e. a traditional possible world plus a perspective.

I am indebted to the members of Herman Cappellen's seminar on relativism for helping me get straight on what I (should) mean here.

[15] The reader is perhaps worried that we are on the brink of an 'anything-goes' view of truth. For suppose that I insist that Mo Vaughn is president, and refuse to recognize any perspective save my own as acceptable. Then won't it be true that Mo is president?

No. *Some* properties are in some sense 'constituted' by interactions between me and the possessor of the property—sexiness and the cool are my running examples. It doesn't follow that *all* properties are. I can insist all I want that I am 5′11″. That does not mean that I am 5′11″, from my own or from anyone else's perspective. Height (alas) is not 'constructed'.

sexy. X is sexy if X plays the role of a sexy person—which X does, if X and I stand in the right relations. Truth enters into the matter only when a particular perspective—in the case of sexiness a certain set of reactions, expectations, and so forth—is assumed to have some special normative force, is assumed to be the perspective from which judgments about the sexy *ought* to be evaluated.[16] Since we may stand in the relevant relations to X while acknowledging that those who do not are not deficient, are not missing anything mandatory in their picture of the world, it can happen that we find ourselves endorsing the claim that X is sexy, but not willing to ascribe it truth. When these two roles for perspective come apart, we lose the '(dis)quotational' aspect of truth: we lose the guarantee that we may always move from the thought that p to the thought that p is true.

Technical Digression

The remainder of this section develops the view just sketched. It can be skimmed or skipped by those with little patience for technicalities. Among the topics discussed are modal judgments of taste ('Reblochon isn't tasty at all, but it would have been if different cows had been bred in the Savoie') and whether predicates of taste ought to be understood as having an 'experiencer' argument place (so that uses of 'Beaufort is tasty' turn out to invariably say something along the lines of 'Beaufort is tasty to such and such a person').

Suppose a simple language with predicates of taste (drawn from a set T), 'normal' predicates (drawn from a set Π), terms, and connectives to be given. Models for such a language will be constructed from a set W of possible worlds, a set P of perspectives, a set U of individuals, and a function F that assigns semantic values to expressions. (Situations are here identified with members of W x P; 'situation' is used below in this way.) A perspective p determines an agent (p_a), a world (p_w), and a set of 'tastes' (p_t). We identify a taste as a pairing of a (n n-ary) member of the set T of predicates of taste with a function from worlds to sets of individuals (sets of n-tuples if the predicate is relational). Intuitively, the taste $<t, f>$ (t in T, f a function from W to subsets of U) is the taste of a person who would stably judge u as it is constituted in w to satisfy t just in case u is in f(w). A perspective contains exactly one taste for each predicate of taste in T.[17]

On the view we are developing it can be that (for example) Reblochon is tasty (because from my perspective it *is* tasty), though it is not true that Reblochon is

---

[16] More accurately and pedantically: truth enters in only when some set of perspectives (which may be a unit set) is assumed to have this role.

[17] Obviously the explanation of the representation is as clumsy as the representation itself. Better stated: the rough idea is that $<$'tasty', f$>$ represents a taste of a person who would judge (under 'appropriate' circumstances) u as constituted in w to be tasty iff u is in f(w). I am assuming that the predicates of taste of the language are 'independent', so that what one such predicate is true of at world w has no effect on any of what at w the other predicates are true of.

tasty (because there are perspectives I acknowledge from which it is not tasty). Let us use 'It is a fact that' so that *It is a fact that S* is equivalent to *S*. Then the semantics for our little language needs to characterize when what a sentence says is a fact in a situation s, as well as when what is said by a sentence is true relative to a set S of perspectives and a situation s. For both tasks we need to invoke the function F that assigns semantic values to expressions. To terms, F assigns members of U. To n-place predicates it assigns a function from situations to appropriate extensions (the extension of an n-ary predicate in a situation being a subset of U^n).[18] This assignment is unconstrained in the case of 'normal predicates'. When t is an n-ary predicate of taste, there is for each p exactly one g (taking W into subsets of U^n) such that $<t, g>$ is in p_t; F(t) is that function h such that for any w in W and p in P, $h(< p,w >) = g(w)$. An atomic sentence states a fact relative to s just in case the relevant tuple (of what's named by its terms) is in the extension of its predicate at that situation; whether truth-functions of sentences state facts at s is determined in the usual way.

Write *[Φ]pw* for *Φ states a fact relative to situation p and w*. (Sometimes I use 'at p and w' instead of 'relative to p and w'.) Intuitively this should obtain iff given the perspective p—that is, given the perspective of p_a—and the (natural) facts determined by w, it's a fact that Φ. If Φ is an atomic sentence whose predicate is normal, the identity of p will be irrelevant, in that *[Φ]pw* iff *[Φ]p'w* for any p, p', and w. If Φ is an atomic whose predicate is a predicate of taste, there is a sense in which it is p alone that determines whether *[Φ]pw*, since p contains a taste which will determine the extension of Φ's predicate at pw for any w. But this does not render the w in *[Φ]pw* otiose in the way in which p is otiose when Φ's predicate is normal. Whether (for example) 'tripe sausages are tasty' is true relative to my (actual) perspective and a world w turns on whether tripe sausages *as they are in w* are tasty *given my actual tastes (which are part of my actual perspective)*. Relative to the actual world and my tastes, the sentence is true, for I like the chewy, somewhat bland taste of boiled tripe; relative to my actual tastes and a world in which boiled tripe has the gustatory properties of bull's liver, the sentence will not be true.

A fully general definition of *what Φ says is a fact in situation s* must incorporate a parameter beyond the situation parameter, since whether it is (a fact that it is) *true* in my situation that tripe sausages are tasty turns not simply on my tastes but on what tastes I acknowledge. Suppose the language to have been expanded to include a one-place operator *T* read 'It is true that'.[19] Let *S* range over sets of

---

[18] This means that what's said by a sentence of the form $F^n a1 \ldots an$, when F^n is a normal predicate, will invariably be absolutely true or false, not relatively true or false or truth-valueless. There is no point in complicating matters here by allowing for the latter possibilities.

[19] Introducing a truth *predicate* doesn't seem worth the effort here; it will be obvious from the account of the operator how (ignoring issues of vagueness and paradox) the treatment of a predicate would go.

perspectives; read $S[\Phi]pw$ as Φ *states a fact at p and w, relative to S.* Writing $|e|_s$ for *the extension of e at s,* we carry over the definition above for the atomic case:

$S[f^n(a1, a2 \ldots an)]pw$ iff $< |a1|_{pw}, |a2|_{pw}, \ldots |an|_{pw} >$ is in$|f^n|_{pw}$.

A sentence is true at pw relative to the set S of perspectives provided that it states a fact relative to p and any member of S:

$S[T\Phi]pw$ iff for any p' in S: $S[\Phi]p'w$.

This definition treats a generalization of the case in which we are primarily interested, the case in which we ask whether it is (a fact that it is) true from a particular perspective p that Φ at p and a world w. One way to distinguish this case is to introduce more structure into our models, by (for example) assigning to each perspective p a set p_S of those perspectives it acknowledges, requiring that p be a member of p_S. (I assume one always acknowledges one's perspective: not to do so would be something like having a belief that one thought was incorrect.) This would allow us to mark the relevant case by saying that a sentence states a fact from a perspective p if it states a fact relative to p_S at p and p_w.

Assume that the (non-epistemic) modals 'necessarily' and 'possibly' are to be regimented as unary operators that play no role in binding; assume that subjunctive conditionals are regimented using binary, non-variable binding operators. As I see it, the primary question about sentences such as

(1) Vegemite could have been tasty.

or about ones of the form

(2) If it had been the case that Φ, then Vegemite would have been tasty.

is (so to speak) what sort of possible situations make them true. Vegemite, I think we can all agree, tastes very, very bad.[20] There are various changes one can imagine in the world such that, were the world so changed, we would sincerely say 'Vegemite is tasty'. That is, there are various changes one can imagine in the world such that, were the world so changed, we would have found Vegemite tasty.[21] In particular, we would have been inclined to sincere use of this sentence in any of the following:

(a) our physiology was different enough from the way it actually is that (though the chemical composition of Vegemite was exactly as it actually is) we found Vegemite tasty;

---

[20] For the moment, I am ignoring the possibility of intersubjective variation within a world concerning whether things are tasty.

[21] I take it that to say that we would have *found* Vegemite tasty is to say that we would have reacted to it a certain way, that it would have *seemed* tasty. I take it that it does not follow from this that (in the relevant circumstances) Vegemite would have *been* tasty, just as the fact that a certain thing might have stably *seemed* red to us in a certain kind of situation doesn't imply that (in that situation) it would have *been* red.

(b) the composition of Vegemite was (just) different enough from what it actually is that (though our dispositions to classify as tasty were exactly as they actually are) we found Vegemite tasty;[22]

(c) we had undergone enough training or acculturation so that (though Vegemite had its actual chemical composition and at the beginning of our training our classificatory dispositions were as they actually are) at the end of our training we found Vegemite tasty.

In which of these cases would it have been true that Vegemite was tasty—that is, would it have been the case that what I say with 'Vegemite is tasty' was true? I don't think that (a) is a case in which Vegemite is tasty; saying that it is strikes me as rather like saying that sunsets might have been gray simply because we might all have been color blind (or that the US flag might have been red, white, and green because we might all have had a different visual system). (b), I think everyone will agree, is a case in which Vegemite is tasty.

About (c) I have mixed feelings. Observe that we will judge someone or something tasty, attractive, cool, handsome, etc. when we do not 'personally' find it/her/him so but know that those whose tastes are considered normal (or those to whom we defer about what 'one ought' find tasty, etc.) judge the person or thing to be tasty, attractive, etc. I think such deferential uses of predicates of taste can be counterfactual. I might be willing to call tasty certain wines delicious not because I find them so but because authorities do, and I might be willing to call tasty certain sorts of wines that don't exist but could have, if I believe that those to whom I defer would have all found them obviously so. Of case (c) I can imagine at least two developments. In one, we are indoctrinated with tastes which we imagine we 'ought' to have but don't; in the other we are brainwashed. In the first case I think it might be true that Vegemite is tasty; in the second not.[23] If your judgments about these cases match mine, then you will agree that when I say 'Vegemite is tasty' what I say ought to be taken as possible—that is, as a possible fact—provided that there is some ('natural') world in which, from my perspective, Vegemite is tasty. This suggests we adopt

$S[$it's possible that $\Phi]$pw iff there's a w′ such that $S[\Phi]$pw′.[24]

---

[22] I assume that the change in composition of Vegemite would not change any of Vegemite's essential properties, so that the stuff would still be Vegemite.

[23] Note that if we give this account of the matter we may say that we are as a matter of fact *mistaken* about whether Vegemite is tasty, since we are committed to the idea that tastes to which we ought to defer—that determine in the case of Vegemite whether it is in fact tasty—are tastes according to which the substance is tasty.

[24] It is generally assumed that the properties expressed by predicates of taste supervene on physical facts, so that (minimally) it is impossible that there be a difference between two worlds, as to whether someone/thing is tasty/attractive/cool, etc., without there being a difference in 'the physical facts' between the two worlds. If we assume that distinct members of W never determine exactly the same physical facts, this sort of supervenience is trivially reflected in the above semantics, in the sense that if we hold constant a perspective p, we don't find that a difference in the physical

A major issue concerning predicates of taste concerns their logical form. One might argue that a predicate such as 'cool' ('sexy', 'tasty', 'handsome', etc.) has *two* argument places, a 'subject' argument place that is overtly filled in sentences such as 'Paraponting is cool', and an 'experiencer' argument place normally filled—usually covertly—with something that names a person to whom the thing whose name fills the subject argument place is said to be cool (or sexy, tasty, handsome, etc.).[25] On this view—call it the binary view—an unembedded utterance of 'Paraponting is cool' makes a claim that would be made more explicitly by a sentence of the form *Paraponting is cool to/for x.* Since unembedded use of the sentence typically makes a claim about the speaker, what is typically said by unembedded utterance of 'Paraponting is cool' is (roughly) what would have been said by something along the lines of 'To/for me, paraponting is cool'. The opposing view—the unary view, defended in this chapter—is that the predicates have only one argument position. On this view, unembedded use of 'Paraponting is cool' ascribes a (non-relational) property to paraponting, not a relation between paraponting and a person.

The strongest argument for the binary view involves what appears to be binding of a variable in the posited argument place. There seem to be readings of

(A) Everyone ordered something tasty.
      Everyone married someone attractive.

on which their uses would not be true simply because everyone ordered something *the speaker* found tasty or everyone married someone to whom *the speaker* was attracted. On the relevant readings, the sentences seem to say something along the lines of

(B) Everyone ordered something tasty to her(self).
      Everyone married someone attractive to him(self).

This seems easily explicable if we suppose that 'tasty' and 'attractive' have an argument place that is usually filled covertly. In this case 'tasty' has a logical form suggested by *X is tasty to y*; the first sentence in (B) is thus regimented

For any person x: there is some object y: x ordered y and y is tasty to x.

The existence of the (B) readings of the (A) sentences seems a bit of a mystery if we suppose that predicates of taste have only a subject argument place.

---

facts makes for a difference as to whether it is a fact that (for example) asparagus is stinky. We *do* find a failure of supervenience in the sense that 'simply' by varying the perspective we take may effect whether (say) asparagus is stinky: there will be models in which, for some S, p, p', and w, the regimentation of 'Asparagus is stinky' states a fact relative to S at p and w but not relative to S at p' and w. Of course, *this* sort of 'failure of supervenience' already occurs when the truth of 'Mary is rich' is said to be relative to a perspective and world.

[25] There will be another argument position on (most) anybody's view which is filled by (the name of) a temporal entity—a time, interval, event, something of the sort. I resolutely ignore this in the remainder of the section.

In working our way up to understanding the sentences in (A), consider those in

(C) Vegemite is tasty to Jean.
   Fred is attractive to Helen.

If we think that predicates such as 'tasty' and 'attractive' have two argument places, we will most likely say that the names ending these sentences fill the second, experiencer argument place of their predicates. However, the sentences in (C) are just the tip of a rather large iceberg, more of which is apparent in

(D) Vegemite is tasty to Jean.
   Fred is attractive to Helen.
   Protest marching is unpatriotic to Howard.
   It's a chair to Carolyn.
   They are red to Park.

Several things should be observed about (D). First off, it's hard to see why one ought to think that the last three sentences in (D) differ either syntactically or (so far as the role of the prepositional phrase (PP) goes) semantically from the first two. Secondly, there is no motivation whatsoever for thinking that 'unpatriotic', 'chair', or 'red' has an experiencer argument position. Thus, if there is indeed no syntactic nor (in the role of the PP) semantic difference between the sentences in (D), then there is a rather strong argument for saying that 'tasty' and 'attractive' lack experiencer argument positions.[26]

This means that the fact that the (A) sentences have readings given by the (B) sentences supplies *absolutely no* evidence for the idea that predicates of taste have two argument positions. Those who think the (B) readings evidence for the binary view must think that when the (A) sentences are used to express the (B) readings there is elision of the relevant argument position and the variable filling it. But the unary view can agree that the (A) sentences have readings suggested by the (B) sentences, and that when the (A) sentences are used to express these readings there is elision of material in which a variable occurs. The advocate of the unary view simply holds that the variable isn't an argument *of the predicates 'tasty' or 'attractive'*.

How could this be? Well, the simplest account is that in the (D) sentences the prepositional phrase *to b* has the semantic properties of a sentence operator *b believes (that)*, so that the first sentence says what is said by *Jean believes that Vegemite is tasty*. If we told this story we would say that the first sentence in (D) has a logical form suggested by

(E) Jean believes [Vegemite is tasty],

---

[26] Of course there is nothing special about the five predicates used in (D); pretty much any grammatical sentence of the form *a is F* can have *to b* annexed to it.

where 'Jean' occurs not as an argument of 'is tasty', but rather as an argument of 'believes'.[27] One then says that the first (A) sentence has (ignoring tense) a logical form suggested by

(F) (Every x: x a person) (Some y: y a thing) [x ordered y and x believes (y is tasty)].[28]

Here 'tasty' has a single argument position. There is indeed an 'orderer' variable in the vicinity of 'tasty', but it is an argument of 'believes', not 'tasty'.

This proposal is demonstrably wrong. First of all, it does not seem to capture the relevant readings of the (A) sentences. Note that if we treat the PP as the operator *x believes that*, something has to decide whether the occurrence of that operator in the first sentence in (B) is to be interpreted as picking out an event before, simultaneous with, or posterior to the event picked out by 'order'. It is hard to see much plausibility in any account which does anything other than have the attitude verb carry the tense of the sentence's main verb, so that the sentence says that everyone ordered something that, at the time of the ordering, they thought to be tasty. But then (F) simply does not mean what the first sentence of (B) means. (F) then means that everyone ordered something that they *thought* to be tasty. But one can be mistaken about this sort of thing. Having never tasted Vegemite, but convinced that one's palate matches that of the Australian gourmand, one might *think* that one will find Vegemite tasty, but be wrong. Because of this, (F) may be true when (D)'s first sentence is not.[29] Secondly, the current treatment suggests that sentences like those in (D) will be ambiguous in a way in which they do not seem to be.[30] For consider

---

[27] Since logical form is a syntactic notion—it's the syntax that is the input to the interpretive process—this is not really correct. The sentence's logical form will be something more like *[To Jean [Vegemite is tasty]]*. The proposal under discussion is one on which the semantic value therein will be what we would assign to an operator with the meaning of *Jean believes that*. These niceties are irrelevant to the points at issue.

[28] Since the view we are considering takes the PP to be an *operator* (something that combines with a sentence, as opposed to a *predicate*, which combines with a name), I have so regimented the sentences from (A) and (B) as (E) and (F). One reason to be unhappy with the present proposal is that 'believes' in English is *not* an operator, as is witnessed by well-known facts about the presence of bound variables and anaphoric pronouns which can occur in the position of the complementizer 'that' and the sentence following it.

[29] Even if one—in my opinion quite implausibly—said that there were readings of the sentence on which the tensing of the verbs was uncoupled, there would still be a problem. For certainly on the current view the (B) sentence has *a* reading on which it says that everyone ordered something that, at the time of the ordering, they believed (possibly wrongly) they would find tasty. But the (A) sentence simply cannot mean this.

[30] The following argument supposes that (1) determiner phrases undergo a kind of movement ('raising'), the possibility of which generates ambiguity when a determiner phrase is commanded by a verb of propositional attitude; (2) on the current proposal, the PP *to Jean* in *Vegemite is tasty to Jean* will be moved to command the position of *Vegemite is tasty*; and so (3) a verb of propositional attitude will govern the position of 'Vegemite' in the just mentioned sentence.

(G) The lottery winner is handsome to John.
    John believes that the lottery winner is handsome.

As is widely appreciated, the second sentence is ambiguous because of the possibility of moving the phrase 'the lottery winner' out of the scope of 'John believes'. The reading obtained by so moving it ('The lottery winner is such that John believes that he is handsome') entails that someone won the lottery; the reading we get without movement does not. There is not a comparable ambiguity in the first sentence; there is no understanding of it on which it can be true although there is no lottery winner. But one expects such a reading if the current proposal about 'to John' is correct. Finally, the current view has a number of puzzling syntactic features. To mention but one: it sits rather poorly with the obvious fact that the PP 'to Jean' is a constituent of the verb phrase 'tasty to Jean', and that there is a syntactic liaison between 'tasty' and 'to Jean' even when the latter occurs at the beginning of the sentence—something which is not true of 'Jean believes [that]' as it occurs in a sentence such as 'Jean believes that Vegemite is tasty'. To appreciate the point, observe that we can do something describable as eliding 'tasty to John' in both

Vegemite is tasty to John, and Draino is tasty to John.
To John, Vegemite is tasty, and to John, Draino is tasty.

by saying

Vegemite is tasty to John, and so is Draino.
To John, Vegemite is tasty, and so is Draino.

But of course we cannot do anything like this to

Jean believes that Vegemite is tasty, and Jean believes that Draino is tasty.

Trying to do so gives us the ungrammatical

Jean believes that Draino is tasty, and [believes that] so is Draino.

An account that does not suffer from the last two problems takes 'to Jean' to be an operator whose argument and output is a verb phrase (VP). On the most wooden implementation of this idea, *VP to Jean* means something like *is thought to be VP by Jean*, and is true of an object iff the object is thought by Jean to be VP. If the PP 'to Jean' in 'The lottery winner is attractive to Jean' operates on the sentence's VP, not on the entire sentence, then even if we move the PP out of the VP (as in 'To Jean the lottery winner is attractive'), the meaning of the PP can only be applied to the VP. So we would expect no ambiguity in sentences like 'The lottery winner is attractive to Jean'. And obviously the current account of 'to John' does not make mysterious the facts about elision mentioned above.

If we say that 'attractive to Jean' means what's meant by 'is believed by Jean to be attractive', we don't solve the first problem mentioned above—that the relevant reading of 'Everyone married someone attractive' means that each married someone who *was* attractive to them, not merely someone whom they *believed* to be attractive. What this shows, I think, is that there is a (somewhat subtle) difference between saying that x is attractive/tasty/a chair/unpatriotic/red to y, and saying that y thinks x to be attractive/tasty/a chair/unpatriotic/red. Roughly and to a first approximation, to say that x is F to y is to say that fleshing out the notion of being an F as it is fleshed out by y, x falls under the notion F. That is, it is to say that from y's perspective x is an F.

How does saying that x is an F to y differ, on this account, from saying that y believes x to be an F? Part of the difference is the sort of difference there is between saying that it is true that x is F and saying that it is valid from y's perspective that x is F. As we know from the last chapter, neither of these entails the other. Recall Didi and Naomi: from Didi's but not Naomi's, perspective Mary is rich. If I share Naomi's perspective on wealth, then I must say that it is not true that Mary is rich, though I must also say that to Didi Mary is rich. Conversely, it is true that Mary is not rich, but not valid from Didi's perspective that this is so.

We cannot say that the distinction is precisely the distinction between truth and validity, for we don't want to say that judgments of taste are in general true or false, either absolutely or relatively. Let us nonetheless use 'extension' for the moment so that *X is in the extension of F, relative to y's perspective* does not imply that *F is true of x relative to y's perspective*. Is there then any difference between the claim *x is an F to y* and the claim *From y's perspective, x is an F*?

It is not altogether clear what the answer is. One can imagine that if Mary is inclined to treat empty cups as ashtrays—not because she has made a mistake about the difference between cups and ashtrays, but because that's just how Mary is—then we will be inclined to say that to Mary empty cups are ashtrays. But Mary might deny that cups, empty or otherwise, are *really* ashtrays—though she still might say, as do we, that for her an empty cup is an ashtray.

One could say that this use of 'to Mary' is continuous with its other uses, and so there is a difference between *x is an ashtray to Mary* and *From Mary's perspective x is an ashtray*—the difference being that when we spell out the meaning of common sense's *to Mary* we find that it has a disjunctive quality that the quasi-technical *From Mary's perspective* lacks.[31] Or one might propose that *to Mary* is ambiguous. Or one might say that the claim about Mary and empty cups is 'loose usage', that is supposed to convey (something like the claim) that Mary behaves as if, from her perspective, empty cups are ashtrays. I do not see that very much hangs on which of these accounts we adopt.

[31] On this alternative, *to Mary S* might be glossed *Either from Mary's perspective S, or Mary behaves as if, from her perspective, S.*

Let us take stock. I suggested that the strongest piece of evidence for the binary view of predicates of taste involves the apparent binding of a variable in certain readings of sentences like 'Everyone ordered something tasty'. I next observed that sentences of the form *x is F to y* are extremely common, and that there is no plausibility whatsoever, as far as many of these sentences go, in the idea that the surface argument of 'to' is in fact an argument of the predicate *F*. This, and the fact that a sentence like 'Everyone ordered something tasty' (on the relevant reading) is naturally glossed as 'Everyone ordered something tasty to him', strongly suggests that in the reading of the sentence that is *supposed* to provide evidence for the binary view, the bound variable that is supposedly an argument of the predicate 'tasty' is in fact *not* an argument *of the predicate* in the first place. I then sketched what seems to be the most plausible account of the semantics of the prepositional phrase 'to Mary' in sentences like 'Watery pasta is tasty to Mary', an account on which it operates on the verb phrase and (consequently) 'Mary' is not an argument of 'tasty'. I conclude that there is no good reason for thinking that predicates of taste are anything other than what they appear to be—predicates with (tense ignored) a single argument position.

5.3

Some will say that there is no 'cognitive disagreement' when you think hang gliding cool and I think it is not. There is a disagreement, but it is not something about which we can really argue: unless one of our assessments is the result of some 'purely factual' mistake, it cannot be resolved by rational means. Those who think this typically do so because they think that (unlike genuine 'cognitive disputes') such disputes arise because of differences in taste or animal attraction or reactions with which we are born or which are trained by various contingencies of social reinforcement. To resolve such a dispute, one or both of the disputants has to change his taste, relinquish or commence being attracted, or otherwise modify his spontaneous reactions to the passing show. But such modifications are not subject to rational control—one does not come to be attracted to someone because of an argument whose conclusion is that one should be; no longer finding something cool is not dropping a belief, but losing a kind of reaction. Telegraphing the worry: basic disagreements about what is cool or sexy (those expressible by sentences of the forms *He/That is/isn't cool/sexy*) turn only on differences in 'taste', 'attraction', 'animal reactions'; this sort of disagreement is attitudinal, not cognitive; and if these disagreements are attitudinal, not cognitive, (pretty much) all disagreements about the hip and the sexy are.[32]

---

[32] Whence the last premise? One might think that the collection of one's judgments, about who or what is sexy or cool, have a structure imposed by the way they are justified if challenged. At the base (the apex?) are those judgments which have no other justification than the response 'But

A minor problem with this argument is that it does not seem true that one cannot come to change one's 'taste' or reactions on the basis of argument. Suppose you find Ethan Hawke unattractive. Am I not arguing with you if I point out that you do find Johnny Depp attractive, and that as Hawke very much resembles the Depp of the early nineties, you *should* find him attractive? (I might go on to observe that your judgment is perhaps clouded by your distaste for the characters Hawke has portrayed.) Suppose you consider what I say, compare the Hawke of *Before Sunrise* with the Depp of *What's Eating Gilbert Grape?*, and come to see the resemblance. Suppose that you *agree* that you should find the one attractive if you find the other so, and that in the fullness of time, and in part as a result of these considerations, Hawke's boyish charm wins you over. Surely my argument *helped* you see a certain kind of inconsistency in your judgment. So argument seems to have an effect on taste, and helps us to render it consistent. If the consistency involved here is somewhat different from that invoked by saying that two beliefs about 'matters of fact' are inconsistent, well, so be it. It is surely kindred, and the sort of inconsistency involved in treating what *should* seem to you to be like cases in different ways is surely as subject to censure—censure from the point of view of *rationality*—as is the inconsistency involved in thinking Angelina to be jolly but not to be jolly.

The major problem with the argument we are considering is its narrow, willful, and downright odd division of judgments. *All* of our concepts are grounded to some extent in propensities to react to the passing show in certain ways—to group the harp, the shade, the bulb as parts of a single thing, while segregating the dust and schmutz on the base as no part thereof; to withhold the label 'water' because though we dimly realize it's 99.44 per cent H_2O, water (it just immediately seems to us) isn't sweet and lemony; to group the tomato with the carrot and not the cherry because—well, that just seems right. Some of these propensities are well-nigh primitive, some are taught to us in childhood, some we learn slowly over years. They are *all*, these propensities to group and react, subject to criticism both by ourselves and others; those of which we have consciousness are all potential targets of training and education. They are no less difficult to alter via argument than are 'matters of taste'. (You can *tell* me that a tomato is a fruit. I may accept what you say, but that in and of itself need not change my feeling that a tomato is a vegetable, not a fruit. I can *tell* you that Hawke is attractive. You may accept what I say—you

he/it/that sort of thing just seems to me to be sexy/cool'. Then there are other judgments, that X is sexy/cool, which can be justified by saying that X is F, and being F is (typically, or in the way X is F) sexy/cool. These latter judgments, of course, can be challenged. If one supposes that (1) judgments in this domain can only be justified in one of the two ways just mentioned, and (2) judgments that have no other justification than '*I* find it sexy/cool' are not really judgments but mere expressions of taste or attitude, then one has the makings of a defense of the final premise.

I do not endorse this picture (especially if it is held that 'judgments of taste' are somehow different in this regard from other judgments). Some discussion of this picture of judgment occurs below.

can think 'I'm sure he's right, but . . .'—but that in and of itself need not change your indifference or worse to his appearance.) Why pick on some of our concepts, such as the concepts of being good-looking or cool, and say that because we are willing to accept variation in their application, they must be 'non-cognitive'?

Perhaps the response will be that these concepts are special in that they are somehow suffused with value or emotion, while the others—the concepts of a lamp, lemonade, or fruit—are not. To judge someone attractive, it might be said, is in part to feel attraction; analogously for the judgment that something is cool. But nothing like this is true of judging a thing a lamp, lemonade, animal, mineral, or vegetable.

Frankly, it is hard to see what the relevance of this is, even if it is true. We are considering whether there is some reason to segregate the judgments about the cool and the sexy, denying them the honorific 'cognitive'. The mere fact, if fact it be, that the concepts of the cool and the sexy are imbued with something attitudinal or evaluative does not put them beyond criticism. It does not mean that we cannot have reasons for and against judgments involving these concepts. It does not mean (as I will argue presently) that such judgments do not stand in logical relations. If someone wants to carve out a niche for judgments about lamps and lemonade and exclude judgments about what is sexy or neat from the niche, well I guess that's Ok. Some people find collecting thimbles interesting, too. But what philosophical or humanly important issue turns on what does or doesn't go into the niche?[33]

5.4

What am I doing when I spontaneously and sincerely say 'That's cool!' in response to something salient—someone motoring along on a Segway, leopard-skin pants,

---

[33] Thus, the primary problem with the objection one paragraph back is that its conclusion doesn't follow from the premise that there is an 'attitudinal difference' between the concept of (for example) a lamp and that of being sexy. That said, it should also be said that this premise is dubious in the extreme. There are two ways to object to it. We can observe that (A) one might judge something cool or sexy without the typical emotional or evaluative accompaniment. Or we can observe that (B) someone's concept of a lamp etc. may be value- or emotion-laden in just the way that the other judgments typically are.

The discussion of thick concepts in Chapter 1 is relevant here. For reasons rehearsed there—recall, for example, our fantasy of St Augustine's liberating the concept of chastity from its Christian patina of the positive—it seems to me that (A) is surely correct. Concepts, especially those with an emotive or value component, are subject to criticism, and one way such criticism can go is for us to retain the concept's boundaries of application while uncoupling its attitudinal aspect.

If that criticism is on the mark, (B) is as well. It is not *essential* to the concept of, say, a balloon that it is arousing. Does this mean that no one can be so invested in the erotic, and in the erotic potentials of a balloon, that their conception of a balloon is such that judging something to be one is connected with emotion and arousal in the same way in which, in those who pass for normal, a judgment that someone is sexy is connected with these things?

a shin-length red-leather cape? I am expressing a belief—that the object in question is cool. That I am expressing a belief is shown by the facts that we can disagree about whether an object is cool, that we give reasons for our own opinion and against others, that we are motivated by the state 'That's cool' gives vent to in ways functionally similar to ways in which other beliefs motivate us.

The belief is indeed one that normally involves appreciating the object, valuing it in a certain way. One of the linguistic jobs of 'cool' *and* 'That is cool' is to express this sort of valuing; thus, if I am sincere when I say 'That's cool', I am committed to its being appropriate to so value the object.[34] But this does not mean that the state isn't a belief, any more than the fact that the concepts normally expressed by racial epithets have an attitudinal component means that sentences in which these terms are used don't express beliefs.

One of the marks of a belief is that it is something that can be evidence or justification for other beliefs. The justification one belief provides for another can be better or worse—airtight, or just compelling, or just plain bad. It is in this observation—that our reasons for beliefs can be graded—that logic is born.

Logic as standardly conceived needs truth. An airtight justification—something that forms a deductively valid argument when what it justifies is taken as conclusion—is normally pictured as one which guarantees truth; a compelling justification, one which makes truth probable. If we forsake truth when it comes to belief about the attractive and the cool, however, we cannot understand the justificatory role of these beliefs in this way. How, then, should we understand it?

We *could* wimp out. For we can make sense of the *relative* truth of the belief that, say, Johnny Depp is attractive. If we fix on an individual or a group of like-minded individuals, then their reactions, considered and otherwise, and their other commitments (for example, their 'theoretical' beliefs about attractiveness) will (vaguely) sort the world into attractive and unattractive, as well as determining a very partial ordering in terms of 'degrees of attractiveness'. It is to this sort of thing that our parochial judgments of attractiveness—those we make when unconcerned with the fact that different groups find different people attractive—are responsible; it is this sort of thing which determines their relative truth. If we call the thing in question a perspective, we may characterize the relative truth of beliefs about being attractive (or sexy, or cool, or tasty) in terms of a perspective. And we can then make use of the ideas in Chapter 4 to define validity: An argument is valid just in case the truth of its premises relative to a perspective guarantees that of its conclusion.

We could characterize validity for the relevant arguments in this way, but I think we should avoid it if at all possible. Part of the burden of the last few

---

[34] Sincere utterance *commits* me to valuing the object. To say this is not to say that sincere utterance *entails* that I value the object.

sections is that it is sometimes inappropriate to think of judgments about who is attractive and what is cool as true or false, since different perspectives, among which there may be no compelling reason to choose, will make these judgments differently. But if we *shouldn't* think of the judgments in question as truth-apt, and we know no way to think of arguments involving them as valid save in terms of their potential truth, it seems that we *shouldn't* think of the arguments as capable of being valid or invalid. But that is to think of the arguments as, well, not arguments. To put the point slightly otherwise: If we shouldn't be evaluating the premises or conclusion of an argument in terms of truth and falsity—if the proper dimension of evaluation is in terms of some other quality Q—then validity for the argument is presumably to be defined not in terms of truth, but in terms of quality Q.

Consider the argument *John is rich; all the rich are attractive; so John is attractive*. Even if the second premise and conclusion are not candidates for truth, because they involve the notion of being attractive, the first premise *is* a candidate for truth. Different beliefs, different claims, involve different sorts of commitments, whose appropriateness is to be evaluated in different terms. Sometimes the right dimension of evaluation is truth, sometimes it is something else. Validity is presumably to be defined, as suggested in Chapters 2 and 3, in terms of 'commitment preservation': valid arguments are those such that whenever the commitments conventionally associated with all their premises are appropriate, so is that associated with the conclusion. The idea that validity is truth preservation is just a special case of such a definition, appropriate when premises and conclusion are all truth-apt.[35]

What does logic look like, on this view? Some of it looks a lot like Austin's *How to Do Things with Words*. For logic will begin by determining what sorts of acts and attitudes are associated by convention with the utterance of our sentences, and what the proper 'dimensions of evaluation' of these are. That is, logic begins by essaying something like Austin's attempt at classifying kinds of speech acts at the end of *How to Do Things with Words*, spelling out the sorts of

---

[35] Claims about wealth (and roundness, and height, and many other notions expressed by the gradable adjectives) may not always be bearers of truth. Suppose Chapter 4's Didi looks upon her differences with Naomi about Mary as not involving any mistake on Naomi's part. Suppose, that is, that Didi's attitude is something along the lines of *That is a way of thinking of wealth; I don't think it's the best way to think about the matter, but it's not as if it is flat-out mistaken*. Then the argument of the first few pages of this chapter may kick in: Didi disagrees with Naomi about p, but acknowledges that Naomi isn't making a mistake. So Didi should not ascribe truth to p, or falsity to Naomi's contrary opinion.

I chose to keep this complication out of Chapter 4 in order to avoid muddying the waters. That chapter argued for one view that clashes with the philosophical orthodoxy: that the truth of a representation may be perspective-relative. This chapter argues for an independent heresy: in effect, that whether a representation is the sort of thing that is to be evaluated for truth or falsity is imposed upon the representation 'from the outside'; that whether a thought is truth-evaluable to begin with is something that can vary across perspectives. It seemed to me best to keep the arguments for these two views separate, and so I have.

commitments one assumes by performing them, explaining what it is for such commitments to be happy or otherwise.[36]

Having done all this, one will go through the sentences of the language in whose logic one is interested, with an eye to ascertaining what sorts of acts, what sorts of commitments are conventionally associated with those sentences, as well as with an eye to determining how (or how much) the acts performed and commitments associated by convention with a complex sentence are determined by those associated with the parts of the sentence and by its grammar. Once one has done this, one is in a position to characterize (deductive) validity: Knowing what commitments are conventionally associated with the premises and conclusion of an argument, one is in a position to say whether and when fulfilling the commitments associated with the premises requires that one has fulfilled those associated with the conclusion. The extent that this is possible for a language is the extent to which there is a logic of the language—the extent, that is, to which the patterns of argument possible in the language have, independently of any particular use, a fixed justificatory force (and thus the extent to which those patterns of argument can be divided, independently of any particular use, into ones whose justification is conclusive and those whose justification is not).[37]

To say all of this is to repeat things that were said in Chapter 3 when we discussed logic and emotivism. As I see it, so long as it is plausible to say that there is a commitment—presumably a commitment to a distinctive kind of valuing—conventionally associated with *is cool* as we use it, it makes perfectly good sense to evaluate arguments we give about what is cool as valid or otherwise—even if it makes no sense to call our claims about the cool true or false.

---

[36] Austin distinguishes among acts that give a verdict, ones which express decision or advocacy, those which commit the speaker to certain future behavior, acts which express reactions to behavior or its products, and those which comment on or relate members of a stream of speech acts. I do *not* propose that Austin's list is the one we should adopt, or even that the classification at which we ought to arrive is likely to look very much like his. But the idea that different utterances may involve quite different commitments, and this is something philosophy and logic need to take seriously, is, I think, Austin's idea.

[37] The emphasis here is very much on the word *extent*: it should be an open question, at least when one begins theorizing about a language, whether the project of theorizing about it as does the formal semanticist or logician is even sensible. For it is perfectly possible that while there are *regularities* connecting speech-act types and sentence types within a population, those regularities fall far short of what is needed for there to be linguistic *conventions* connecting speech-acts types (or propositions, or types of propositions) and sentence types. After all, one might be inclined to interpret a sentence type in a certain way, or adopt a sort of interpretation as an initial interpretive hypothesis (in the absence of countervailing evidence), without having the sorts of expectations which are necessary to establish a convention, on most any standard account of what is necessary for linguistic convention.

I don't see why language use *must* rest on anything stronger than interpretive inclination. If it does not and the semanticist's goal in studying natural language is to depict how conventional regularities issue in validity, then there may not be all that much for the descriptive semanticist to do with natural language. (Which is not to say that she could not trade in her descriptive project for a normative one.)

Most of this chapter has been devoted to sketching a story about thinking or saying that something is cool which is consistent with the idea that such thoughts and sayings *aren't* properly said to be true or false. It is, of course, possible to ascribe truth or falsity to them if one (for example) gives one's own perspective and only one's perspective normative authority in the matter of what is and isn't cool. But normally we do not do this, for we recognize that different people may differ without error about such matters as what is cool, or tasty, or attractive. It is apt and appropriate and not in the least a mistake for me to value something as cool, provided I am stably disposed to so value it and my valuing coheres in the right way with my other commitments in the way discussed in Section 5.1. It is apt and appropriate and not the least a mistake for you to deny that the thing I take to be cool is so if you are stably disposed to not so value it or so valuing it would not cohere with your other commitments.

There are many ways to live a life, and we are all busy living our own, each with commitments that certain sorts of things are and aren't valuable. These commitments are often in conflict across persons. Sometimes the conflict is not one which one side 'ought to win', because neither side is superior to the other. It is worth reminding ourselves of this banality, because these commitments help shape how beliefs and sayings are to be evaluated. There need be nothing wrong, nothing mistaken about either of two contrary commitments to what is worth admiring, enjoying, despising, disliking. And so there need be nothing wrong in the beliefs and statements that reflect such commitments.

What Can Be Said?

I.1

Towards the end of his paper on truth Kripke wrote:

> It seems likely that many who have worked on the truth-gap approach to the semantic paradoxes have hoped for a universal language, one in which everything that can be stated at all can be expressed. . . . the present approach certainly does not claim to give a universal language, and I doubt that such a goal can be achieved. . . . there are assertions we can make about the object language [studied in the paper] which we cannot make in the object language. For example, Liar sentences are *not true* in the object language . . . but we are precluded from saying this in the object language by our interpretation of negation and the truth predicate. . . . The ghost of the [Tarskian] hierarchy is still with us.[1]

If we think of the language as one thing, and the acts we perform in speaking the language as another, then Kripke is, I think, wrong. One way to say something is to deny a claim. What is to stop us from speaking the language Kripke studies, asserting some of its sentences, denying others? It is straightforward to extend the language in Section 2.5 so that it contains its own Kripkean truth predicate and validates denials of liar sentences. Speaking *that* language one can certainly say what the status of the liar is.

According to Kripke, 'is [a] true [sentence of English]' is only partially defined on the set of English sentences: there are sentences which are in neither the extension of 'true' nor its anti-extension (the set of things of which it is false). Kripke takes the extension and anti-extension of 'true' to be determined in stages as follows. Start with an interpreted propositional language—call the model interpreting it M—in which truth-value gaps may arise; assume that the connectives are given the strong Kleene treatment. Now add a truth predicate 'T' to the language, as well as constants 'a', 'b', etc. and quotation names to the language; call the resulting language L. Extend M to a model $M(0)$ as follows: the constants name sentences of the (extended) language; 'S' names its interior; the extension and anti-extension of 'T' are empty. $M(0)$ makes no *ascriptions* of truth or falsity true or false, though of course it makes many sentences true, others false.

Consider the model obtained from $M(0)$ by putting the sentences $M(0)$ makes true into 'T''s extension, those $M(0)$ makes false into its anti-extension; call this $M(1)$. What $M(0)$ made true (false), $M(1)$ makes so. But some ascriptions of truth that were without truth-value in $M(0)$ are now themselves true or false. Consider now the sequence of models one gets by iterating this procedure, using the rule:

(R) $M(n + 1)$ is the model one obtains from $M(n)$ by making the extension of 'T' the set of sentences which $M(n)$ makes true, the anti-extension of 'T' the set of sentences which $M(n)$ makes false.

---

[1] Kripke (1975: 79–80).

One can carry this sequence into the transfinite in the following way: After following the procedure infinitely many times (at a limit ordinal, as they say), construct a model by making the extension of 'T' the set of those sentences which have been put into the predicate's extension at *some* point in the preceding sequence of models; analogously for the predicate's anti-extension. Then go back to using rule (R). In this sequence the extension of 'T' at each stage includes its previous extension; likewise for 'T's anti-extension. Thus, one must eventually reach a point where these sets stop growing. That is, one must eventually reach a point where the set of sentences which are true (i.e. are made true by the model) is the same as the set of sentences to which one can correctly ascribe truth. At this point—the so-called fixed point—we have arrived at a model in which 'T' is a truth predicate for the language.

We want to add a truth predicate to our language using Kripke's method. Before we do, however, we should address some issues about truth and force. If I am saying something when I deny that Jo is bald by uttering 'Jo is not bald', I can be correctly reported as having said something, presumably by uttering 'Richard said that' and then echoing the words I used. Adopt for present purposes a conventional view of attitude ascriptions, on which they involve a two-place predicate ('believes', 'hopes', etc.) whose second argument place is typically filled by a 'term' formed from a complementizer, such as 'that', and a sentence. To regiment such ascriptions in a language like that of Section 2.5 we would introduce (besides names and 'said') a complementizer—let it be 'that'—which combined with unforced sentences to yield terms for the regimentation of the likes of 'Alfred believes that snow is white'. We would *also* allow 'that' to combine with forced sentences, so that our language allows for sentences along the lines of

(1) a said that not Fb.

which we would use to report a denial. A first approximation of the semantics of (1) has it true just in case whatever *a* names produced an utterance whose force (in the language he was then speaking) was the conventional force of 'not Fb'.[2] That is, (1) is true iff what *a* names uttered something which expresses the second-order commitment conventionally associated with 'not Fb' in the language of (1).

It is not just after a verb of attitude that something of the form *that S* may occur; it can also occur after 'It's true'. But things such as 'not Fb' do not make truth-evaluable claims. The idea that things of the form *that S* pick out something not truth-evaluable is, of course, quite against the grain of entrenched philosophical common sense. I have already made clear why I think we ought to go against the grain here, and won't pause to further defend this. What does call for some discussion is the combination of things like 'that not Fb' with a truth predicate. And this impacts what we say about the sentential truth predicate, at least given a desire that sentences of the form *It is true that S* and *'S' is true* should run in tandem.

It would seem that if a can *say* that S, we can entertain the thought that it is *true* that S. Likewise, if we can use S to say something, it would seem that we can use *'S' is true* to say something. So if (1) is in order, so are

---

[2] (I) completely ignores subtleties connected with the hyperintensionality of contexts like 'says that . . .'.

(2a) It's true that not Fb.
(2b) 'Not Fb' is true.

This doesn't mean that such sentences are possibly true. If 'that not Fb' in (2a) picks out the claim—i.e. second-order commitment—made by uttering 'Not Fb', and that claim isn't the sort of thing which can be true or false, then (2a) itself is either false or without truth-value. The same sort of thing applies to (2b). I will take sentences such as the (2)s to be without truth-value. Since they are not even candidates for a truth-value, I also take it to be always appropriate to deny them. These stipulations are a matter of convenience—matters seem to run most smoothly in what follows if one so proceeds. So far as I can see, nothing hangs on this decision.

Consider now (an interpreted version of) the propositional language of Section 2.5; add to it constants, quotation names, and a truth predicate 'T'; stipulate that applying the predicate 'T' to any constant or quotation name results in an unforced sentence. A moment's reflection should make it clear that we can straightforwardly apply Kripke's procedure for defining truth to this language. The only novelty here is the presence of forced sentences. But since these are not assigned truth-values by the semantics, they will sit on the sidelines as we progress through the sequence of models which define 'T'. We can prove—we will sketch a proof below—that we reach a fixed point at which 'T' is a truth predicate for the language: in which, if S is an unforced sentence of the language which is true (false, undetermined), $T('S')$ is true (false, undetermined).

If we speak this language—call it P—we do not have to be embarrassed about being prepared to seriously utter absolutely any instance in our language of the equivalence schema

(E) 'S' is true iff S.

—S unforced—even when S is a sentence which, because of vagueness or pathology, is without truth-value. For any such sentence is appropriate—indeed, any such sentence is a logical truth, since it will be appropriate in any model of the language.[3] Modest extensions of the language allow us to express all sorts of things which are commonly held to be inexpressible. For example, a sentence such as

(3) This is a sentence of P, and this is not true in P.

is a declarative sentence, even given that its 'and' and 'not' are force indicators. (It's not as if the sentence is, say, interrogative or imperative.) So

(3') x is a sentence of P, and x is not true in P.

with 'and' and 'not' construed as force indicators, is a predicate. Add it to the language and interpret it in the obvious way. It is now a non-truth predicate for P, in the following sense: A sentence of the form

(3'') t is a sentence of P, and t is not true in P.

---

[3] We are at the moment operating with the definition of appropriateness given in Section 2.5. That definition undergoes modification below, when we add an appropriateness predicate to the language.

is appropriate iff (what) t (names) is a sentence of P which is not true.[4] That is, such a sentence has conventionally associated with it a second-order commitment which is appropriate if and only if (what) t (names) is a P-sentence either false (viz. one with a true negation) or without truth-value.

This is not to say, of course, that such a sentence is *true* if and only if (what) t (names) is a P-sentence which is not true; we cannot, for familiar reasons, have such a predicate in P, which after all has ideology enough to create paradoxical sentences. But there is really no reason we *need* such a predicate. Why, after all, think that we need such a predicate, save because we think that if it is a fact that a sentence of a language is false or without truth-value, we should be able to say in the language that it is so? But we *have* in P a predicate which allows us to say this sort of thing: (3″).

Languages like that being sketched are not ones in which one can 'give the semantics of the language in the language', for the language does not even contain quantifiers, much less the syntactic ideology necessary for this. But it should be clear that by adding quantifiers and ideology we can at least start to do this sort of thing. Since we can incur second-order commitments without committing to the truth of any proposition, it would seem there is a perfectly good sense of 'give the semantics for a language in the language itself' in which we can start doing this: not by making assertions, but by making the appropriate claims—i.e. incurring appropriate second-order commitments—about the language. For example, suppose we extended the language with quantifiers and syntactic ideology, and added a vague predicate like 'bald', interpreting this last as a predicate defined only on some of the objects in the domain. We can surely correctly—i.e. appropriately—say in the language that

(J) For any individual object u and singular term t of our language: if t names u in our language, then:

(1) the sentence *t is bald* is true (in our language) iff u is bald;

(2) the sentence *t is bald* is **not** true (in our language) iff u is **not** bald;

(3) otherwise, the sentence is not true (i.e. if (u is not bald and u is not **not** bald), then the sentence is not true).

Here all of the connectives save boldface 'not' are understood as force operators; boldface 'not' is truth-functional. An utterance of (J) quite precisely characterizes the semantic facts about sentences of the form *n is bald*; when we know that the commitment (J) expresses is appropriate, we know all there is to know about the conditions under which such sentences are true, not true, and otherwise.

I.2

I have spoken of second-order commitments as being appropriate or otherwise. Appropriateness is not truth: it is appropriate to deny a liar sentence, but that appropriateness is not a reflection of the liar sentence's truth or falsity, and the denial itself is not truth-valued.

---

[4] If we think of the words of 3″ as retaining their English senses, then it is fair to say that 3″ literally *says* that t is a sentence of P that is not true.

Still, appropriateness is in some important sense a semantic notion, and one would want a semantic theory to characterize the conditions under which sentences (strictly: the associated second-order commitments—SOCs, for short) are appropriate or otherwise. Indeed, if we are speaking a language whose claims we both assert and deny and want to do as much of the language's semantics within it as possible, we will want the language we speak to contain its own appropriateness predicate.

Such a predicate threatens to produce something very much like the liar. Suppose that 'Ap' is a predicate of the language, and $Ap(a)$ is appropriate—i.e. has associated with it an SOC which is appropriate—iff a names a sentence of our language which has associated with it an SOC which is appropriate.[5] Isn't this trouble? For presumably the status of the SOC associated with a sentence S will be that of the sentence $Ap('S')$. Thus, any instance of

(4) $Ap('S')$ iff S.

will be c-valid. But just as we can construct a sentence which says of itself that it is not true, given a truth predicate, a negation operator, and sufficient sentence-christening power, so we can construct a sentence which 'denies of itself that it is appropriate', given an appropriateness predicate, a denial operator, and sentence-naming technology of sufficient strength:

(5) Not $Ap(5)$.

Given the identity '(5) = "Not $Ap(5)$"' and this instance of 4:

(4') $Ap('Not Ap(5)')$ iff Not $Ap(5)$.

identity elimination yields

(4'') $Ap(5)$ iff Not $Ap(5)$.

And (4'') is problematic. The problem is not a problem with truth: (4'') is not a candidate for truth to begin with, as its principle operator is a force connective. But (4'') c-follows from premises which are apparently themselves appropriate, and so must be appropriate. But it is not.

This argument does not show that a language cannot contain its own appropriateness predicate. It assumes that any instance of (4) is appropriate, given that S and $Ap('S')$ always have the same 'appropriateness status'. But we know that this *sort* of inference is not generally valid. For example: S and the sentence 'S' *is true* invariably have the same 'truth-value status'. It doesn't follow that any instance of S ↔ S' *is true* is itself true. In particular, when S (and thus an ascription of truth to S) is neither true nor false, the biconditional will also be without truth-value. Analogously, if there can be 'appropriateness gaps'—if it can be neither appropriate nor inappropriate to assume the second-order commitment associated with a sentence—then instances of (4) themselves may be neither appropriate nor inappropriate. If, in particular, (5) suffers from an appropriateness gap, then (4') should too. Thus, the argument just rehearsed does not show that the language cannot contain an appropriateness predicate for itself.

---

[5] Lexicalizing force—introducing operators whose utterance encodes force—simplifies things by making it possible to make both the truth and the appropriateness predicate apply to the same sorts of things.

Is it coherent to suppose that a sentence('s SOC) might be neither appropriate nor inappropriate? One might well doubt that it is, given the way in which we introduced the notion of appropriateness. When we introduced the notion, we proceeded roughly as follows. Fix a (possibly partial) assignment of truth-values to the 'non-semantic' atomic sentences of the language. If a(n unforced) sentence S comes out true on that assignment, it's appropriate and *not S* is inappropriate; otherwise, S is inappropriate and *not S* is appropriate. Appropriateness is then assigned to (unforced and) forced compounds in such a way that when all the subsentences of a compound are appropriate or inappropriate, so is the compound. Since every atomic sentence starts out as appropriate or not, how could appropriateness gaps (AGs, for short) arise?

But the language of Section 2.5 does not contain an appropriateness predicate. For such a language, appropriateness *is* determined as above, and AGs can't arise.[6] Once we introduce an appropriateness predicate, however, we should not be surprised that appropriateness gaps can occur, given the obvious analogies between truth and appropriateness. Just as the truth predicate is truth-disquotational for sentences with truth-values—i.e. $S \leftrightarrow$ 'S' *is true* is true provided that S has a truth-value (and so the sentences flanking the biconditional will have the same truth status if true or false)—so the appropriateness predicate is 'appropriateness disquotational': S iff 'S' *is appropriate* is appropriate, provided that S does not suffer from an AG (and so the flanking sentences are either both apt or both inapt). A language with a predicate, like 'is true', which is truth-disquotational, an operator, like '-', which reverses truth-value, and sufficient sentence-naming ability can construct sentences, like the liar, the truth-teller (b: 'b is true'), and so forth. In such a language, truth-value gaps must arise. A language with a predicate which is appropriateness-disquotational, contains an operator, like 'not', which reverses appropriateness, and sufficient sentence-naming ability can construct sentences like (5), the self-appropriator (c: 'c is appropriate'), and so forth. In such a language, appropriateness gaps must arise.

One expects the extension of 'appropriate' to be determined in a way parallel to the way the truth predicate's extension is determined. If the truth predicate is Kripkean, a truth-value cannot be assigned to a sentence of the form *a is true* or of the form *a is not true* before a truth-value is assigned to the sentence named by *a*. This prevents liars, truth-tellers, and the rest from receiving a truth-value.[7] If appropriateness is determined in an analogous fashion, then sentences of the form *a is appropriate* and *a is not appropriate* can be assigned the status appropriate or not only after the sentence named by *a* receives such a status. And this will prevent sentences such as (5) from being decided as appropriate or otherwise.

I.3

I'll sketch what seems the most natural way of introducing an appropriateness predicate.[8] To keep things simple, we continue with the sentential case. The language contains

---

[6] This is perhaps too facile. Perhaps atomic sentences without semantic vocabulary can suffer from appropriateness gaps. I will just ignore this possibility.

[7] In the minimal fixed point. We can, of course, stipulate that some of these sentences—in particular, the truth-teller—are true.

[8] Anyone familiar with Soames's elegant discussion (1999) of Kripke (1975) will recognize that the presentation in this section is modeled on Soames's.

atomic letters, truth-functional '$-$' and 'v', the force operators 'not' and 'or', constants, quotation marks and the predicates 'Tr' and 'Ap'. We stipulate

1. Constants are terms, as is any result of quoting a sentence.
2. Any atomic letter is an unforced sentence.
3. Applying '$-$' to an unforced sentence, or 'v' to two unforced sentences, yields an unforced sentence.
4. Applying *not* to a sentence, or *or* to two sentences, yields a forced sentence.
5. Applying 'Tr' or 'Ap' to a term yields an unforced sentence.
6. Nothing is a term or sentence save in virtue of (1) through (5).

We call the resulting language LTA.

I.3.1

The hierarchy of models. We define a sequence of models for LTA, adapting the technique of Kripke (1975). The initial model, $M(0)$, consists of a function D and a tuple $M(0)_E = <M(0)_{T+}, M(0)_{T-}, M(0)_{A+}, M(0)_{A-}>$. D maps the terms of LTA onto its sentences (mapping quote names, of course, to their interiors); it also assigns truth-values to some or all of the atomic letters of the language. $M(0)_E$'s members are, respectively, the extension of 'Tr', its anti-extension, the extension of 'Ap', and its anti-extension. In $M(0)$ all of them are empty.

The definitions of truth and appropriateness in a model (given below) determine relative to D and $M(0)_E$ a tuple $M(0)_V = <M(0)_{W+}, M(0)_{W-}, M(0)_{G+}, M(0)_{G-}>$. These are, respectively, the wffs which are true, false, appropriate, and inappropriate in $M(0)$. Analogously for models $M(i)$ latter in the sequence to be defined. When convenient, we speak of this latter tuple as also being part of the model.

Given a model $M(i)$, $M(i + 1)$ is the model consisting of D along with the tuple $M(i + 1)_E = M(i)_V = <M(i)_{W+}, M(i)_{W-}, M(i)_{G+}, M(i)_{G-}>$. That is: $M(i + 1)$ is obtained by holding D constant and making the extensions (anti-extensions) of 'Tr' and 'Ap' the sets of wffs which were made true (false) and appropriate (inappropriate) in $M(i)$. When i is a limit ordinal, $M(i)$ is the result of pairing D with the quartet of sets which result from taking unions of the extensions and anti-extensions of 'Tr' and 'Ap' at levels below i. We call the first $M(i)$ such that $M(i)_E = M(i)_V$ —i.e. the first fixed point in the sequence— *F(0)*.

We now wish to define a second sequence of models which will again culminate with a fixed point. To define the first such model, $M^*(0)$, we first define, for ϕ a sentence of our language, the *family* of ϕ as follows:

If ϕ is an atomic letter, the family of ϕ is $\{\phi\}$.

If ϕ is *Tr(a)* or *Ap(a)*, the family of ϕ is the set of what a names plus the members of its family.

If ϕ is $-\psi$ or *not* ψ, the family of ϕ is the family of ψ plus ψ.

If ϕ is ψ v χ or ψ *or* χ, the family of ϕ is the union of the families of ψ and χ along with ψ and χ.

Say that a wff ϕ is *safe* for $M^*(0)$ when it is unforced and its family contains no occurrence of 'Ap'. Let the model $M^*(0)$ be the result of pairing D with

$< F(0)_{T+}, F(0)_{T-}, F(0)_{A+}, F(0)_{A-} \cup S >$, where S is the set of wffs which are safe for $M^*(0)$ and which are absent from the extensions and anti-extensions of 'Tr' and 'Ap' in $F(0)$. If an unforced wff is safe for $M^*(0)$ and is without a truth-value in $F(0)$, it will never receive a truth-value, and thus its use is inappropriate. Adding these wffs—call them the *initial wffs for $M^*(0)$*—to $M^*(0)_{A-}$ is recording that they will never be assigned a truth-value, and are thus inappropriate.

We now proceed as above, obtaining $M^*(i + 1)$ from $M^*(i)$ by making the extension of 'Tr' in $M^*(i + 1)$ the set of wffs made true in $M^*(i)$ (and so on, for the predicate's anti-extension and for 'Ap''s extension and anti-extension); we take unions of extensions and anti-extensions from lower levels at limit ordinals to form models at the limit. We call the first fixed point in this new sequence *F(1)*.

I.3.2

Definitions of truth and appropriateness. Truth in a model M(i) is defined much as it is in Kripke (1975), using a strong Kleene treatment of the truth-functional connectives. Forced wffs, since they are not candidates for truth or falsity, are never assigned a truth-value. Making things explicit: As noted above, we use $M(i)_{W+}$ to name the set of wffs true in M(i), $M(i)_{W-}$ to name the set of wffs false in M(i), etc. Then, where M(i) is any of the models described in the previous section (including those in the sequence from $M^*(0)$ through $F(1)$):

1. If p is an atom of LTA,   p is in $M(i)_{W+}$ iff $D(p) = t$
   p is in $M(i)_{W-}$ iff $D(p) = f$
   Otherwise, p does not have a truth-value in M(i).

2. If p is *Tr(a)*, and *a* names q,   p is in $M(i)_{W+}$ iff q is in $M(i)_{T+}$
   p is in $M(i)_{W-}$ iff q is in $M(i)_{T-}$
   Otherwise, p does not have a truth-value in M(i).

3. If p is *Ap(a)*, and *a* names q,   p is in $M(i)_{W+}$ iff q is in $M(i)_{A+}$
   p is in $M(i)_{W-}$ iff q is in $M(i)_{A-}$
   Otherwise, p does not have a truth-value in M(i).

4. If p is $-q$,   p is in $M(i)_{W+}$ iff q is in $M(i)_{W-}$
   p is in $M(i)_{W-}$ iff q is in $M(i)_{W+}$
   Otherwise, p does not have a truth-value in M(i).

5. If p is $q \, v \, r$,   p is in $M(i)_{W+}$ iff (q is in $M(i)_{W+}$ or r is in $M(i)_{W+}$)
   p is in $M(i)_{W-}$ iff (q is in $M(i)_{W-}$ and r is in $M(i)_{W-}$)
   Otherwise, p does not have a truth-value in M(i).

6. If p is a forced wff,   p does not have a truth-value in M(i).

The wffs which are initial for $M^*(0)$ are, in effect, stipulated to be inappropriate when $M^*(0)$ is constructed. Thus, the following definition of *p is appropriate in M(i)* begins with a clause which establishes this stipulation:

If M(i) is $M^*(j)$ for some j and p is initial for $M^*(0)$, then p is inappropriate (i.e. is in $M(i)_{G-}$) in M(i). Otherwise, whether p is appropriate or inappropriate in M(i) is determined by the following rules:

1. If p is atomic,

p is in $M(i)_{G+}$ iff $D(p) = t$
p is in $M(i)_{G-}$ iff $D(p)$ is not t.

2. If p is $Tr(a)$ and a names q,

p is in $M(i)_{G-}$ if q is forced. Otherwise:
p is in $M(i)_{G+}$ iff q is in $M(i)_{T+}$
p is in $M(i)_{G-}$ iff q is in $M(i)_{T-}$
Otherwise, p is neither app. nor inapp. in $M(i)$.

3. If p is $Ap(a)$ and a names q,

p is in $M(i)_{G+}$ iff q is in $M(i)_{A+}$
p is in $M(i)_{G-}$ iff q is in $M(i)_{A-}$
Otherwise, p is neither app. nor inapp. in $M(i)$.

4. If p is $-q$,

p is in $M(i)_{G+}$ iff q is in $M(i)_{W-}$
p is in $M(i)_{G-}$ iff (q is in $M(i)_{W+}$ or q is in $M(i)_{G+}$)
Otherwise, p is neither app. nor inapp. in $M(i)$.

5. If p is $q \vee r$,

p is in $M(i)_{G+}$ iff (q is in $M(i)_{W+}$ or r is in $M(i)_{W+}$)
p is in $M(i)_{G-}$ iff both q and r are in either $M(i)_{W-}$ or $M(i)_{G-}$
Otherwise, p is neither app. nor inapp. in $M(i)$.

6. If p is *not q*,

p is in $M(i)_{G+}$ iff q is in $M(i)_{G-}$
p is in $M(i)_{G-}$ iff q is in $M(i)_{G+}$
Otherwise, p is neither app. nor inapp. in $M(i)$.

7. If p is *q or r*,

p is in $M(i)_{G+}$ iff at least one of q, r is in $M(i)_{G+}$
P is in $M(i)_{G-}$ iff both q and r are in $M(i)_{G-}$
Otherwise, p is neither app. nor inapp. in $M(i)$.

I.3.3

Fixed points. Let M and M' be two models in the hierarchy. M'_E extends M_E provided that each member of the first is, pointwise, a superset of each member of the second; M'_V extends M_V if the same relation holds between them; M' extends M when M'_E extends M_E and M'_V extends M_V. Notice that by the construction of M(0) and M*(0), $M(1)_E$ extends $M(0)_E$, and $M^*(1)_E$ extends $M^*(0)_E$. Given this, from

(I) For any models M and M', if M'_E extends M_E, then M'_V extends M_V.

it follows that

(II) Both the fixed points F(0) and F(1) exist.

For, since $M(i + 1)_E$ is $M(i)_V$, I guarantees that if $M(i)_E$ extends $M(i - 1)_E$, then $M(i + 1)_V$ extends $M(i)_V$. So M(j) must extend M(i) when $j > i$. This monotonicity entails (II).

We prove (I) by an induction on the complexity of a wff p, showing that if M'_E extends M_E, then if p is in a given member of M_V, it is in the corresponding member of M'_V. The proof is somewhat tedious, because there are four cases to consider for each possible form of a wff. Since the denotation of terms does not shift across models, in what follows we write such things as *a is in $M(i)_{T+}$*, instead of the somewhat more cumbersome *D(a) is in $M(i)_{T+}$*.

Suppose that M'_E extends M_E; call this assumption E. *Basis.* When p is a propositional letter, p's status with respect to whether it is true or false, and to whether it is appropriate or inappropriate, is fixed by whether it is true or otherwise, which is in turn fixed by D, which does not vary across models. So, trivially, if p is in M_{W+} ($M_{W-}, \ldots$), it is in M'_{W+} ($M'_{W-}, \ldots$). Suppose that p is of the form *Tr(a)*. Then

If p is in M_{W+}, then a is in M_{T+} (truth definition = TD), so a is in M_{T+} (by E), and so p is in M'_{W+} (definition of truth = TD).
If p is in M_{W-}, then a is in M_{T-} (TD), so a is in M'_{T-} (E), so p is in M'_{W-} (TD).
If p is in M_{G+}, then a is in M_{T+} (definition of appropriateness = AD), so a is in $M = _{T+}$ (E), so p is in $M = _{G+}$ (definition of appropriateness = AD).
Suppose p is in M_{G-}. If a is forced, p must be in M'_{G-} (TD). If *a* is unforced, then a is in M_{T-} (AD), so a is in M'_{T-} (E), so p is in M'_{G-} (AD).

Suppose that p is of the form *Ap(a)*. Then

If p is in M_{W+}, then a is in M_{A+} (TD), so a is in M'_{A+} (E), so p is in M'_{W+} (TD).
If p is in M_{W-}, then a is in M_{A-} (TD), so a is in M'_{A-} (E), so p is in M'_{W-} (TD).
If p is in M_{G+}, then a is in M_{A+} (AD), so a is in M'_{A+} (E), so p is in M'_{G+} (AD).
If p is in M_{G-}, then a is in M_{A-} (AD), so a is in M'_{A-} (E), so p is in M'_{G-} (AD).

Use both force operators and truth functors to determine logical complexity. *Induction step.* The induction hypothesis (IH) is that if M'_E extends M_E, then for any sentence S of logical complexity less than n, if S is in M_V, then it is in M'_V. Again assume that M'_E extends M_E and call the assumption E. Suppose that p is of length n. If p is $-q$, then

If p is in M_{W+}, then q is in M_{W-} (TD), so by IH q is in M'_{W-}, so p is in M'_{W+} (TD). Analogously, if p is in M_{W-}.
If p is in M_{G+}, then q is in M_{W-} (AD), so q is in M'_{W-} (IH), so p is in M'_{G+}. Analogously, if p is in M_{G-}.

The argument for the case in which p is $q \lor r$ is similar enough to the last that it can be left as an exercise. Suppose p is *not q*. Here, p cannot be in M_{W+} or M_{W-}, as it is forced.

If p is in M_{G+}, then q is in M_{G-} (AD), so by IH q is in M'_{G-}, so p is in M'_{G+} (AD). Analogously, for the case in which p is in M_{G-}.

The case where p is *q or r* is routine.

I. 3. 4

Consistency. It is not altogether obvious that in F(1) no wff has incompatible properties—that, for example, there is no p that is true and inappropriate, or false and appropriate. So it is worth proving:

(III) In each model M, no wff in M_{W+} is in M_{W-} or M_{G-}; no wff in M_{G+} is in M_{W-} or M_{G-}.

Consider first the sequence from M(0) to F(0), and the status therein of those wffs whose family does not contain a sentence in which 'Tr' or 'Ap' occurs. A routine induction on logical complexity shows that (III) holds for these wffs in these models. Using that result to prove the basis, one can then show by induction on the number of occurrences of 'Tr' and 'Ap' in a wff that the theorem holds for all wffs in the set of models. Given this, the theorem holds at $M'(0)$, and thus another induction aping the two inductions just mentioned shows that the theorem holds in the sequence from $M'(0)$ to $F(1)$.

I. 3. 5

Sample applications. Consider the wffs

(a) $-Ta$
(b) Ta

Neither of these wffs is made true or false in any model through $F(0)$, and thus neither is made appropriate or inappropriate either. Thus, each is added to $A-$, the anti-extension of 'Ap' in $M^*(0)$, and each is stipulated to be inappropriate (i.e. to be in $M^*(0)_G$). Thus, in $M^*(0)$ the wffs

(c) not $-Ta$
(d) not Ta

are appropriate. Furthermore, in $M^*(0)$, since a and b are in $A-$, the wffs

(e) $Ap(a)$
(f) $Ap(b)$

will be *false*, since the relevant sentences are in the anti-extension of 'Ap'. Thus,

(g) $-Ap(a)$
(h) $-Ap(b)$

are both *true* in $M^*(0)$ and $F(1)$. Thus, in $M^*(0)$ and $F(1)$ we can say *truly* what the status of a liar sentence such as (a) is: we can say, truly, that it is inappropriate. Finally, note that in any model in which 'a' names '$-Tr(a)$', c and g will both be appropriate. Thus, the sentence

If $a = $ '$-Ta$', then (not $-Tr(a)$ iff $-Ap(a)$).

will be a logical truth, in the sense of being c-valid.[9] Thus (speaking a little loosely), when we truly say that a liar sentence such as a is inappropriate, we say something logically equivalent to what we say when we deny that the liar is true.

What prevents paradox from occurring in the language? Let us look at a simple attempt to construct a paradoxical sentence:

(i) $-Ap(i)$

If we try to ape canonical derivations of a contradiction from the strengthened liar using (i), we will have to employ both

---

[9] We assume: 'iff' is introduced so that *p iff q* abbreviates *not(p or q) or not(not p or not q)*; analogously for 'if . . . then'; '=' means equality.

(j) −Ap(i) iff not Ap(i)

(k) −Ap(i) iff Ap('−Ap(i)')

One might think that these should both be appropriate (so that 'not Ap(i) iff Ap(i)' would be): (j), one might think, should hold because, quite generally, a sentence is inappropriate iff it is not true; (k) because −*Ap(i)* is true iff it is appropriate. But in fact neither (j) nor (k) is appropriate. The principle that a sentence is inappropriate iff not true holds only for sentences whose family is 'Ap'-free; sentences such as (k) will be neither appropriate nor inappropriate when their flanking formulas suffer from an appropriateness gap.

Finally, consider the wff

(l) not Ap(l)

What is its status in the final fixed point for the language? It should be clear that it is neither appropriate nor inappropriate (and neither true nor false). For (l) is not safe for the model based on the first fixed point (as it contains 'Ap'), and thus will not be declared inappropriate therein. (And obviously it can't become so before this model.) Given this, its appropriateness will continue to be undecided through the second fixed point.

Will (l) lead to a paradox-like situation? It would if the schema

(m) Ap('S') iff S

were c-valid. And this schema would be valid, if every wff was declared appropriate or inappropriate in the second fixed point. But this does not happen. So far as I can see, (l) leads to no paradox-like problems.

To generalize the preceding to a first-order language requires generalizing the notion of the family of a wff, in order to adequately characterize the class of sentences declared inappropriate in the construction of the model M*(0). The way to do this, I think, is to make the family of a wff a class of (atomic) predicates: The family of an atom contains the predicate from which it is constructed; the family of *Tr(a)* contains the family of (what is named by) *a* as well as (what is named by) *a* itself; etc. In the construction of M*(0), we put a sentence in the anti-extension of 'Ap' if its family is 'Ap'-free and the sentence's truth-value has not been decided in the fixed point on which M*(0) is based. I leave an investigation of the details to anyone who has gotten this far.

I.4

Perhaps you feel like echoing Kripke:

there are claims we can make about the object language which we cannot make in the object language. For example, sentences such as a = 'not Ap(a)' are *not appropriate* in the object language . . . but we are precluded from saying this in the object language by our interpretation of denial and the appropriateness predicate. . . . The ghost of the hierarchy is still with us.

Well, no and yes.

Surely we *can* say in the language of sentence a that it is not appropriate. Why shouldn't there be a kind of speech act—call it *rejection*—not definable in terms of assertion, denial, or the other speech acts introduced in Chapter 2, which is sometimes voiced with the idioms of negation? After all, if it is possible to introduce an appropriateness predicate, sentence (a) is a perfectly good sentence, and we can *see* that the claim that it makes isn't right. In saying that this claim 'isn't right' we aren't asserting anything—if we were, contradiction would ensue.[10] In saying that a isn't appropriate, we can't be denying anything either. So we must be doing something else.

There is no reason that rejection must be 'lexicalized'—either with a construction conventionally marked to express it, or via a predicate for classifying utterances which achieve it—any more than assertion or denial need be. (Which came first, warnings or 'warning'?) Neither need we have a well-developed concept of rejection—or of denial as something distinct from the assertion of negation—in order to reject a denial. That a particular utterance is a denial, as opposed to the assertion of a negation, or is a rejection, as opposed to an assertion or denial—this is surely often a matter of what interpretation of the utterance makes the most sense of it.

Rejection must be like assertion and denial insofar as we can speak of a rejection as 'getting it right' or 'getting it wrong'. Getting it right when one rejects something can't be a matter of truth or appropriateness; it must be a matter of the thing being rejected having yet some *other* property, *being fit* we might call it. And so it does look like we are still haunted by the hierarchy. For one suspects this process will never stop. Fitness is as much a semantic property as appropriateness; so we have to introduce a fitness predicate, if we want to say everything there is about semantics. But then there will be a sentence that says of itself that it's not fit. In evaluating it, we will be driven again to yet a higher level, and so on and on. If one tells the story I am telling, one must be at peace with the idea of an endless sequence of *sui generis* semantic properties evaluating an endless sequence of kinds of denial. Since each property in the sequence is *sui generis* with respect to the earlier ones, no language can express all the facts, semantic or otherwise.

Is this problematic? What seems most problematic about the hierarchy of truth predicates associated with Tarski's work on truth is the idea that there is a property—that expressed by the use of 'true sentence of English'—about which it is impossible to adequately theorize. On the standard way of applying Tarski's ideas about truth to natural languages, we understand 'true [in English]' as (at least potentially) infinitely ambiguous, since a Tarskian truth predicate cannot be true of a sentence in which it occurs.[11] There is, on this view, no understanding of 'true English sentence' on which it is true of . . . well, every true English sentence.[12] Do we encounter *this* sort of problem on the current account?

Well, it doesn't seem that we do. Truth in L, on the Kripkean approach we've hijacked here, is of course defined in L. And so is appropriateness in L. There's no reason to think that the same thing won't be true of fitness in L or any of the other residents of the semantic stable. Neither does the charge, that we are unable to adequately theorize about the property of truth (or about the others) seem to be correct. The point here is perhaps seen most clearly if we consider the language discussed in Section I.1 above, which extends the (semantic-vocabulary-free) language of Section 2.5 simply by the addition of a truth

---

[10] I assume, of course, that an assertion is apt iff what's asserted is true.

[11] This is an upshot of Tarski's procedure of only defining *true sentence of language L* in a ('richer') language than L, so that such a predicate is never a part of the language of whose sentences it is potentially true.

[12] A particularly forceful development of this sort of worry is found in McGee (1991).

predicate. In this language, we are not only able to define truth, we are able to do such things as say that its liars are not [denial] true, and (using, of course, forced sentences) to give an accurate account of the conditions under which (unforced) sentences are true and false. We can, in this language, theorize about truth in the language.

It seems—though I have nothing like a proof for this—that something cognate is true of the language of the last section and the properties of both truth in that language and appropriateness in that language. Speaking that language *and* performing acts such as the above-posited act of rejection, we should be able to adequately theorize about both truth and appropriateness in the language. The language, of course, isn't 'semantically closed'. Its sentences will be fit or unfit, but—lacking a fitness predicate—one isn't able to ascribe fitness to sentences. But the language *does* seem able to 'state all the facts' about the truth, falsity, appropriateness, and inappropriateness of its sentences.

So far as I can see this sort of thing will continue as we rise in the hierarchy: For any finite set of the properties in the sequence that begins 'truth, aptness, fitness, . . .' a language can contain predicates which characterize each of the properties (ones which have the properties' extensions and anti-extensions), and its speakers can, by performing the appropriate speech acts (whose performance may or may not be associated with lexical items) indicate exactly how these properties are distributed to the sentences of the language. The apparent infinitude of semantic properties makes semantic closure impossible. But it would seem that it *is* possible—if the sort of thing just indicated does indeed continue as we ascend the hierarchy—to say as much as there is to say about the distribution of any finite collection of semantic properties to a language's sentences. Since in some fairly clear sense we can focus on only finitely many semantic properties anyway, we can, that is, say all there is to say about all of the semantic properties that we can or could actually get a fix on. And perhaps that's all one could ever want or need, in the way of semantic effability.

Relativism and Contextualism about Knowledge

II.1

The relativism defended in Chapter 4 is hardly shocking. It doesn't, for example, entail that thinking or saying makes it so. In placing the relative within the range of variation allowed by our practices of accommodating and negotiating meaning, it confines it to an arena in which we recognize that there may be legitimate differences of opinion, different opinions each of which, in the right situation, may be correct. My relativism is so boring that one might wonder whether it's of much interest. Does it give us some traction on any philosophical issue?

It does: it provides an effective answer to objections to contextualism about knowledge ascriptions. Indeed, it increases contextualism's plausibility.[1]

According to the contextualist, the relation expressed by 'knows'—and thus what is said by a sentence like 'George knows that he has hands'—depends upon the 'standards of knowledge' supplied by the context of the sentence's use. A representative version of the view, which I'll presuppose in what follows, has it that

(a) knowledge that p requires being able to rule out scenarios in which p is not true, where ruling out a scenario generally requires giving good evidence that it doesn't obtain;
(b) what scenarios one needs to rule out in order to know varies across contexts.

What determines when one needs to be able to rule out a scenario in order to know? Many contextualists point to the salience of a scenario: simply raising the possibility that (say) our current experience is a product of imagination and not of perception seems to put us in a position where we aren't entitled to claim to know p (p a claim justified only if our experience is veridical) unless we can give reasons to think that our experience is not merely a product of our fancy. Though it doesn't figure very much in the contextualist literature, it seems that our interests and purposes in ascribing knowledge can also contribute to determining whether one needs to be able to rule out a scenario before knowing.[2]

Why should salience of counter-possibilities and our interests be factors in determining whether someone has knowledge? Well, the first seems required by (a) above. Knowing p just *is*, in part, being in a position, when someone says 'Well, for all we know, q (and if q then not p)', to say 'Don't worry about q, because . . .'. As for the dependence of

---

[1] Examples of contextualist views about knowledge are Cohen (1999), DeRose (1995), and Lewis (1996).

[2] That knowledge turns on interests has been much discussed in recent anti-contextualist literature—see, for example, Hawthorne (2004) and Stanley (2006). But there is nothing about contextualism that would rule out ascriber interests as influencing the truth of knowledge ascriptions. *Au contraire.*

knowledge on interests: We use what we know to figure out what we ought to do. Thus, the standards we need to meet in order to count as having knowledge bear on action: the more flexible we need or want to be in acting, the less certainty we can demand for the beliefs on which we base our calculations of expected benefit. Our interests and purposes help shape how we manage this trade-off between what we require for knowledge and how flexible we are in action, by helping us decide what sorts of contingencies we ought to be able to rule out before using a belief as a basis for deciding how to act.

That these things are factors in determining whether someone has knowledge is, if not a truism about knowledge, at least a truth. And, so far as I can see, contextualism about knowledge best makes sense of them.[3] This alone makes it an attractive philosophical position. It also offers insight into what is going on when we consider skeptical arguments to the effect that since for all we know q (q being some doubt-casting claim, such as that we are brains in a vat), we can't know p (p being some claim we would normally claim to know, such as that we have hands). Such arguments are unsettling in part because (a) before we confront them we are quite confident that we know the relevant p, but (b) afterwards we uneasily think that perhaps we *don't* know it. If contextualism is correct, then these reactions are to be expected because they are correct: until the salience of the doubt-casting scenario is raised we *do* know the relevant p; after it is raised, we don't.[4]

---

[3] There are 'invariantist' views of knowledge which *acknowledge* them. The invariantist holds that the extension of 'knows'—and thus what counts as knowledge—doesn't shift across contexts. Invariantists say that whether X knows p depends upon *X*'s interests and purposes: if X's interests make it important that he be able to rule out a particular scenario before he may claim to know p but he can't rule the scenario out, then from *nobody's* perspective does X know p.

The invariantist holds that whether X knows p turns on the interests and standards operative *in X's* context. The contextualist, on the other hand, sees questions about knowledge turning on the interests and standards operating in the context in which the question *Does X know p?* arises. So for the contextualist it might be that while *from X's perspective* X doesn't know p, X does know p *from some other perspective*. On the invariant view, the interests of the person who asks *Does X know that p?* are irrelevant to the question's answer. Hawthorne (2004) and Stanley (2006) defend versions of this view.

The problem with such invariantism is that on it, knowledge isn't determined by one's epistemic situation. Suppose that Mary and Jeff have exactly the same evidence, acquired in exactly the same ways. Suppose that their methods of acquiring evidence are equally reliable, and that their situations in the world are relevantly similar. (If knowledge about birds is under discussion and one is, for example, in a place where there are birds that look like goldfinches but aren't, so is the other.) So the two are in exactly the same epistemic situation, so far as being able to rule out various challenges to whether it is the case that the bird in the garden is a goldfinch. Indeed, if you were to challenge each in a particular way (you observe, let us say, that the bird's wing seems to have a red band, which goldfinches don't have), each would respond, with the same justification, in the same way (each would, let us say, respond that it's not a red band but the setting sun's light). Surely the identity of their epistemic—that is, their evidential and justificatory—situations makes it the case that if one knows the other does. The contextualist can agree with this, for the contextualist would say that if we ask if the two know, the answer is determined by applying *our* standards of evidence to each one's claim to know. But the invariantist cannot agree, as it may be that Jeff's interests demand that he be able to rule out some challenge to knowledge which Mary's interests deem irrelevant.

[4] This is not to say that contextualism 'solves' all the problems which skepticism raises. In particular, one feels that once skeptical scenarios are introduced, there is a question as to whether we 'really' know the claims the skeptic says we don't know. Given what the contextualist says about knowledge, this would seem to be a question about whether the standards for knowledge the sceptic's challenge introduces *ought* to govern or be applied to our everyday claims to know.

II.2

I have been extolling the virtues of contextualism about knowledge. But the view is liable to the same sorts of objections concerning disagreement as is contextualism about the gradable adjectives. Contextualists hold that the truth of 'I know that I have hands' is determined by the standards for knowledge operative when the sentence is used. Consider a variant of Chapter's 4 example, The Report. In it, Didi uses 'knows' with low standards for knowledge, low enough, we may suppose, so that she qualifies as knowing that she has hands. Naomi uses it with high standards, high enough, we may suppose, so that Didi does not qualify as knowing that she has hands. It would seem that given contextualism about 'knows', Didi speaks truly if she says 'I, Didi, know that I have hands'; Naomi speaks truly if she says 'Didi doesn't know that she has hands'. But Didi says that she, Didi, knows that she has hands; Naomi says that Didi does not know that she has hands. Since each speaks truly, it follows that Didi knows that she has hands, and that Didi doesn't know she has hands. Contradiction.

This, of course, is just an epicycle on one of the objections to contextualism about wealth that we discussed in Section 4.4[5]. If we embrace relativism, we can respond to it in just the way we responded to the original objection. Given the banality on which it rests—that (ignoring issues about tense) whenever someone assertively utters the English 'Didi knows that she has hands' they say that Didi knows that she has hands—the contextualist must deny that both Didi and Naomi spoke the truth. I can evaluate sentences such as 'Didi knows that she has hands', 'It is true that Didi knows that she has hands', or 'What Didi said is true' for truth. In doing this, I interpret 'knows' and 'true' using the standards of *my* context, to determine who knows what and what is true. No matter what those standards might be, they won't make Didi know something but not know it; nor will they make the claim that Didi knows she has hands true and not true.

It is a mistake—a mistake contextualists about knowledge have committed—to formulate contextualism so that it implies that what Didi says with a sentence such as 'Didi knows that she has hands' is true just in case according to Didi's standards of knowledge Didi knows that she has hands. What Didi says with this sentence is true—i.e. has the property I ascribe (here and now) with 'true'—just in case Didi knows that she has hands—i.e. just in case she has the property I ascribe to her (here and now) with 'knows that she has hands'. Once the contextualist accepts the banality that whoever utters 'Didi knows that she has hands' says that Didi knows that she has hands, he must use a relativized notion of truth to formulate contextualism. Contextualism about knowledge ought be formulated as the view that whether a use of 'Didi knows that she has hands' is valid—i.e. is true relative to the conversational context in which it occurs—turns upon the standards of knowledge supplied by that context. Once contextualism is so formulated the puzzle above disappears, in exactly the way it disappears for contextualism about wealth.

Jason Stanley claims that this response won't fly.[6] The claim occurs in the course of an argument that once the contextualist embraces relativism he can't account for the

---

[5] It is (a version of) an objection to contextualism by John Hawthorne mentioned there.
[6] Stanley (2006).

'factivity of knowledge', the banality that whatever one knows is true. Stanley interprets the contextualist who is a relativist (henceforth, for brevity, the contextualist) as holding that truth is to be evaluated relative to a possible world, a particular time, and a 'judge'. As Stanley puts it, the 'circumstances of evaluation' for a contextualist are made up of a world w, time t, and judge y.[7] If one thinks of matters this way then the banality that one knows that p only if p is true may be put so:

(F) x knows at t that p at $< w, t', y >$ only if p is true at $< w, t', y >$.

This won't work says Stanley:

Suppose that John is in a low standards situation with some evidence for his true belief that p, and Hannah is in a high standards situation, where more evidence is needed than John possesses in order to know that p. Then, by relativist lights, relative to $<w, t, John>$, John knows that p, and relative to $<w, t, Hannah>$, John doesn't know that p . . . we have disagreement about whether John knows that p, but both parties are correct. . . . [It is] deeply implausible that John and Hannah each is merely lucky to be right. . . . if they are both correct, then John *knows* that he is right, and Hannah *knows* that she is right. That is, in the envisaged case, John knows that John knows that p, and Hannah knows that John doesn't know that p. A neutral observer can then point out that John knows that John knows that p, and Hannah knows that John doesn't know that p (as I have just done). If [the principle (F)] were correct, it would then follow that John knows that p, and John doesn't know that p. But that is a contradiction. So [(F)] is false.[8]

This '*reductio*' of (F) is just a variant of the objection discussed above. The contextualist will reply that whether a claim is true relative to a perspective (or judge or context) depends upon the standards operative from *that* perspective (that the judge is using, that the context provides); that the person to whom knowledge is ascribed may have different standards is neither here nor there. No matter what the standards of the 'neutral observer', they will make no claim both true and false. So the observer will *not* be able to observe that John knows q and Hannah not q. The neutral observer can of course observe that John's self-ascription of knowledge (that he knows p) and Hannah's denial that he has that knowledge are both valid—true in the contexts in which each is made. But no inconsistency arises from *this*.[9]

---

[7] Judges are not the parameter I've suggested the relativist needs, but that won't effect matters; let's just pretend for the nonce that truth is relative to the person judging, instead of a particular set of standards operative in a potential context of judgment.

[8] Stanley (2006: 146).

[9] In Stanley (2006) Stanley suggests that a relativist will respond that what John *knows* is that relative to his own standards he knows that p; *mutatis mutandis* for Hannah. He then observes that this response does not present the two as genuinely disagreeing.

The imagined 'response' is simply irrelevant to Stanley's original objection, which was to account for the factivity of knowledge while maintaining relativism. (F) does this perfectly well. (Notice that in the story accompanying Stanley's objection, whenever *John knows that p* is true relative to a world, time, and judge, so is *It is true that p*.) The relativist can and will say the things in Stanley's imagined response, but she will not identify the claim on which John and Hannah disagree with anything like the claim that according to John's standards he knows p. What they disagree about is simply whether *John knows that p*.

In an earlier draft of Stanley (2006) Stanley anticipates the response to his objection in the text. Against that response he wrote:

The relativist might reply that [A] from the standpoint of relativism, there is no observer z such that John knows that John knows that p relative to z, and Hannah knows that John doesn't know

Stanley makes a second, more interesting objection to relativism about knowledge. To set the stage for it, recall that we often represent a proposition as a function from 'circumstances of evaluation'—the things relative to which a proposition is true or false—to truth-values. Possible-worlds semantics represents a proposition as a function from possible worlds to truth-values: The proposition that during 1982 Al was fickle gets represented as the function that maps a world w to truth just in case during 1982 Al was fickle in w. Those who think that propositions may differ in truth-value not just across worlds but from time to time within a single world represent propositions as functions which map a world and a time to a truth-value: the proposition that Al is fickle, to this way of thinking, should be represented as the rule which assigns truth to a world w and a time t just in case Al, at time t in world w, is fickle.

If you represent propositions as functions you'll say that a sentence is true at a circumstance X just in case the proposition the sentence expresses maps X to the true.[10] The sentence 'During 1982 Al was fickle' is *in fact* true—true *at the actual world*—just in case the claim that during 1982 Al was fickle maps *the way things actually are* to truth. And this is the case just in case Al was, *as things actually are*, fickle in 1982. Note now that there are operators (like 'possibly' and 'necessarily') whose meanings 'shift' the circumstance that is relevant to whether what a sentence says is true:

It could be that S is true at world w just in case the claim that S is true *at some world.*
Necessarily, S is true at world w just in case the claim that S is true *at every world.*

One might argue—David Kaplan once did argue—that tenses are best understood as playing such a shifting role, and therefore propositions should be thought of as functions from worlds and times to truth-values. After all, Kaplan observed, it seems that

It was true that S is true at a time t (in a world w) just in case the claim that S is true *at some time earlier than t* (in world w).

---

that p relative to z. In other words, [B] *there is no one with respect to which [sic] the relativist account of the intuitions we have been discussing is correct.* But to concede that the relativist explanation of the intuitions we have been discussing is false for everybody surely does not amount to a compelling defense of relativism. (Labels added.)

But why think that [A] amounts to [B]? Stanley seems to have been thinking something like this: (1) The relativist holds that John may know *John knows that q*, while Hannah knows *John doesn't know that q*. So (as knowledge implies truth), (2) it must be true from the relativist's point of view that John knows that q and John doesn't know that q. So (3) if relativism is correct, there must be some perspective relative to which John knows he knows that p and Hannah knows he doesn't.

But (1) isn't implied by the view sketched above (or the view developed in Richard (2004), to which Stanley objects). The clear-headed relativist will introduce and explain what it is for a claim to be true in a context (from a perspective, for a judge), in part by relating that notion to the notion of truth full stop—that is, the relativist will give the sort of account of truth and truth given in Chapter 4. He will then say that the claims, *John knows that q* and *John knows that John knows that q* may be true for John while the claims *John doesn't know that q* and *Hannah knows that John doesn't know that q* are true for Hannah. *This* is the relativist's view, and it is perfectly effable. If the relativist is right, his view is not just true for him, it's true full stop (and thus 'true for everyone'.)

10 If we were being prissy here, we would say that a use of a sentence *in a particular context* at a particular world was true if and only if the proposition expressed *in that context* was true at the world. I suppress the fact that the context of use may affect what a sentence says when it's irrelevant to the issue at hand.

It will be true that S is true at a time t (in a world w) just in case the claim that S is true *at some time later than t* (in world w).[11]

If what a sentence says is to be evaluated for truth relative to circumstances that systematically vary with respect to a parameter P—a possible world, a time, a place, whatever—one expects that there will be operators whose role is to shift that parameter as do modals and (according to Kaplan) the tenses. After all, if our claims vary in truth-value as the values of the parameter P shift—if a claim might be true at (a circumstance with) p, false at (one with) p*—then we will have reason to want to convey that a particular claim, while not true here at p, is true at p*, or that it isn't true at any P of a particular sort, etc. Conversely, one expects that if there *aren't* operators whose role is to shift parameter P, then quite probably parameter P doesn't play a role in individuating circumstances of evaluation. This observation brings us to Stanley's objection.

The relativist thinks that claims are true relative to a possible world *and* a set of standards (or kindred parameter). This implies that language provides expressions whose role is to shift this parameter. If there aren't such expressions, that is good evidence that truth isn't relative to that to which the relativist says it is relative. But, says Stanley,

> it is hard to see how the . . . relativist about knowledge could countenance the existence of such operators, if she is to preserve her claim to be providing a more charitable account of our intuitions about knowledge ascriptions. Suppose O-j is an operator on the judge feature, one that evaluates the content of the embedded sentence at the judge feature corresponding to j. Then, the . . . relativist would countenance the truth of claims such as 'O-j John knows that the bank will be open, but not O-h John knows that the bank will be open.' I cannot think of any natural language stand ins for such operators that are linked to some notion of truth, and would make it acceptable to countenance the truth of instances of these claims.[12]

Surely natural language is loaded with such operators. Consider

From John's perspective, relative to Hannah's standards, it's true for Bob, given low standards, if we adopt very strict standards for knowledge/for being rich/for being flat, then . . . [13]

Stanley anticipates such a response. He argues that since these sorts of operators can be acceptably applied to pretty much any sentence whatsoever, to say that they express

[11] See Kaplan (1989*a*, Sect 3). There is an extensive literature on whether the tenses are best understood as operators (on something temporally neutral) or as quantifiers (over times, or intervals, or some other temporally ordered entity). A critical summary of some of it is given in King (2003).

I should perhaps say that I do not (contrary to what I once thought) think that the tenses are circumstance-shifting operators. Indeed, I don't think that the modalities are such operators; I think the whole kit and caboodle are (restricted) quantifiers. For discussion see Richard (forthcoming *b*).

[12] Stanley (2006: 150–1).

[13] Stanley says of the operator 'According to John', in 'According to John, John knows that the bank will be open' that it doesn't have anything to do with relative truth; it 'just mean[s] that if asked, John would accept the claim that he knows that the bank will be open'. I imagine he might say the same sort of thing of some of the phrases on this list.

It's true that on *one* use, 'According to John', 'From John's perspective', and other expressions of this ilk are variants of 'In John's opinion'. But there surely *is* another use of such expressions on which they have a meaning along the lines of 'It's true for John', 'If we accept John's standards for wealth, we must agree that', and so forth. (Relevant here is the discussion (in Chapter 5's technical digression) of the interpretation of prepositional phrases such as 'for John' and 'To Mary' in sentences such as 'To Mary, it's a chair' and 'It's tasty for John'.)

relative truth commits us to saying that pretty much any sentence whatsoever is only relatively true. The crux of his argument is this. Consider a sentence like

(C) By the standards of chemists, the stuff in the Hudson River isn't water, and someone with no lab experience doesn't know that hydrogen is an element.

The effect of 'By the standards of chemists' on each conjunct must be the same, says Stanley. Its effect on the second conjunct is to require very strong standards for its truth. So it has the same effect on the first one. So, if 'By the standards of chemists' can shift the standards of truth for knowledge claims, it can do the same for other sentences. So every, or pretty much every, sentence will possess truth-values only relatively, as we can always come up with an operator that will shift the standards for a sentence's truth in a way that changes its truth-value from our own perspective.[14]

Let's allow for the moment that 'By the standards of chemists', when it's used to indicate relative truth, has the same effect on 'the stuff in the Hudson River isn't water' as it does on 'someone with no lab experience doesn't know that hydrogen is an element'. What is the effect it has? As I see it, it shifts *those standards whose variation can in fact effect the truth of a discourse*. What are those standards? Well, not just *any* variation of standards or opinions will have an effect on truth. I have suggested that we find relative truth when we have an area of discourse where we recognize that our concepts can be developed in different ways, and when we are prepared to accommodate and negotiate over different ways of fleshing those concepts out in the course of a conversation. The notions expressed by words which are subject to the sort of conversational accommodation discussed by David Lewis—those expressed by gradable adjectives and, if contextualism about knowledge is correct, verbs like 'knows'—are the primary examples of such notions.

Given that this is what operators of the form *on X's standards* work on when they are used to convey the relativity of a truth, there are genuine and severe limits to what can be relatively true. We do not, for example, recognize that it is up for serious negotiation as to when the Revolutionary War ended, or whether Ben Franklin was the first Postmaster General, or whether water condenses on cool surfaces.[15] It is just plain false, absolutely false, that on very loose standards the Revolutionary War was still being waged in 1791. There is no agent or perspective which is such that it's true for that agent or from that perspective that Mo Vaughn was America's first Surgeon General.[16] There are, perhaps, some people who *think* that Mo was the first. But there is no way of thinking of political offices such that, on that way of thinking of them, (it is true that) Mo was the first.

What about the claim that the stuff in the Hudson River isn't water? Well, we can certainly negotiate what is to count as water for certain purposes; we will accommodate various uses of 'water' if doing so makes sense. Is it really the case that by the standards of chemists the Hudson River isn't water? The question just isn't concrete enough to answer. Chemists, like everyone else, use different standards on different occasions, depending on

---

[14] Stanley, 151–2.
[15] There is, of course, a *kind* of negotiation we allow over these things. We allow, when it's necessary to be very precise about dates, *stipulation* about the *exact* time an event begins and ends. But it's simply not up for grabs as to whether the Revolutionary War was still going on in 1796.
[16] Vaughn played for the Red Sox from 1991 until 1998.

their interests and purposes. One would have to have a particular situation with particular people in mind, in order even to begin to consider the question.

A rough test for whether a use of an operator such as 'On Kekulé's standards' or 'On Kekulé's way of looking at things' is supposed to be capturing the fact that something is *true* relative to a certain perspective is whether it can be expanded with '—and those standards are one permissible way to look at the matter—' or '—and his is one permissible way of thinking of things—'. I in fact doubt that by the standards of chemists for knowledge—when those standards are one permissible way of thinking about knowledge—those without lab experience don't know that hydrogen is an element. Be that as it may, no one with a wit of sense is going to say that there is any reasonable way of looking at history on which it is true that Mo Vaughn was a nineteenth-century doctor. It is *not* true, no matter who X might be, that by the standards of X concerning office holding—X's standards for who holds what office being one permissible way of looking at office holding—it is true that Mo Vaughn was once Surgeon General.

There is no reason to think that saying that operators like 'On Niels Bohr's standards' allow us to express judgments about relative truth leads to the view that 'everything is relative'.

II.3

Contextualists about 'know' typically point to the gradable adjectives in explaining their position, suggesting that the verb's semantics is cognate to that of the adjectives. Stanley claims that 'knows' doesn't pattern semantically with context-sensitive expressions to begin with.[17] He makes the following observations in support of his claim.

(i) Modals are generally held to be context-sensitive: even fixing the sense of a modal (to, say, physical possibility), its reading can shift within a conversation. An example: suppose A is discussing future developments in technology, and B doesn't realize this. We may have

A: So I could fly from NY to London in an hour!
B: Impossible—even the Concorde can't do that.
A: I didn't deny that; I was talking about future technology.

We don't have such shifts with 'knows', as witnessed by the bizarreness of

A: I know that's a zebra.
B: Couldn't it be a painted mule?
A: Uh, I guess.
B: So you admit you were wrong when you said you knew it was a zebra?
A: I never said I knew that it was a zebra.

Stanley argues that if 'knows' were context-sensitive in the way the modal is, then its content would shift in this conversation, as B's observation effectively raises the standards for knowledge. But then, if contextualism is true, A's use of 'I know that's a zebra'

---

[17] Stanley (2004; 2006: ch. 3).

expresses different claims at the beginning and end of the conversation. So A's last utterance would, if contextualism were true, be acceptable.

(ii) The possibilities for propositional anaphora are different with 'knows' than with other contextually sensitive expressions. While

It's raining here. If I'd been inside, that/what I just said would still have been true.

is acceptable, this is not:

I don't know I have hands. . . . Hey, I can open the door; I know I have hands. But what I said earlier still holds.

(iii) Some expressions, such as 'For all I know', act like quantifiers over contexts. A use of

For all you know, I'm a robber.

seems true just in case in some context 'epistemically possible' for the addressee, the speaker of that context is a robber. Thus, 'For all you know' neutralizes the context-sensitive 'I' so that it does not have its normal contextual interpretation. The interpretation of 'know' does not so shift within this operator. Even if you are unsure what standards for knowledge are operative in the context, and so are unsure whether Fred counts as knowing that he has hands, there's no felicitous reading of

For all you know, Fred knows that he has hands.

(iv) Gradable adjectives, modals, and quantifier phrases can have their standards for application or extensions shift within a sentence, as witnessed by

(T) That butterfly is small, and so is that elephant.
       That field is flat, and so is that rock.
       In Syracuse there are many serial killers and many unemployed men.
       I can't bench-press 100 pounds, but I could with regular training.

This isn't the case with 'knows', as witnessed by the infelicity of

(T′) Bill knows he has hands, but not that he isn't a brain in a vat.
        Bill doesn't know that he's not a brain in a vat, but he knows he has hands.

It seems to me that rather than undercutting contextualism about 'knows', Stanley's observations actually make it more plausible. For in each case what Stanley observes about 'knows' is also true of gradable adjectives. Stanley's first point is, in effect, that when a modal such as 'could' is used by different speakers in 'A could fly to Europe in a half hour' to express different sorts of physical possibility, we treat the uses of the sentence as saying different things. He observes that we don't treat uses of 'A knows that that's a zebra' as saying different things even when it is clear that different standards of knowledge are presupposed by the user. The observation about 'knows' is correct. But exactly the same sort of thing is true of 'rich' and other gradable adjectives. The following dialogue is exactly as bizarre as the zebra dialogue in (i) above:

A: He is rich [It is flat].
B: He can't afford a house on the Vineyard [it's really sort of bumpy].
A: I see your point.

B: So you admit you were wrong when you said he was rich [it was flat].
A: I said no such thing.[18]

Similar points hold concerning propositional anaphora. True,

I don't know I have hands. . . . Hey, I can open the door; I know I have hands. But what I said earlier still holds.

is unacceptable. But so is

She's not rich. . . . Oh, yeah, I guess I do think that *he*'s rich, and she and he make about the same. So I guess she is rich. But what I said earlier still holds.

As far as operators such as 'For all you know' are concerned, Stanley himself points out that they do not have the sort of effect on gradable adjectives which they have on words like 'I'; once again, 'know' and the gradable adjectives pattern together.

Finally, there are the examples (T) and (T'). These are allegedly examples in which the content of a contextually sensitive expression shifts across uses within a single sentence. In thinking about these examples we should distinguish two kinds of context-sensitivity. The word 'tall' is context-sensitive insofar as it requires a reference class—something is tall for a tree/building/two-year-old; nothing is tall *simpliciter*. Other adjectives, while perhaps not requiring a reference class in order to get assigned an extension, clearly accept one. I may call a field flat and obviously be comparing it to the fields in Bucks County, or call a pond flat with the clear intent that we evaluate what I say relative to the class of naturally occurring large bodies of water. A quite different sort of context-sensitivity results from the fact that (even after a reference class is determined) candidates for the extension of a term such as 'flat' or 'rich' are ordered by the degree of the relevant property (flatness, wealth), with the extension of the term being determined by 'how one draws the line' within the ordering—such line drawing being something that can be done differently in different contexts.

Call the first sort of context-sensitivity comparative, the second extensive. I think once we see the distinction, we also see that Stanley's first two examples are examples of comparative, not extensive, sensitivity. The first sentence, for example, is OK if understood so:

That butterfly is small for an animal, and that elephant is small for an elephant.

It's not OK—and not an example of what Stanley wants it to be an example of—if it's understood as

---

[18] Stanley argues (2006: 55–6) that 'rich' really does pattern with 'could' and not 'know' here. He argues that the last remark in the 'rich' version of this conversation can be made felicitous by 'adding background context'—e.g. by changing A's last remark to

A: I didn't say that he is rich; I wasn't considering that level of wealth.

But, says Stanley, this sort of contextualizing won't render the last comment in the zebra conversation felicitous.

Frankly, I don't find that this sort of 'contextualization' makes A's last remark any more acceptable. Indeed, if I were B and A said that, I would probably say something like

B: Of course you said that he was rich; it's the fact that you weren't thinking clearly about what it takes to be rich that made you say the stupid thing you did, you twit.

But then I am somewhat rude.

That butterfly is small for an animal and that elephant is small for an animal.

But it is no part of the agenda of the contextualist about 'knows' to say that the verb is context-sensitive in every way in which terms such as 'flat' or 'rich' are context-sensitive. What the contextualist about knowledge holds is that the standards for knowledge accompanying a knowledge ascription are relevant to its truth-conditions. As this talk about standards is usually fleshed out, differences in standards are, very roughly, differences in how reliable one is in distinguishing cases in which what one is supposed to know obtains from ones in which it doesn't. This is a kind of extensive sensitivity. And, in fact, if we look at sentences involving gradable adjectives which could be true only if we 'draw the line' differently for different uses of an adjective, we get the same feeling of bizarreness which Stanley notes accompanies sentences such as 'He knows he has hands, but he doesn't know whether he is a handless brain in a vat'. Consider, for example,

This rock is flat, but that one isn't (said of two rocks which are more or less indistinguishable).[19]

In short: contrary to what Stanley alleges, our intuitions about (semantic) acceptability and bizarreness are exactly what one would expect, if the contextualist claim, that 'knows' has a semantics like the gradable adjectives, is correct.

---

[19] Contextual variation in the interpretation of the modals seems to me more like comparative than extensive sensitivity. (The sorts of shifts involved don't seem to involve 'drawing a line' on an ordering of worlds, but rather selecting a set of worlds relative to which to determine possibility.) Insofar as this is so, variants of the remarks just made apply to 'I can't bench-press 100 pounds, but could if I trained'. This is also relevant, of course, to Stanley's first objection to assimilating the contextual sensitivity of 'knows' to that of the gradable adjectives.

References

Almog, J., Perry, J., and Wettstein, H. (1989) (eds.,) *Themes from Kaplan* (Oxford University Press).

Appiah, Anthony (1990), 'Racisms', in Goldberg (1990).

Ayer, A. J. (1936), *Language, Truth, and Logic* (Gollanez).

Barwise, Jon, and Perry, John (1983), *Situations and Attitudes* (MIT Press).

Blackburn, Simon (1984). *Spreading the Word* (Oxford University Press).

——— (1993). *Essays in Quasi-Realism* (Oxford University Press).

——— (1998), *Ruling Passions* (Oxford University Press).

——— (2004), *Lust* (Oxford University Press).

Burge, Tyler (1979), 'Semantic Paradox', *Journal of Philosophy*, 76: 169–98; repr. in Martin (1984).

Cohen, Stewart (1999), 'Contextualism, Skepticism, and the Structure of Reasons', in Tomberlin (1999).

Davidson, Arnold (2001), *The Emergence of Sexuality* (Harvard University Press).

DeRose, Keith (1995), 'Solving the Skeptical Problem', *Philosophical Review*, 104/1: 1–52.

Devitt, M., and Hanley, R. (2006) (eds.), *The Blackwell Guide to the Philosophy of Language* (Blackwell).

Dreier, James (1995), 'Expressivist Embeddings and Minimalist Truth', *Philosophical Studies*, 83: 29–51.

——— (1999), 'Transforming Expressivism', *Nous*, 33: 558–72.

——— (2006), 'Negation for Expressivists', in Shafer-Landau (2006).

Foot, Philippa (1970), 'Morality and Art', in Foot (2002).

——— (1979), 'Moral Relativism', in Foot (2002).

——— (2002), *Moral Dilemmas* (Oxford University Press).

Frege, Gottlob (1918), 'Negation', repr. in trans. in Geach and Black (1970).

French, Peter, et al. (2001) (eds.), *Midwest Studies in Philosophy*, xxv, (Blackwell).

Garcia, J. L. A. (1996), 'The Heart of Racism', *Journal of Social Philosophy*, 27: 5–45.

Geach, Peter (1965), 'Assertion', *Philosophical Review*, 74/4: 449–65.

Geach, Peter, and Black, Max (1970) (eds.), *Translations from the Philosophical Writings of Gottlob Frege* (Blackwell).

Gibbard, Alan (1990), *Wise Choices, Apt Feelings* (Harvard University Press).

——— (1993), 'Reply to Blackburn', *Philosophical Issues*, 4: 57–63.

——— (2003*a*), 'Reasons Thick and Thin: A Possibility Proof', *Journal of Philosophy*. 100/6: 288–304.

——— (2003*b*), *Thinking How to Live* (Harvard University Press).

Goldberg, David (1990) (ed.), *Anatomy of Racism* (University of Minnesota Press).

Grice, H. P. (1967), 'Logic and Conversation', in Grice (1989).

——— (1989), *Studies in the Ways of Words* (Harvard University Press).

Hacking, Ian (1999), *The Social Construction of What?* (Harvard University Press).

Haldane, J., and Wright, C. (1993) (eds.), *Reality, Representation, and Projection* (Oxford University Press).

Hale, Bob (1986), 'The Compleat Projectivist', *Philosophical Quarterly*, 36: 65–84.

Hawthorne, John, and Zimmerman, Dean (2003) (eds.), *Philosophical Perspectives*, xvii (Blackwell).

Hawthorne, John (2004), *Knowledge and Lotteries* (Oxford University Press).

Hornsby, Jennifer (2001), 'Meaning and uselessness: How to Think About Derogatory Words', in French et al. (2001), 128–41.

Horwich, Paul (1998*a*), *Meaning* (Oxford University Press).

——— (1998*b*), *Truth*, 2nd edn. (Oxford University Press).

Hursthouse, R., Lawrence, G., and Quinn, W. (1995) (eds.), *Virtues and Reasons* (Oxford University Press).

Johnston, Mark (1989), 'Dispositional Theories of Value', *Proceedings of the Aristotelian Society*, supp. vol. 63: 139–74.

——— (1993), 'Objectivity Refigured: Pragmatism without Verificationism', in Haldane and Wright (1993).

Kaplan, David (1989*a*), *Demonstratives*, in Almog et al. (1989).

——— (1989*b*), *Afterthoughts*, in Almog et al. (1989).

Kennedy, Chris (1999), *Projecting the Adjective: The Syntax and Semantics of Gradability and Comparison* (Garland).

Kennedy, Randell (2002), *Nigger* (Pantheon).

King, Jeff (2003). 'Tense, Modality, and Semantic Values', in Hawthorne and Zimmerman (2003).

Kripke, Saul (1975), 'Truth', in Martin (1984).

Lewis, David (1979), 'Scorekeeping in a Language Game', in Lewis (1983).

——— (1983), *Philosophical Papers*, i (Oxford University Press).

——— (1996), 'Elusive Knowledge', in Lewis (1999).

——— (1999), *Papers in Metaphysics and Epistemology* (Cambridge University Press).

McDowell, John (1998), *Mind, Value, and Reality* (Harvard University Press).

McGee, Vann (1991), *Truth, Vagueness, and Paradox* (Hackett).

Martin, Robert (1984), *Recent Essays on Truth and the Liar Paradox* (Oxford University Press).

Moravscik, Julius (1990), *Thought and Language* (Routledge).

Parsons, Charles (1984), 'The Liar Paradox', in Martin (1984).

Parsons, Terence (1984), 'Assertion, Denial, and the Liar Paradox', *Journal of Philosophical Logic*, 13, 137–52.

Postow, Betsy (1979), 'Dishonest Relativism', *Analysis*, 39: 45–8.

Richard, Mark (1990), *Propositional Attitudes* (Cambridge University Press).

——— (2002), 'On an Argument of Williamson's', *Analysis*, 60: 213–17.

——— (2003) (ed.), *Meaning* (Blackwell).

——— (2004), 'Contextualism and Relativism', *Philosophical Studies*, 119: 215–42.

——— (2006), 'Propositional Attitude Ascription' in Devitt and Hanley (2006).

——— (forthcoming *a*), 'Indeterminacy and Truth Value Gaps'.

——— (forthcoming *b*), *Meaning in Context: Collected Papers* (Oxford University Press).

Rorty, Richard (1998), *Truth and Progress* (Cambridge University Press).

Scanlon, Tim (1995), 'Fear of Relativism', in Hursthouse et al. (1995).

Shafer-Landau, Russ (2006) (ed.), *Oxford Studies in Metaethics*, i (Oxford University Press).

Soames, Scott (1999), *Understanding Truth* (Oxford University Press).

Stalnaker, Robert (1974), 'Pragmatic Presupposition', in Stalnaker (1999).

_____ (1999), *Context and Content* (Oxford University Press).

Stanley, Jason (2004), 'On the Linguistic Basis for Contextualism', *Philosophical Studies*, 119: 119–46.

_____ (2006), *Knowledge and Practical Interests* (Oxford University Press).

Tomberlin, James (1999) (ed.), *Philosophical Perspectives*, xiii (Blackwell).

Unwin, Nicholas (1999), 'Quasi-Realism, Negation, and the Frege–Geach Problem', *Philosophical Quarterly*, 49: 337–52.

_____ (2001), 'Norms and Negation: A Problem for Gibbard's Logic', *Philosophical Quarterly*, 51: 60–75.

Urmson, J. O. (1968), *The Emotivist Theory of Ethics* (Oxford University Press).

Wellman, D. T. (1977), *Portraits of White Racism* (Cambridge University Press).

Williams, Bernard (1985), *Ethics and the Limits of Philosophy* (Harvard University Press).

Williamson, Timothy (1992), 'Vagueness and Ignorance', *Proceedings of the Aristotelian Society*, suppl. vol. 66: 145–62.

_____ (1994), *Vagueness* (Routledge).

_____ (2000), *Knowledge and its Limits* (Oxford University Press).

Wilson, Mark (1982), 'Predicate Meets Property', in Richard (2003).

_____ (2006), *Wandering Significance* (Oxford University Press).

Wittgenstein, Ludwig (1958), *Philosophical Investigations*, 3rd edn. (Macmillan).

Zimmermann, Aaron (2007), 'Against Relativism', *Philosophical Studies*, 133: 313–48.

Index